PENGUIN BOOKS

TRAIN TO INDIA

Maloy Krishna Dhar was born in Kamalpur, Bhairab-Mymensingh in East Bengal and migrated to West Bengal with his family during Partition. After obtaining a Masters in Bengali Literature and Language and Comparative Literature from Calcutta University, he worked as a college teacher and a junior reporter. He joined the Indian Police Service in 1964 and worked with the Indian Intelligence Bureau (IB) for three decades.

After retirement from a service that honed his ability to observe and understand people and their motivations, he has had an extremely successful career as a freelance journalist, contributing to all the major English dailies. He is also a best-selling author and his landmark books include *Open Secrets: India's Intelligence Unveiled, Fulcrum of Evil: ISI-CIA-Al Qaeda Nexus, Black Thunder: Dark Nights of Terrorism in Punjab* and *We the People of India: A Story of Gangland Democracy.*

Dhar also manages the website www.maloykrishnadhar.com where research articles on security, terrorism and internal and international security are regularly updated.

GW00480573

TRAIN TO INDIA
MEMORIES OF ANOTHER BENGAL

MALOY KRISHNA DHAR

PENGUIN BOOKS

An imprint of Penguin Random House

PENGUIN BOOKS

USA | Canada | UK | Ireland | Australia
New Zealand | India | South Africa | China

Penguin Books is part of the Penguin Random House group of companies
whose addresses can be found at global.penguinrandomhouse.com

Published by Penguin Random House India Pvt. Ltd
7th Floor, Infinity Tower C, DLF Cyber City,
Gurgaon 122 002, Haryana, India

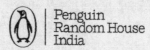

Penguin
Random House
India

First published by Penguin Books India 2009

10 9 8 7 6 5 4 3 2

The views and opinions expressed in this book are the author's own and the
facts are as reported by him which have been verified to the extent possible,
and the publishers are not in any way liable for the same.

ISBN 9780143065463

Typeset in Minion by InoSoft Systems, Noida
Printed at Repro Knowledgecast Limited, India

www.penguin.co.in

To the memory of my parents
Debendra and Sushama

Contents

Contents

Author's Note

Memorization of history often leads to the historicization of memory. The former is bland reality without any imagination; the latter process mixes up memory with remote history, mythological tidbits, prejudices and love and anger. The memories of the last sixty-five years—1944 to 2009—are a part of current history, and of my life, but I have never allowed them to be historicized with borrowed ingredients of social, ethnic, cultural or religious bias.

Events moved so fast between 1945 and 1950 that I did not have the luxury of growing up gradually, learning leisurely and forging the steel inside through the usual slow process of maturing. Events forced me and the other children around to mature at a faster rate and catch up with the pace of history that was churning like a cyclone and changing our lives mercilessly.

Our composite and culturally sublimated society developed cracks. The small joys of life turned to very big liabilities. Our common folk deities like Olai Chandi (the deity of cholera), Bon Bibi (of forests), Sheetala (of small pox), Manasa (of serpents) and our Peer Dargah (a holy shrine of a Sufi saint) were suddenly divided on communal lines. We Hindus were not encouraged to visit the Dargah and the Muslim women were strictly prohibited from taking part in the worship of folk deities derived from Hindu and animalistic pantheons.

Our songs were common. My father and his companions used to sing the same bhatiali, bhawaia, mahishali and boat songs. They were equally adept in murshedi songs and qawwali. Hindu pat (scroll) paintings depicted exploits of Hindu deities and Ghazi pats described the exploits of Muslim heroes. These were our common cultural heritages. Suddenly Hindu and Ghazi pats started spitting venom and decrying Hindu and Muslim holy practices and persons. Our culture and tradition was split into many pieces.

The political events moved at such a fast pace that the seams of our social bondages could not absorb those shockwaves. We started falling apart. Hatred replaced love, scowl replaced smile, social exchanges ceased and gradually violence was imported and imposed by politically inspired separatists. We ceased to be one people.

As the spate of violence spread, we bled physically and emotionally. The cancer of violence turned virulent after the Direct Action of 1946. We took the first journey to the princely state of Tripura, temporarily avoiding the violence that gradually infected our areas. The lure and love for the soil prompted us to return soon. Some amongst us did not lose hope and pursued the dream of unity. But their dreams were sold in the markets of political expediency and communal segmentation. Uprooting is an irredeemable disaster that was compounded by the bloodshed all around us. The ambience of hatred and violence brought me three gifts: I came closer to my father and understood the person he was and the values he stood for; I did not swap love for hate for my Muslim friends; and I matured overnight, prepared to face the torrents of violence.

I was baptized in blood while making the first aborted effort to escape my village and the knife and blood syndrome haunted me even after landing in an uncertain India, a supposed homeland. It took time to develop a bond with the new home, new peoples and I could abandon the blood-knife complex only at that critical moment when I lost the last anchor—my father. His death propelled me to undertake a new journey and rediscover that my tryst with blood, hatred and revenge was not tailored for me. There was a poet, a troubadour and a loving creature in me, inherited from my father.

The journey of hatred had finally become a journey of love and faith in humanity. That is the real story of my journey aboard the Train to India.

Parts of the story of the Great Exodus enacted in India were narrated by my father, a staunch supporter of revolutionary action, and my mother, a silent powerhouse who excelled in the art of absorbing pain. She had mastered the art of unmasking the games of hatred that were invented by kings, masters, political poker players and religious toads living in their isolated wells.

Their narration and suffering had prepared me to expect the worst, to anticipate the darkness of eternal void and to prepare for a new light of hope, thirst, and a desire to explore. As my mother said, 'In the beginning there was light', and this light was the essence and source of life. She propelled me towards another journey to discover the light we were forced to flee from.

My parents did not share with me the horrific events that followed the Independence movement and the Congress and Muslim League's determined plans for

India. I watched their anxious faces and often collected tidbits from Rahman and his daughter Lutfa. Later I was to learn more about the story of the Great Human Exodus that was interpreted as the victory of the struggle for Independence, victory of the dream of securing a Promised Muslim Homeland in Hindustan.

There were other dimensions to the Great Exodus. The stories of trains travelling between India and East Pakistan carrying human bodies—dead and live—and the miseries of millions have been relatively less chronicled than the events in Punjab. This is a story by a real-time traveller who had to take two train journeys to a new India from his old India in the eastern flank of the country. Some great literary minds like Sadat Hassan Manto and Khushwant Singh have chronicled some aspects of the great tragedy that was enacted in the western flank of India.

This is not an attempt to chronicle the Great Human Exodus but what I saw myself and what I learnt from my parents and their contemporaries.

The tragic events did not start with the political division. It started with the gradual and increasing devastation of the lives of the people. The story cannot be told without describing the emotional, cultural, linguistic and traditional bondages of the people who were forced to turn swords and guns against each other after being poisoned by political and religious fanatics.

Telling a story long after it unfolded has certain advantages and disadvantages. People don't relish ruminating over the hoary past. However, distance adds not only a romantic hue; it also helps shed bias and idiosyncratic views.

It has taken me over fifty years to understand that with my train journey to India, a light has not been extinguished. The theatre changed, the lights and props changed—instead of the Meghna and Brahmaputra, I had reached the banks of the Ganga and Yamuna.

The forced train journey to India had implanted in me a deep hatred for any people who killed in the name of religion and political separation. I hated the political manoeuvres of the Congress and the Muslim League and I hated the people I thought were responsible for my father's distress and premature death. Hatred, violence, anger and distrust had virtually numbed my mind for a while.

It took me over half a century to understand that we were all victims of a history that was imposed on us by the colonial powers and the political hunger of leaders who felt that religion alone was a factor to impose nationhood on groups of people.

As I recovered from the deeply entrenched bias and hate, I realized that I had been chasing the life, friends, and almost everything that I was forced to leave, and which had enriched my inexhaustible treasure box of memories. There was no scope for hatred, there was no room for political and geographical division, and there was no weapon that could divide minds.

Train to India is a part of that treasure box—a journey back towards the light and time, and the people who were forced to redraw the geography of my country. The story unfolds from light to darkness and the rediscovery of the unbroken chain of light and life.

one

In the Beginning

The Great Exodus took survivors across imaginary lines drawn on cartographer's maps, which promised them no home, land or manna from heaven. They waded through rivulets of blood and hillocks of skeletons but failed to negotiate the barrier of history. The Muslims of the subcontinent had a Promised Land after a brief cohabitation with their Hindu subjects for a mere period of 650 years. The British had earned the right to divide after a brief rule of about 170 years.

We, the supposed original inhabitants of India, had not received any promises. We, the Hindus and Muslims fought a common enemy, the slave masters who ruled us, with the assurance that we would have a Common Land, Our Own Land—Hindustan. It was not to be. We were being told that religion was the universal constant that determined the history and geography of a people.

The story of the Great Human Exodus has not been recorded faithfully. Hindus and Muslims wrote their respective histories, some perverted mutilation of history called the history of Hindustan and Pakistan. Historians, who evaluate and present history from their own perspective, often rationalize human tragedy with their own interpretations. We were offered Congress, communist, Hindu, Muslim, swadeshist and several other versions of history. They dared not chronicle the pains of the Great Exodus because they were busy cushioning their chairs.

～

In the beginning, there was *srishti-sthiti-binashanag shaktibhute sanatani*—the Eternal Energy that caused creation, assured preservation, and inevitable destruction. The eternal energy of creation had endowed my village and part of Bengal with the sweet melodies of nature.

We, the Bengali speaking people living in our tiny corner of the universe and India were there with our rivers, the Meghna and Brahmaputra, the memorable Teetas Beel, Satmukhi Beel (the lake with seven inlets and outlets), paddy fields, orchards full of flowers, fruits, spices, ducks, herons, cranes, Bengal robins, finches and parrots, goats, cows and ponds full of fish.

I had my very own pets: Chandana the parrot, Pintu the white goat, Tomtom the dog and Sonai the duck. Mother had Victoria, the all-white furry cat.

There was everything—my primary school, our teacher Dhiru Acharya, friends Lutf-un-Nissa (Lutfa), Jasimuddin (Jasim), Saifullah (Saifi), Mehboob Alam, Haripada, Mani and scores of cousins. Living next to the wild, moody and surging Meghna and Brahmaputra rivers, only a dead soul could escape the turbulent love of creation.

Bhairab, our lively railway station connected Calcutta, Dhaka and Mymensingh with the southernmost tips of east Bengal. There was the wonderful Anderson Bridge over the Meghna, the only bridge to span the turbulent river. The station unravelled new surprises, day in and day out, besides bringing in new faces and carrying away some known faces to destinations beyond the horizon. The station was our telescope to the outer world.

I dreamt of riding a train through the land I saw on the global map in the Bradshaw travel guide of India. It made me dream of boarding a train to explore other parts of India.

One fine morning in January 1945, as a boisterous child of six, I had my dream journey to Brahmanbaria, a town in Tipperah district. That short journey was preceeded by my obdurate persistence to accompany our family retainer Dhiru Saha. He had told me, in his exquisite poetic language, of the beauty and charm of Kanan Devi, the film actress, and the magical world of the Meghdoot cinema hall at Brahmanbaria. My nagging persistence led to admonitions but finally, mother yielded. She pushed eight annas (fifty paise) into my pocket and reminded me that Dhiru's social mores were different from ours. Her decision irked a few elders and evoked the awesome admiration of my young cousins and friends. I took the dream journey with Dhiru, who figured in our lives like the occasional cyclonic hailstorm, mostly enjoyed and often rued.

Dhiru was a romantic. He gave me a nice rickshaw ride to the wonder world of Meghdoot, spoke about the beauty of young lasses, dumped me near a flower vendor and reappeared with a garishly dressed girl. I can't recall her name. She caressed me like an affectionate mother, ran her fingers through my hair and offered me a coloured ice cone. She accompanied us to the cinema hall where I was enchanted by the unreal world of celluloid fantasies. I did not notice the physical closeness of Dhiru and his girlfriend. Kanan Devi's charms disappeared behind the silver screen and Dhiru sternly warned me not to mention the girl to anyone in the family.

I had plenty to babble about to my friends of my wonderful journey to the forbidden world of a cinema hall, the goodies I ate and the girl who had bewitched Dhiru more than Kanan Devi did.

Stories flew like wild fire. My story, garnished with imagination and many a twist had reached the inner chambers. My adventure finally landed me in the court of Grandpa Chandra Kishore, Dad Debendra, Uncle Birendra and the many women members of the family. Grandpa pronounced that I should be punished with three cane strokes, Dhiru with ten, and an amount of twelve annas should be deducted from his grand monthly salary of five rupees for his acts of blatant indiscretion.

Mother Sushama got a scolding from Grandma Chandrakanta for her frivolous act of indulgence in permitting me to see an adult movie called *Mane Na Mana* (Mind Unfettered).

My mother was different. She did not mind her kids taking steps out into the uncertain world outside our village Kamalpur. She suffered quietly, served the needy and violated the strictest codes of Chandra Kishore. She was a sort of social rebel.

That was the first of some other train journeys to other parts of my country that was soon to become a new India, from my niche in the old India. Our railway station was a stage, and trains and tracks unravelled the drama scripted by people who were not part of our life. However, these train journeys to India were not mere village stage-dramas. These were a human drama; a part of a cruel Indo-drama which did not end with the Great Exodus. Ours was a different kind of Exodus. There was no Promised Land, no Father of the Nation leading his people and no Commandments.

November 1944

Our peaceful rural community, emotionally bonded together by centuries of love and care, lived together peacefully until the harmony was shattered by several events. Newspapers and radio brought in horrific stories of political sword-fencing between major political parties, the reappearance of Netaji Subhas Chandra Bose in the eastern war theatre and the formation of the Indian National Army (INA), Japanese advances and communal divide. The Bengali tradition of armed resistance against the British was rekindled with the news of Netaji's Indian National Army gaining a foothold in Indian territory.

We were young but the fires around heated up our tender lives. My conscious and discerning memories of our surroundings and our friends were not the only treasures embedded on the canvas. Our railway station presented a confusing collage. Strange people descended on our lands— white, black and Indian troops. Some trains carried them to unknown southern destinations.

The trains unloaded heavy long barrelled guns and a couple of tanks. The British troops set up positions next to the ice factory owned by our family. Some troops encamped in a mango grove about a kilometre east of our homes. They patrolled in jeeps and often glared at us.

One dusky evening Lutfa ran to my part of our sprawling dwelling, 'There's a big problem Krishna. The *gora sipahis*, those white soldiers chased me. I ran as fast as I could.'

'Why? You haven't done them any wrong'

'They are demons. They have started paying hefty prices for chicken, duck and everything in the market. The affluent Muslim League leader Kala mian is visiting the camp frequently. And your cousin Dukhia is supplying them with wet rations. 'You're a kid, you won't understand. Dukhia is taking some low caste girls to the camp to those very soldiers who chased me.'

Dukhia was the apple of our grandfather's eye. He was often deputed by grandpa to torture share-croppers and bonded labourers. He was feared as the designated general of the old patriarch.

A week later, a British officer accompanied by an Indian junior, Kala mian and Dhukia came calling on Chandra Kishore. Although not a recognised zamindar, our family was widely regarded as a *mahashay*, aristocrats with huge landed and business interests. The eastern building was decked up with sofas and chairs and someone managed to procure a garland for the senior officer with metal stars on his shoulder pips.

Family elders and elders of the Hindu and Muslim community of village Kamalpur and the surrounding villages assembled in the hall. After welcoming the officer Grandpa delivered a speech in the King's English offering unqualified support to the King Emperor and his forces.

The officer spoke in broken Hindi with lots of English words thrown in. Dhiru Acharya, our school teacher, translated his speech into our local Bengali dialect: 'My government and I are happy with you people. I have no complaint against the Muslims. Some Hindus, followers of Bose are creating trouble. Congress is not cooperating. I request you zamindar sahib to direct your *royats* and your tenants, to support the King's army against that traitor Bose. I would recommend you for a British honour. I believe in this village itself there is a revolutionary group. I warn you Kishore sahib that I would not spare anyone, even if they belong to your extended family.'

Sweets and sherbet were served. Grandpa wanted to serve whisky to the British officer but he declined saying that some evening he would drop in for a drink.

~

Things changed very fast. We lived in a period of confusion—confusion of the political skullduggery of the Congress, the Muslim League and Hindu Mahasabha leaders, rebellious anger generated by the followers of Subhas Bose and confusion in the minds of the staunch British loyalists. There was no one to lead the confused Hindu and Muslim masses.

The world around us was crashing down with much more ferocity than the tidal waves of the Meghna River that devoured acres of land and human habitat while on its journey to confluence with the Bay of Bengal.

The Second World War, the family elders told us, had devastated millions of homes and the British Lion was about to emerge victorious, as usual. The sun, Grandpa Chandra Kishore said boastfully, would never set below the horizons of the Empire of the descendants of the Queen. He did not wait for the news of the fall of Berlin and the surrender of Japan. Dressed in a silken dhoti and punjabi, the traditional male Bengali long kurta, he led a delegation of the loyal subjects of His Majesty

King George VI's representative, to the district collector of Mymensingh, to express solidarity with the Allied Powers.

But some of our clan members including his wife Chandrakanta did not agree with Chandra Kishore and his loyalists. She secretly supported a few young daredevils of her family who were with the resistance movement that was started by the Bengal Provincial Volunteers, a remnant of the rebellious movement started by Netaji Subhas Chandra Bose. Subhas was the first people's general mandated by the freedom fighters of India to fight a historic war against the British occupation forces. Some of our clan members secretly supported his call: 'Give me blood, I will give you freedom'. My father, a Benares and Calcutta trained ayurvedic medic was associated with one such group headed by Uncle Satish and his band of revolutionaries.

Our Meghna-Brahmaputra basin witnessed a large deployment of the British Indian Army on either side of the vital Anderson Bridge at Bhairab. The white, black and brown soldiers milled around our small railway station and purchased whatever they could, including village women.

Some members of the family pointed fingers at Dukhia, the favourite grandson, who was born after his father's premature death. Dukhia dropped out of school and turned entrepreneur at the young age of seventeen, supplying rations to the British forces and village lasses for the hungry soldiers. We, the young brigade were fully aware of his patriotic duties rendered faithfully to the Crown. The family elders dared not say anything against the favourite grandson.

Lutfa, the daughter of bonded labourer Rahman headed our young brigade. At eleven, five years older to me, she had more worldly knowledge than I did. She moved around the troop deployments and counted the trains that carried soldiers and armaments to the Sylhet warfront which was opened up to contain likely Japanese and INA thrusts to the plains of Bengal and Assam.

Along with the troop concentration, a dirt airstrip had been developed overnight near Kuliarchar, a prosperous village ten miles northwest of our village. We could see the planes zooming in and out over our homes but we were not allowed to travel the forbidding distance to see the planes.

We scurried around at the behest of the nationalist underground fighters to ferret out information about British and American troop movements. Our group of close friends included Lutfa, Jasim, Haripada, Saifullah and Mani. Our lack of knowledge was compensated for by curiosity, courage for and an uncertain sense of thrill.

Independence, Lutfa told our squirrel brigade, was our birthright and we were equal partners with our struggling elders. I often wondered at her wisdom and courage, but followed her blindly as a loyal soldier. She was the cleverest of us and never tired of telling us that the seasoned army and police officers just thought of us as innocent children. A biscuit or lozenges were often our reward.

Lutfa was regarded as an imprudent village belle, daughter of a serf, having access to most kitchens and nooks and corners of most households and helpful by nature. Later I realized that Lutfa had the most balanced head on her frail body. I was mesmerized by Lutfa, the eternal firewalker. She compromised with circumstances only as a measure to hit back uncompromisingly. She was a master of guile. Her courage often stung me to action.

∽

Rumours more than solid information propelled some of our elders to celebrate the Japanese and INA offensive. Very few outsiders were invited, and kids like us were shooed away from the *chandimandap*, the community centre. But the teen brigade, an ensemble of country bumpkins led by Lutfa fleeted around their meeting places like curious sparrows. We waited anxiously to serve water, tea and snacks, and occasionally filled the clay pots with molasses and scented tobacco.

We also had many other daring duties to perform. Aunt Mudrajita, the first woman graduate from our village, didn't mind giving us a break or two by deploying our juvenile brigade to ferry messages between the revolutionary bands that had taken up arms in support of the INA. Her clever ploy worked fine. We moved around freely from village to village, defying the spy network of Kalimuddin Biswas, a sub-inspector of police of the district intelligence department. His stool pigeons, some of them our blood relations, fished around the village lanes to pick and cook up intelligence against the enemies of the King Emperor of India.

Our brigade scurried around, often playing odd village games, almost under the noses of Kalimuddin's networks. Lutfa often diverted their attention by offering them water and snacks. The watchers, rooted to their posts for hours on end didn't mind accepting Lutfa's sweetened rice balls, syrupy jalebis and other tidbits. She charmed them with small talk and pretended to volunteer sensitive information. Her stories frequently, I had no doubt, filled in the daily diaries of the petty informers and sent them scurrying on wild errands.

National fervour and patriotism, however, didn't fill everyone in our family with missionary zeal. We were not united in opposing the British war efforts. While Uncle Satish and Altaf Hussain led a gang of poorly armed desperadoes and often sabotaged the movement of British Indian troops and their supply lines, cousin Dukhia patronized the British. Another cousin, second removed, had even enlisted in the Royal Air Force as a corporal, and carried out bombing operations from Kuliarchar base against the advancing troops of the Indian National Army. Most of our elders didn't see anything wrong in their actions. They were either insensitive or expected patronage from the Crown. They always smelt a rat in the stealthy activities of my father and his band of subjects disloyal to the Empire.

∽

One fine afternoon Lutfa brought in a piece of startling information. She had offered some coconut candy to a police informer on the prowl and pumped out vital information on the transit schedule of a special goods train to the eastern frontier, via Sylhet, carrying consignments of artillery shells and assorted weapons.

Lutfa dropped the news nonchalantly to Aunt Mudrajita and kept sucking on a mango.

'Where did you get this information from?' asked Mudra.

'That pot bellied Irfan. He keeps snooping on all of you.'

'Are you sure that the train would pass by at midnight?'

'Sure, if Irfan's information is correct.'

'Fine.' Aunt Mudra paid four annas for the information and said, 'Come and see me after supper.'

A quarter of a rupee could buy us a fortune. We rushed to the shop of the weaver Jagannath and spent the money on candies, balloons and sherbet. We assembled at our favourite hideout behind the bamboo grove and enjoyed the rare treat. Aunt Mudra was no fool to invest four annas on our brigade, Lutfa reasoned.

'There must be something big in Irfan's story.' Lutfa switched over to sucking a piece of green tamarind garnished with salt and hot green chilli. 'What do you think Krishna? What do they do with all these bombs and shells?'

'Before I say anything give me a piece of salted hot tamarind.'

Lutfa obliged and took out some luscious pods of green tamarind, two green chillies, and a dollop of salt by unfolding a bulging knot of her sari. 'I think there is a war.'

'Why? Why do they have to fight and kill?' asked Saifullah.

'War is a religious duty,' proclaimed Haripada, the son of our family priest. 'My father says that Lord Krishna had ordained so to Arjuna.'

'Phoo!' Lutfa spat out a tamarind seed. 'That can't be true. How can God ask people to fight and kill? Isn't Krishna a God?'

'I presume he is. But all the epics are full of war stories.'

'That's because men have written those books, not women,' Lutfa announced with a laugh.

'What's the difference?' I asked peevishly.

'Shut up,' Lutfa suckled at a lollypop loudly. 'Women have better things to do.'

Our early lesson in the philosophy of war and peace and gender speciality was cut short by shuffling footsteps. We took cover behind young bamboo shoots and foliage.

'Lutfa,' we heard the whispering voice of Aunt Mudra coming through the rustling of the bamboo leaves, 'are you there?'

'Yes.'

'Why are you hiding? Aren't you afraid of snakes and jackals?'

'It's our secret hideout. Snakes are good friends,' Lutfa added nonchalantly, 'anything we can do?'

We crawled out of the bamboo bush. Anyway, it was about time to quit our secret rendezvous. No one was allowed to stay out of the house after sunset, thanks to the absence of electricity and the abundance of snakes, jackals, the odd panthers and monitor lizards in the adjoining jungles. We were not particularly afraid of goblins, ghosts and jinns, as we had mastered the mantra to overcome those dark bloodthirsty creatures.

We came out and faced Aunt Mudra, who was anxiously stretching her neck to locate us behind the thick foliage. 'Come, you and Lutfa, follow me.'

She led us to a small shed which was the permanent maternity shack of our extended joint family. Some aunt, sister or daughter-in-law kept that room occupied throughout the year, adding new progeny to our extended family tree.

'Listen Lutfa,' Aunt Mudra whispered, 'you and Krishna go out after supper and contact Satish and Altaf. They should be in the riverside sand caves.' She handed over a full rupee and a small torchlight.

Excitement gripped my mind like the flute on the lips of a maestro. My blood surged through my arteries like the full-bosomed monsoon Meghna river.

'Fine.' Lutfa took a bite of her delicious green tamarind concoction, 'What do we do there?'

'Just give this letter to Satish. Take care, no one should see you.' Aunt Mudra disappeared in the descending darkness.

Lutfa looked at me questioningly. I knew what she meant. My mother would not allow me to go out after supper. She would sit down under the wicker lamp to teach me English and arithmetic. That was the usual time for her to corner me with all her questions about my studies. Lutfa didn't have that problem. Daughter of a bonded labourer and a Muslim girl child, she wasn't supposed to venture anywhere near the temple of learning. I often thought that Lutfa attended some sort of a school behind my back. How else could she know so many things about almost everything?

'Don't worry, I'll come. Keep the torch with you.' I tried to reassure her.

Lutfa hid the letter and the torch under a haystack and advised me to join her at seven, soon after Ramdeen, the night watchman, struck the metal bell with his hammer to announce the time.

I threw the usual tantrums during dinnertime, declined to eat and went to bed with the plea that I had a bad stomach cramp. Mother administered a herbal concoction and served food to the rest of the joint family. I slipped out, shared hot fish curry and rice with Lutfa, and retrieved the letter and the torch before heading for the Brahmaputra.

Lutfa was an expert field rat. She led the way through the darkness dragging me by the *gamocha*, the thin cloth towel that worked as a belt around my waist. We crossed the banks of Gagan deeghi, a mini lake and climbed the railway embankment. Lutfa flashed the tiny torch as we negotiated a small forest patch and the cremation ground.

'Don't you think it's too risky?' I asked.

'What's so risky? We've been to that hideout before.'

'I'm not talking about that. I mean the ghosts. They can attack us. Those longhaired, toothy and pitch black ghosts who suck blood.' I stammered as I spoke.

'Don't be silly. There are no ghosts. Just chant the name of Lord Rama. He'll save you from the evil spirits.'

Lutfa started muttering the name of the Hindu god and I followed her. We rolled down a sandbank and landed on the wet mud of the riverside. The entire place looked eerie, covered with tall grass and assorted foliage. The sandbanks were dug up at places by wild jackals that foraged the riverside in search of crabs, small fish and floating corpses. Lutfa encouraged me to go deep into the jackal holes, often spanning a couple of hundred metres.

'Wait.' Lutfa gestured with her left hand and entered into a big sand hole. She returned in two minutes and asked me to follow. I climbed into the gaping hole and landed in a big cave. Its walls and floors were lined with bamboo thatch and candles provided the bare minimum lighting. I had never been to this secret joint of the freedom fighters.

Lutfa moved around freely. She had access to the most secretly guarded niche that included my grandpa's iron chest buried deep under the floor of his bedroom. Lutfa had strange stories to tell about the chest and its contents. Gold and gems, some earned, some plundered and some acquired through questionable means. Lutfa was different. I had implicit faith in her abilities to make things happen out of impossible situations. I followed her inside the cave that was more of a foxhole, enlarged by the volunteers as a hideout. With two openings, they never had to gasp for oxygen.

Lutfa stopped at a bend and called out to Uncle Satish in a whisper. Two youth appeared from behind the shadows and flashed a torch on her face. 'What do you want?' someone asked in a surly voice.

'Call Uncle Satish. There's a message for him.'

'From whom?'

'Why should I tell you? Call uncle.'

One of the dark shadows disappeared and the other stood guard. Uncle Satish appeared from another tunnel. He took us to a corner and read the letter under the narrow beams of the flashlight. 'Are you sure about the timings?'

'Yes,' Lutfa replied, 'the train passes around 2 a.m.'

'Okay. Take care. Return by a different route. Tell Mudra to wait behind the fruit bushes.' Uncle Satish disappeared behind the shadows of his companions.

We climbed out of the caves, took a detour through the paddy fields, avoided the railway colony, and reached home well after 8 p.m. I went to bed straight away not to sleep, but to fool my mother, who, I knew, was sure to hit her bed by 9.30.

Lutfa came at ten sharp, woke me up by throwing small pebbles on my bed, and dragged me along to a remote corner of our cowshed.

'What are we doing here?' I asked.

'Shh . . .' Lutfa signalled silence and whispered, 'I know what they're up to. Wait. We'll follow them.'

'What's the great mystery?'

'Shh . . .' She dragged me behind a bush. Aunt Mudra arrived first. She was joined by two other burka-clad women. The three female figures walked past the cowshed and disappeared inside the chasm of the dry canal bed.

'Where are they heading for?'

'Follow me.' Lutfa followed the shadows at a discreet distance. I trailed her rather reluctantly. I wasn't sure if I was doing the right thing by chasing shadows at a time when I was supposed to dream sweet dreams.

Aunt Mudra and her burka-clad companions climbed up the canal banks and headed towards Jagannathpur, the village eight acres south. The rail tracks took a sharp right turn near Jagannathpur before heading towards the sub-divisional town of Kishoreganj. The track passed through a dense forest. We never ventured to that notorious forest, the one favoured by the legendary dacoit Ramzan Ali and a couple of striped Royal Bengal tigers.

The team headed by Aunt Mudra squatted on the track and started dismantling some nuts and bolts. One of the women spoke for the first time. 'Give me the spanner and remove that fishplate.' It was Uncle Satish's voice. There was no mistaking it.

'I've removed two. Now let's wait for the train. Where are the other volunteers?' The other mysterious voice replied.

'They should be somewhere nearby. Ramzan is expected to send his son Suraj to help.'

'Is he reliable?' asked Mudra.

'He's with us in this game of fighting the British. We'll overrun the police station and the small army picket once we get these weapons.' Altaf Hussain chuckled happily.

We were just about twenty yards away from them. I pushed Lutfa. 'It's time we go home. Mother would kill me if she finds my bed empty.'

'Wait,' Lutfa placed her ears on the ground and held her breath, 'I hear some approaching footsteps.'

'Could be Ramzan and his gang. Let's run.'

'No. Wait.' Lutfa ran like a doe and soon returned. 'It's not the dacoit Ramzan. It's the police and Dukhia is guiding them.' Lutfa clutched my hand and we ran in the direction of Aunt Mudra's hideout.

She wasn't pleased to see us. 'What the hell are you doing here?'

'Run aunty, run fast. A police party is heading for this location. Dukhia is with them.' Lutfa managed to blurt out.

One of Mudra's companions removed the veil. Uncle Satish peeked out of it, 'How did you know?' he challenged.

'We saw them coming. You run, I'll manage.' Lutfa didn't wait for them. She grabbed some green twigs and leaves, and dumped them on the track that had been tampered by uncle Satish. I helped her. We finished the cover-up operation in five minutes and ran back to the safety of our beds.

We woke up late, very late for the primary school run by Dhiru Acharya, the stern disciplinarian. My fellow students milled around the courtyard in excitement.

'What's the problem? Hasn't the teacher come?'

'He's there. But a police party is in the classroom. They've summoned all who count in the village,' replied cousin Mani.

'Why?' I feigned ignorance.

'Don't you know? There's been a rail accident at Jagannathpur and the dacoit Ramzan has looted all the weapons of the British army,' cousin Mani added boastfully.

Aunt Mudra and an array of servants entered the building with trays of snacks and sherbet.

Grandpa Chandra Kishore, seated at the head table, an imposing photo of King George VI hanging over his head, politely helped the minions of the law with liberal helpings of snacks.

'Daroga sahib,' grandpa started in his inimitable oily voice addressing the officer in charge, 'I've sent a telegram to the

Collector Bahadur to set up a permanent police camp in my village. I can't allow the anarchists and revolutionaries to disturb the laws of the King Emperor.

'Your point is well taken. We can't allow these terrorists and dacoits to get away with this. The empire is too powerful to succumb to such small pinpricks.'

Lutfa came in carrying two hukkas, one for the Hindu and the other for the Muslim officers. She fanned the blazing charcoal pieces that allowed the officers to have satisfactory puffs at the specially blended Motihari tobacco.

'Shall I bring some tender green coconut water for you sir? You must be thirsty. The cool sweet water would refresh you.' Lutfa added.

'Why not?' prodded Aunt Mudra. 'Get some green coconuts.'

Grandpa maintained a dignified silence and allowed the young Muslim girl to have her way. The irresistible charming girl had become a part of his life too. She had inherited from her father Rahman the proprietary right to blend the homegrown tobacco with molasses, fragrant condiments and liberal doses of opium. That was our grandpa's favourite concoction.

The police party left after a lavish lunch with an elaborate gourmet menu. All of us heaved a sigh of relief, especially Lutfa and me.

Soon after the departure of the police contingent, another high-powered team descended on us. The District Collector, an officer of the Imperial Civil Service, and the Superintendent of Police, a member of the Imperial Police camped at the revenue administration building. A large number of youth, mostly Hindu, were arrested and consigned to the Dacca prison. Aunt Mudra and Uncle Satish were spared thanks to our family status. Father Debendra was in Calcutta and was not a suspect. Grandma Chandrakanta, from behind a muslin veil, assured the Collector that her family would never support disruptive activities.

The rail accident and the plundering of weapons by dacoits were about to become another folk tale, to be sung by mothers at bedtime. For me, however, it was far from a story about the exploits of a gang of dacoits. I was vaguely aware that arms and ammunitions were in the hands of a band of revolutionaries who were committed to liberating the country from British rule. I suspected my father was one of them.

Lutfa didn't disappoint me. It was a rainy afternoon. Overcast skies, clouds hanging over treetops and strong winds sent panic signals; another cyclone was on its way. The cows were driven inside the sheds, the ducks to their coops and the children under light quilts. The elders chanted the names of numerous gods and goddesses and Rahman kneeled on a mat to say special prayers.

Mother pushed me under a quilt and squatted before the family deity, Mangal Chandi, invoking her mercy. She was soon engrossed in reciting a longish composition believed to be a sure prescription against all natural and manmade calamities. Seasonal cyclones in our part of the Meghna basin were as feared as the horrendous goblins that reigned over the night and knocked at every door.

Lutfa had no fear of goblins like *brahma daitya* (Brahmin ghosts) and *mamdo bhoot* (Muslim ghosts). She knew the magic mantra Rama that scared away all evil spirits. She turned up amidst strong winds and drizzling rain and crouched below my window pelting small pebbles at my quilt. I peeped out. 'What's the matter?'

She put her right index finger on her lips and signalled me to sneak out of the house. Mother was busy reciting her mantras and invoking her goddess.

'It's a severe cyclone, Lutfa.'

'So what?' She tugged at my gamocha and said, 'recite after me: *Bismillah ur Rehman e Rahim.*'

'What does it mean?'

'It's another way of calling Rama and asking him to blow away the dark clouds.'

I chanted the mantra after her and Lutfa guided me through the wooded banks of our family pond. I thought both Rama and Bismillah had gone to sleep under heavy quilts or our chanting was not loud enough. The storm hit us with wild ferocity accompanied by blinding lightening and darting rain. We were wet like wretched ravens. Lutfa dragged me through the sugarcane field and finally reached a clearing. Uncle Satish and four others were squatting under a waterproof canvas smoking cigarettes. 'What's the message?' he asked.

Lutfa spoke in a cool voice, 'Father says the weapons have been cached at Chandiber village, under the debris of the old mosque.'

'Any policemen?'

'Kalimuddin's men have disappeared. But Uncle Dukhia is on the job. He visited the military camp this morning. His men are everywhere. The camp commander has given him a motorcycle to shuttle around.' Lutfa shared her inputs like an expert. 'Pick up the weapons tonight and here's a letter from Aunt Mudra.'

We huddled under the canvas and waited for the storm to abate. My excitement ran high. The chance of being scolded and slapped by mother for defying her orders and braving the cyclonic storm failed to frighten me. Neither was I afraid of my cousin Dukhia.

'Give this to Mudra and tell her that we'd be at Chandiber tonight.' Uncle Satish handed over a heavy cloth wrapped packet to Lutfa.

'What's in it?' she asked.

'Just give it to Mudra. Now go.'

We walked through mud and slush and trudged back home. I insisted on avoiding the lizard's nest. Lutfa smiled and took a detour through a bamboo bush and the olive and chalita groves. She buried the packet under sodden bamboo leaves.

'Pick up the olives,' she commanded and started picking up ripe and green olives that had littered the soggy ground.

'Hey you two,' a rude voice shouted. 'What the hell are you doing here?'

We looked up. Cousin Dukhia, a powerful torch in his hand and a mahogany black goon behind him accosted us.

'Collecting olives,' Lutfa replied calmly. 'Some are ripe. Would you like some?'

'Don't act smart. Why did you go to the sugarcane field?'

Lutfa looked up and replied with ready wit. 'Not the sugarcane field. Been to the canal to lay fish traps.'

'Fish! What bloody fish?' my cousin's shadow shouted.

'Any that gets caught into the trap. How do I know which fish would be in?' Lutfa dodged the mahogany looking ruffian and resumed picking olives.

Cousin Dukhia suddenly grabbed Lutfa's wet hair and slapped her face with his muddy palm. 'You daughter of a miserable servant. How dare you talk to me like that? Tell me where you've been. And you stupid fellow.' He stepped towards me menacingly.

I ducked and ran. Lutfa wriggled free and joined me. Cousin Dukhia cried out obscenities and chased us. Fleet-footed Lutfa ran straight to Aunt Mudra's bedroom. I hit the bed.

Dukhia had smelled blood. He rushed in, stood under the huge litchi tree, and called out to Rahman. Busy in cutting haystacks for cattle fodder Rahman came out. The hurricane lantern in his hand failed to repel the thick darkness but it was sufficient to lighten up the ugly and angry contours of Dukhia's face.

'Anything I can do master?' Rahman asked in his usual docile voice.

'You bloody *goolam,* bonded labour, daring to insult me?'

'Master, I've met you for the first time in three days. When did I insult you?'

'Your whore of a daughter did.' Dukhia roared like a ferocious jackal.

The drama and din woke the others some of whom, including Aunt Mudra came out. Lutfa stood behind her. Grandpa wasn't in the habit of coming out of his room after 7 p.m. post his opium session but Dhukia's shrill cries disturbed his slumber. 'What's going on?' he roared out rather sluggishly. The evening opium dose had slowed down his speech.

'This goolam and his daughter have insulted me. He should be punished, here and now.'

'Katia,' grandpa shouted at a Garo tribal, 'tie Rahman up against the bottle palm tree and give him forty lashes.'

The grand patriarch retreated into his private chambers. Katia, a six foot dark demon started dragging Rahman to the nearest and thickest palm tree. My father intervened. 'What's his fault?'

The entire family gathering was mortified at the temerity of my father. Who was he to challenge the order of the supreme patriarch? Uncle Birendra, by far the closest ally of my grandpa intervened in a loud voice. 'Who're you to challenge father's orders?'

'You can't punish a man for nothing. What's his fault? Did you ever try to find out what that little girl did?'

'She's a terrorist. She helps gangs of swadeshi revolutionaries. She's a collaborator of Satish and that gangster Altaf. How can our family allow such seditious creatures to roam freely?' Dukhia blurted out with frustration in a loud voice.

'Enough is enough,' Grandma Chandrakanta stepped in, 'Katia, leave Rahman alone. And you Dukhia, I warn you not to broadcast our family secrets. Your British masters are bound to go eventually, mind you my words. Don't play into the hands of collaborators.'

Grandpa was the supremo but our grandma was the godmother of the family. She was our ultimate anchor. The old patriarch never challenged her. He simply didn't have the guts.

Dukhia limped back to his quarters like a wounded jackal followed by that mahogany-coloured shadow of his.

'All of you go in. I don't want any discussion on what happened.' Grandma Chandrakanta spoke in a soft but firm voice and disappeared into her room.

Katia recoiled like an earthworm and Rahman re-entered the shack to complete his chore, cutting haystacks for the bovine members of the extended family.

∾

After the freak cyclone and equally terrible Dukhia drama subsided, we feasted on rice and fish for dinner and retired early. I woke up gingerly as Aunt Mudra shook me gently. I had no idea of the time. 'Shoo . . . ' Aunt Mudra gestured with her index finger, 'follow me.'

We tiptoed out of the room and proceeded along the areca nut-lined dart road towards Chandiber village. 'Where's Lutfa?' I asked nervously.

'She can't come tonight. Show me the way to the old mosque.'

'Follow me.' I jumped out of the dirt road and followed a shortcut through millet and sugarcane fields.

'Let's follow the road,' Mudra protested. I reminded her of that evening's encounter with Uncle Satish and Dukhia. If he was true to the salt of his masters, he should be on the prowl. And Kalimuddin, the chief police sleuth wouldn't hesitate to respond to Dukhia's emergency call. She nodded in appreciation.

An unknown young man emerged out of a bearberry bush with a long barrel revolver in his hand. 'Bande Mataram.

Hail the Motherland.' He greeted us with the slogan of the freedom fighters.

'Bande Mataram,' Aunt Mudra replied. 'Where are Satish and the others?'

'We're here.' Uncle Satish and his gang materialized out of the thick dark night. They disappeared behind the walls of the mosque and I was asked to wait outside. I couldn't control my curiosity. I climbed a broken wall and peeped down. Mudra, Satish and ten others were seated around candlelight. Each of them held weapons which glistened under the dim light. Uncle Satish was talking of attacking the lone platoon army picket near the ice factory below the Anderson Bridge.

The young man who had greeted Aunt Mudra spoke in an animated voice. His idea was to overrun the police station and loot the weapons. They talked at length and finally settled on blowing up two vital spans of the bridge. That was more important than killing a few soldiers. The bridge was the only lifeline between Dacca and Calcutta and the rest of estuarine Bengal, especially the vital district of Sylhet, which acted as the steady supply artery to the Burmese front.

Excitement made me oblivious of fast approaching footsteps. Uncle Satish stood up with a rifle in his hand and looked out through a hole in the wall. No, it wasn't an enemy contingent, it was Lutfa. 'Run, they're coming.'

'Who?' asked Aunt Mudra.

'Dukhia, Kalimuddin and many policemen. They're armed.'

Uncle Satish gave a terse command to his group to take up their positions and fire on his command. Aunt Mudra intervened. She advised the group to retreat, conceal the arms and ammunition, and wait for a better opportunity. Dukhia, she said, was a despicable viper and his grandpa wouldn't hesitate sacrificing anything and everything to protect his dearest grandson and his British title.

The group picked up their weapons and melted into the dark night. Three volunteers whom I didn't know stayed put. Lutfa was asked to assist them to load the heavier weapons on a boat berthed at a nearby canal.

Aunt Mudra signalled and asked me if I could guide her back through a safer route. I knew the safest route that passed through the courtyard of Brajen Acharya, a paramedic, and the backyards of the fishing community.

As we crossed the water-filled ditch and climbed a fence to enter the courtyard of the carpenter Atul Sutar, the fireworks started. Gunshots rang out repeatedly breaking the stillness of the night. We ran like mad dogs and finally made it to the safety of our compound. Aunt Mudra entered her room and advised me to get back under my quilt.

'What about Lutfa? I should guide her back.'

'Don't bother. Lutfa knows how to melt into the nearest Muslim village. They don't suspect the Muslims of Chandiber,' Aunt Mudra assured me with her soothing voice and a full rupee coin. The silver coin did not hold its usual attraction. I hid behind the thickest palm tree and waited for Lutfa. Despite my anxiety and will power, I dozed off.

~

The next morning the people of Kamalpur and the neighbouring villages rushed towards the abandoned mosque. Military personnel had joined the police force and mounted an assault on the terrorists. Cousin Dukhia and his acolytes receded to the rear lines and started haranguing the villagers. 'Encircle the enemies of His Majesty the King Emperor,' he commanded but no one paid attention to his rabid exhortations.

Grandpa Chandra Kishore stood under a guava tree and ordered Katia to prepare his hukka. He didn't appear to be perturbed. He enquired briefly about his cousin's son Satish and his own niece Mudra and went into his opium-induced slumber, with occasional puffs at his hukka.

The firing stopped after about ten minutes. The army personnel crawled up the broken walls and dragged out three dead bodies. I was told that they were classmates of Uncle Satish from Dacca University, and were involved in revolutionary activities.

One of the soldiers dragged Lutfa out by her hair and forced her to lie prostrate on the ground. A police sepoy handcuffed her and cousin Dukhia kicked her repeatedly. Kalimuddin grabbed Lutfa by her hair and made her sit on a wooden bench.

'Who are these dead people?' he boomed out.

'No idea.' Lutfa replied in a composed voice.

'Who're the other gang members?'

'What gang are you talking of?'

'Were Satish and Altaf there with the gang?'

'Who is Satish and who is Altaf? I don't know them.' Lutfa shook her head.

Kalimuddin banged her back with a mighty slap. Lutfa stumbled and fell on the ground. Another kick from Dukhia followed. 'Are you a member of the terrorist and swadeshi gang?'

'Yes.'

'Where are the looted weapons?'

'Won't tell you.' Lutfa tightened her lips.

'Tell me why have you done this? Why have you fired on the police force?' Dukhia kicked her again.

'Bande Mataram.' Her feeble but determined voice shouted back at Dukhia and other agents of the Crown, 'We're fighting for independence.'

'Hang your bloody independence.' Dukhia hurled another kick at her groin.

'Allah is great. He will give us freedom. Bande Mataram.'

No one dared echo her mantra of self-determination and independence. I nudged closer to her but my mother whisked

me away. I squirmed out of her arms and rushed towards
Rahman who was sitting on the ground, his arms extended
and palms cupped towards the sky. He was praying to Allah
for his only daughter Lutf-un-Nissa.

Kalimuddin and his police force aided by the soldiers and
Dukhia dragged the 'dreaded terrorist' Lutfa towards the police
station. She didn't look back and refused to respond to my
cries as I ran alongside the mighty police force alternately
shouting the name of Rama and Bismillah. Her eyes were
magnetically locked somewhere on the horizon. The crowd,
some in a festive mood, some in pain followed the party.

Newspaper reports and village rumours depicted Lutfa as
a martyr. Some reports depicted her as a bandit queen, an
accomplice of Altaf, the brigand.

But I knew the real story. Rahman too was aware of
her links with the revolutionaries. But being bonded labour,
Rahman wasn't attuned to the cult of protesting. He took
me to Brahmanbaria jail to meet Lutfa only once. She was
lodged in a solitary cell. That's how dangerous enemies of
the Empire were treated.

'How're you Lutfa didi?'

'I'll be free soon. Independence isn't very far off.' I missed
Lutfa.

Subsequent events moved so fast that our lives were
incapable of keeping pace with the fierce cyclone of history
in the making: the reported death of Netaji on 18 August
1945, America's barbaric act of dropping nuclear bombs on
Hiroshima and Nagasaki, Japan's surrender, and the end of
the Second World War.

∽

20 August 1945.

Father returned home from Calcutta late in the night.
He travelled by river ferry to avoid the police dragnet. Four

unknown faces accompanied him. I was in bed tucked under a thin kantha, a comforting light cotton quilt, reading a fairytale, *Thakurmar Jhuli*. We loved these traditional grandmother folk tales.

'Sushama,' I heard father whispering, 'I've brought some guests. Please serve them some food.'

'Nothing special at home except rice and dal.'

'That's enough. Subhan mian,' he addressed one of the strangers, 'come inside. No one should see you. We leave soon after dinner.'

The guests hustled in silently. Each of them carried pistols and bulging sling bags. 'Hey Akram,' the man called Subhan whispered, 'take care of the bags. All are live bombs. No accident inside Deben's house.'

I was acquainted, courtesy Lutfa, with words like bombs, pistols and rifles. As they washed up and settled down to eat some rice, lentil and dry fish curry, I scurried out of bed and took out a bomb with a protruding wick that looked like a coconut. The pungent odour smelt like rotten eggs.

'We're leaving, Sushama,' Father said, 'take care.'

'When will you be back?'

'There's a mission in Sylhet. I should be back in three days if things go well. My dear, take care of the kids if I don't return. I'm sorry that you married a stupid like me.'

'Take care. They say Netaji is dead.'

'We don't believe it. Japan has surrendered but Netaji will continue to fight.'

'He is brave but the British are stronger. Our Congress leaders have also betrayed Netaji.' I saw her touching my father's feet, turning away from him and wiping her eyes. Mother sat before the image of goddess Chandi and chanted mantras that I did not understand.

I woke up a little late and anxious. Where in Sylhet had my father gone? To fight a war against the British? Aunt Mudra, who listened to All India Radio regularly and read

the *Statesman* avidly, announced that the British had trounced
the Indian National Army, recouped the Azad Hind gains in
Manipur and that the Japanese had surrendered. Could my
father and a few freedom fathers face the British might and
defeat them?

Saifullah, my classmate from a neighbouring village,
Jagannathpur, and mother's reminder that it was time to
leave for school disrupted my contemplative mood. Walking
past the railway station, we traversed the narrow paddy field
pathways.

'You look serious Krishna. What happened?' Saifullah
asked.

'I can't stop thinking about Lutfa,' I replied.

'Where is your dad?'

'He's gone to Calcutta.'

'Dudu mian says he's a dacoit. Your dad fights the British.'
Saifullah referred to Dudu mian, headman of Jagannathpur
and a Muslim League stalwart.

'Look Saifi,' I reported as if I was a senior counsel, 'my
dad is not a dacoit. He helps freedom fighters. He has gone
to Calcutta for a political meeting. Tell Dudu that he should
not support the British.'

'Are we going to be free? Dudu mian says Hindus and
Muslims require different kinds of freedom—Hindus for
Hindustan and Muslims for Pakistan. Where would you
go?'

'Hindustan or Pakistan, I would stay here in my village.
Where would you go?'

'Same here. My village is my world.'

Our small political talk ended there. We had matured a lot
politically after Lutfa's arrest and the gangs including Aunt
Mudra's, dispersed. Saifullah ducked and dragged me behind
a shrubbery of thorny bushes.

'Look on your left. Dudu mian and Subhan Ali's gangs have
lined up with deadly weapons. They were on either side of

a railway culvert that ran over a gravel road to Bhariabpur village. Both the gangs were armed with lethal weapons: long swords, spears, bows, arrows and some handguns. Dudu mian's group was shouting '*Allah ho Akbar, ladke lenge Pakistan*' (we'll take Pakistan after fighting). The mixed Hindu and Muslim gang of Subhan Ali was shouting 'Bande Mataram, *azad Bharat zindabad*' (long live free India).

We had very little time to think. The school was still 300 metres away and our pathway almost skirted the battlefield chosen by the supporters of Pakistan and Hindustan. We ran as fast as we could and landed behind the thatched houses of Rani Bazaar. It was the official red-light district patronized by men belonging to all conceivable religions and political hues, the loved, hated and romanticized abode populated by women from who knows from where.

'Run in,' a female voice hustled us in, 'they have started fighting.' She was a middle-aged woman, not much older than my mother. Saifullah whispered into my ears. 'These are bad women. Let's run towards the school.' His steps froze as an armed crowd rushed past us shouting 'Allah ho Akbar.'

The woman shoved us in and closed the door. 'They're going to attack the Hindu traders. It's a bad day. Stay put and get back home when things settle down.' She offered us some sherbet and sat by my side. 'Nice kid. What's your name and where are you from?'

'Krishna. Dhar family, Kamalpur.'

'And you?' She asked Saifullah.

'Saifullah, from Jagannathpur. And you?' Saifi asked in a doubtful voice, 'Are you Hindu or Muslim?'

'Don't know. How does it matter? Enjoy the sherbet and go home in peace. In here, there is no Hindu or Muslim. We're in a common business.'

'What's your business?' I asked.

'No need to know till you grow up. Just go home and don't go out till your elders allow you.' She lit a bidi and looked out through a small window. 'These mad Hindus and Muslims will ruin us all. Hindustan and Pakistan . . . spoiling my earnings for the day.'

'Did you say something?' I asked.

'No dear. You're from a big home. Tell your elders to stop this madness. They fight for their spoils and we starve. Now get out and run for home. I hear the police announcing curfew.' She pushed us out as calmly as she had dragged us in.

We rushed out, climbed down the slope and ran towards the railway station. 'Why did you say she's a bad lady?' I asked as we ran.

'She's a *randi*.'

'What's a randi?'

'Bad women. Ask your mom. Now get to the station and run for home. No school tomorrow. See you in a day or two.' Saifi crossed the rail tracks like a hopping rabbit, crossed the dry canal and ran towards his village. I wondered about bad bazaar women. A shout from Purno Sangma disrupted my contemplative mood. I scurried to the safety of our part of the village, wading past a mixed armed crowd of Hindus and Muslims headed by Purno, a hefty Garo retainer of the family.

'Rush back home,' Purno shouted. 'It's a riot.' Purno was a tall tough fellow and the commander of the small private army of our family which lorded over the tenant cultivators and bonded labourers.

I obeyed and ran home. Mother hustled me in and pushed me inside a small room, ten feet by eight feet, guarded by a small force headed by Rahman Sheikh and a few other family retainers. Armed with swords, *ramdao*, those long scimitars with curved heads at the top, and spears they kept a sharp look out for invaders. With fifteen odd kids in the room, and the doors and windows closed, we felt suffocated. We were told to keep quiet. The army of Muslim League raiders was on their way.

Rahman opened the door after about two hours and warned us of dire consequences if we ventured out to the football ground or anywhere near the railway station.

Late in the day, Uncle Birendra returned from Bhairab market and announced that the skirmish between Dudu's and Dhala's group of Pakistan protagonists had been defeated by the mixed undivided Hindustan crowd headed by Subhan Ali and Joinath Dhar, one of our uncles, third removed. Dudu mian's gang suffered five casualties from pellet wounds and three of the Subhan group suffered sword blows. It was a victorious day for the undivided Hindustan protagonists.

The family elders and the women folk squatted around the radio set to listen to the main political events of the day. H.S. Suhrawardy, the premier of Bengal, delivered a speech that sounded ominous with veiled threats, followed by a speech by Kiran Shankar Roy, a leader of the Congress Party. He spoke about peace between Hindu and Muslim communities and even indicated that Sharat Bose, the brother of Netaji Subhas had convened a meeting of the Hindu and Muslim leaders to discuss the preparation for a blueprint of a united independent Bengal.

Cousin Adhir, about eighteen years older to me, and a student in Calcutta, gathered us around the cemented platform near an ancient banyan tree. He lit his favourite Scissors cigarette and asked, 'What did you understand from today's events?'

'Hindustan and Pakistan,' replied my cousin Mani. He was supposed to be the cleverest of the lot who invariably scored above eighty in his school arithmetic papers.

'Correct. We Hindus are for Hindustan and the Muslims are for Pakistan. Soon there will be a great Hindu and Muslim war.' Adhir added.

'What would happen to Rahman and his son Jasim?' I asked referring to Jasimuddin, Lutfa's brother.

'Hindus will kill Muslims and Muslims all Hindus. We all go to Calcutta. That city is sure to be in Hindustan.'

I was not convinced. Lutfa was a Muslim yet she fought for our independence. Altaf, Subhan and Paran mian were my father's colleagues in his revolutionary activities. Rahman Sheikh was my best guide and teacher, and Jasim and Saifi were my best friends. I felt dejected. But there was no one around to whom I could unburden my heart. Father was away to Sylhet and mother was free from her family chores only after nine at night. My elder brother Benoy was busy with his studies. He was a serious and sincere student unlike me.

'Better not go to school for a few days. Let your dad return from his business tour. Study at home.' Mother spoke as she ran her fingers through my hair.

'What is a bad bazaar woman, Ma?' I asked.

'Who told you that?'

'Saifi.' I narrated the incident of our brush with that bright looking woman, 'She was good, Ma. She gave us shelter and offered us sherbet. How could she be bad?'

'No woman is bad, son,' she patted me affectionately. 'Men force women to become bad.'

'How?'

'You'll know when you grow up.'

'What's Baba fighting for if we've to go to Hindustan and leave our village?'

'Ask him when he comes home.'

❧

Father returned after four days, rather late in the night. Akram and two others accompanied him. His friends dispersed after dinner. I heard Mother talking to him in a low voice.

'It's time you paid attention to your family. Your brothers are planning to shift to Calcutta and Agartala, the capital of the Hindu kingdom of Tripura. Your elder son is in Dacca, our daughter and her family are at Kendua. She is expecting another baby.'

'The Muslim League is proposing the merger of Sylhet with Pakistan. We have to stop it.'

'You haven't inherited the burden of the whole nation. Netaji is gone. Congress is planning to partition the country. Suhrawardy has overshadowed your idol Fazlul Haq. He's the premier now. You can't fight alone.'

A long spell of silence followed.

'I know Sushama. There's a madness in me. I don't know when to stop. What should I do?'

'I suggest you get in touch with the Congress leaders. Seek a political career with them.'

'How can I abandon my friends? They're my trusted fighters. We've grown up together. I can't leave this soil just because a few Congress and Muslim League leaders want the entire nation on their dinner plates.'

'Look, the poison of religion has infected most of the people. They've brought religion to the centre stage of national politics. You alone can't prevent this. Sail with the wind when you're rocked by a storm.'

'Okay. Let's go to Kendua to look up our daughter Parul. On our return, I'll visit Dacca and take directions from Hemanta da.' Hemanta Bose was a Forward Block leader.

The story of our brief visit to Kendua and Mymensingh ended on a tragic note. Parul, our eldest sibling died while the doctors were performing a Caesarean section to remove a dead baby from her womb. Our sorrow was compounded further when our brother-in-law turned up with his baby daughter and son and informed my parents that he was going to his parental home to marry another woman. Our parents were overwhelmed with grief.

'Why should he marry again?' I asked Ma as I slipped into her bed.

'We women are helpless. They treat us as chattel. They maltreated my daughter for a dowry of just five acres of land. Now she is gone. Don't ever maltreat a woman. Remember all are born from a mother's womb. *Janani janmabhumisha swargadapi gariasi* (mothers and the motherland are more exalted than heaven).'

The grand idea of janani and janmabhumi did not sink in until the magnitude of the tragedy hit us. I witnessed my mother suffering silently after Partition, our forced evacuation from Pakistan to an unknown corner of Hindustan, and my father's sudden death. The meaning of both janani and janmabhumi dawned on me much later. The cutting of the umbilical cord does not separate a mother and a son; and the redrawing of political maps does not alter the essence of janmabhumi.

two

First Train Out of India

14 April 1946.

Much later in life, I learnt about the Big Bang theory about the creation of the universe. Human history is witness to such manmade bangs, which brought down civilizations, created new cultural and national histories and newer changes in the geophysical features of the planet.

The first bang, a mini one, had disrupted our lives in a shattering explosion. That was the beginning of major political and societal changes in our village on the banks of the Meghna and the Brahmaputra. As a seven year old, disturbing happenings in the country worried me but failed to rein in my playfulness. Communal tensions were simmering under the surface and the historical ties that united us—Hindus and Muslims—started crumbling.

The first manifestation came in the form of a blatant act of indiscipline by Dhala who was in charge of our cattle herd of about fifty. Assisted by two Hindu attendants he tended and milked the cows. We always thought of him as an uncle and part of our family. We called him Dhala kaka.

One dark monsoon evening when the rays of the setting sun painted the low clouds with innumerable colours Jatin, Dhala's assistant ran to grandfather's door. He was trembling.

'What's happened Jatin?' Katia, Grandpa's personal valet asked.

'The heavens have fallen.'

'What bloody nonsense! Out with the facts.'

The story narrated by a trembling Jatin sounded absurd and impossible. Dhala mian had stolen a tender calf and killed it for the Id festivities. He had warned Jatin of dire consequences if he told anyone.

Seven in the evening was opium time for Grandpa. But the indomitable patriarch and self-styled zamindar stood up and shouted, 'Katia, get that *haramzad*. The bastard must be punished for an unpardonable offence. From where does a goolam get such guts?'

Katia ran with a small force to the western part of the village that was inhabited by Muslims and low caste Hindus. He returned with Dhala within an hour. But Dhala was not alone. A sizeable group of Muslims headed by Dudu mian, the flag bearer of the Muslim League followed him.

Grandpa's dispensation of justice was instantaneous. Punish Dhala with twenty lashes, Katia was ordered, and Uncle Upendra was asked to file a complaint for theft. The dictator ordered the cancellation of three bighas of land granted to Dhala's family. In the court of a landlord, such punishments were the norm but this time voices of protest rang out loudly.

Dudu mian intervened. 'You can't do that, *karta*. Once we have Pakistan, which will be soon, all your lands would be ours. You can't punish Dhala for a minor crime. Eating beef is a part of our religion. Take money as compensation. You've no right to forfeit his land grant.'

Chandra Kishore exploded. 'Upen,' he ordered his fourth son, 'throw them out and inform the police.'

Dudu mian was devastated and cried out 'Allah ho Akbar' repeatedly. Debendra walked up to Dudu and comforted him by saying that Dhala would have to accept the punishment for stealing a calf. However, he should not whip up communal frenzy. He turned towards Chandra Kishore and did the unthinkable. 'You can't whip Dhala. Let's hand him over to police for the crime.'

'Who're you to intervene?'

'Well! I'm your son, but I've a duty to the people.'

'What bloody people? I am the master. My order shall prevail.'

'Whipping is illegal.'

'What? You dare to challenge me? Upen, draw up my will, I want to disinherit this rebellious son of mine.' The gathering was stunned.

Mother stepped in and implored Grandma Chandrakanta to intervene. 'No,' Grandpa refused to relent, 'today he's encouraging Dudu and Dhala and tomorrow he'll fight His Majesty's government. I don't want a black sheep in my family.'

Soon after, my father got a tin-roofed house constructed at the far end of the family pond, far enough from Chandra Kishore's homestead. Gradually it sank into our minds that we were separated from the main family just because of a few words uttered by a displeased father. No one had the guts to stand up to him and his paid and unpaid private army.

It gave very little comfort to anyone when Dhala was arrested by the police and released after about fifteen days in informal custody and some bone-breaking beatings. We heard on the grapevine that Dhala was released on the intervention of a Muslim League leader from nearby Brahmanbaria town. Dhala soon emerged as the number two man of Dudu mian and a flag bearer of the militant Muslim forces.

∽

The 7 p.m. radio bulletin on 20 April created a commotion in the family. At the western court building of the premises occupied by grandpa, Uncle Birendra tuned the only family radio, an old German Grundig, to catch All India Radio's broadcast of the day's most important news bulletin. Most adult male members surrounded the radio, the women folk took back seats and we children were shooed out.

The news broadcast was of no interest to us children. However, the size of the gathering impressed us—about ninety adults crammed into the big hall. Their glum faces signalled alarm. Jasim, the son of our family retainer Rahman was the only member of our group to walk in and out of the room. He had important duties to perform—filling the earthen hookah clay pots with molasses-treated Motihari tobacco, serving water and fanning grandpa with a palm-leaf fan.

'What's happening Jasim?' I asked.

'Big problem Krishna. *Kanit Mison* (the Cabinet Mission) has told Gandhi and Jinnah that we Hindus and Muslims have to live together.' Jasim replied in a grave voice.

'What is Kanit?'

'Kanit is a big white man from London.'

'What would happen to our independence fighters?'

'You ask too many questions. We'll fight the British. Your father is fighting, his group is fighting, Netaji is fighting. Don't worry.' Jasim disappeared with two tobacco-filled clay bowls.

That night, after an early supper, four of us assembled behind the croton bush, our nearest rendezvous. Jasim enlightened us by delivering a small lecture on the struggle for independence by Netaji, Gandhiji, Jinnah and others. We would soon be free from British rule. The Cabinet Mission was looking into the places where Muslims and Hindus would live.

'Why do we require separate places?' I asked Jasim. 'You and I live in the same village.'

He sucked on a piece of dried green mango and replied, 'I don't really know. Perhaps now onwards we Muslims can live in your part of the village.'

Jasim referred to the system created by our ancestors to settle people in our sprawling village according to caste and religion. Our part of the village belonged exclusively to our extended family and a couple of assorted Hindu castes that serviced the upper castes and other common villagers like fishermen, carpenters, blacksmiths and barbers. Only Rahman Sheikh, our bonded labour and his family were allowed to live in a plot of land on the far side of the family pond. The rest of the lower caste Hindus and Muslims were settled on the western side of the village across the railway line.

We did not doubt what Jasim said. A boy of ten, he was not as mature as Lutfa was, but he was as clever. Often my window to the world was through his eyes and mind.

Cousin Mani added his bit. 'None of you are correct. Brother Adhir knows better. He says India will be partitioned. Hindus would live in Hindustan and Muslims in Pakistan.'

I protested, 'We have been living together for years. How can one fellow called Cabinet Mission decide where we should live? I won't go anywhere. This is my village and Lutfa, Jasim and Saifullah are my friends.'

'You're a fool. Do you know how much I score in arithmetic? Who doesn't know you're a dud in arithmetic? Do you want to challenge Adhir, my big brother and a student in Calcutta?'

I digested the dig with humiliation. Mani was correct. I was notoriously weak in arithmetic, never scoring more than forty. Well! I did well in Bengali and English.

We were confused. Would we have to live separately? What would be the shape of Hindustan and Pakistan?

That night father returned from Dacca around ten p.m. where he had gone to attend a meeting of the Bengal Provincial Volunteers (Forward Block), a revolutionary group with which the legendary names of Panchanan Chakravarti, Hemanta Bose and Satya Gupta were associated. Debendra, an accredited ayurvedic medic, practiced more in peripheral revolutionary activities than in the science of indigenous medicine.

After dinner, he sat down at the edge of his bed and told mother that the news of Netaji Subhas's death was incorrect.

Congress leaders were conniving with the British to declare him dead. He was safe in Russia and was likely to reappear soon and take command of the country.

'Would the Congress and British allow him to return?' mother asked.

'That's a problem. Jawahar is playing into British hands.' Then the penny dropped. 'The most disturbing is the Cabinet Mission's attitude. They want to give Dominion status and Congress is ready to grab it. I doubt if Jawahar would agree to share power with Jinnah. He is a power monger. I must prepare the boys for a decisive fight against the British.'

'Why? Netaji is not there. Your friends are busy with political power games. Your dad has disinherited you. Take care of your family. We need the money.'

'My dear, soldiers of liberation don't bolt the field even if the General has fallen. I don't mind being disinherited. I'm fighting for the inheritance of the people of India. Netaji should be back any time. We must fight.'

'As you wish. But take care of your children.'

'You're there. You're my strength.'

∾

Father left home two days later. I saw him boarding a train for Calcutta. Mother did not shed tears. She visited three neighbouring villages and convened meetings of Hindu and Muslim women to teach hygiene, basic childcare, sewing, and making marketable handicrafts from palm and coconut leaves. She and a few other women of our village cluster formed an association to maintain communal peace.

Grandfather Chandra Kishore hated my mother for her daring acts of lifting the veils of societal sanctions, educating women, and encouraging people with ideas of social changes.

I went back to school and to the world of Jasim, Mani, Saifi and Rani. The ever-busy railway station reverberated with activity and our football team captained by Rani continued to score goal after goal against the teams of neighbouring villages.

Rani, though a girl of about thirteen was our team captain and leader of most of our outdoor activities including pinching coconut and other fruits from neighbour's gardens. There was no shortage of fruits in our own gardens, but fruits stolen from the neighbour's gardens tasted sweeter, lemonier and more pungent. Life went on and we did not bother about political events. However, the shadows of political events did not stop chasing us.

Jagannath Jola from the community of weavers, *julaha*, who lived next to the railway station created a commotion sometime in early July. He waved a Bengali newspaper, which carried a picture of an emaciated person with a sharp face and a cap on his head. The lead story quoted him, 'We shall have India divided, or we shall have India destroyed.'

The rest of the news story was not intelligible to us kids. Jagannath shouted like a possessed person, 'We want Hindustan. Mahatma Gandhi zindabad, Netaji Subhas zindabad.' He succeeded in attracting a small crowd.

Dudu and Dhala were not far behind. They also gathered a big Muslim crowd and raised slogans, 'Qiad-e-Azam Jinnah zindabad, Fazlul Haq zindabad, Suhrawardy zindabad, ladke lenge Pakistan.'

Both sides started throwing stones and assorted missiles at each other. We ran for cover. Jasim dragged me inside the compound of the sub-registrar's office and entered the premises of a Muslim employee. 'Stay here. No one will harm us at my aunt's house.'

We peeped out through the thatched bamboo perimeter fence. A tall imposing person flanked by a gun wielding escort walked in and straightaway dragged Jagannath Jola out of his teashop and slapped him. 'No one raises slogans for Gandhi or Hindustan, Jinnah sahib is bringing Pakistan for us. We Muslims own this country.'

The gang headed by Dudu and Dhala forged ahead and showered blows on Jagannath. The rest of the Hindu crowd dispersed. The small vending stalls owned by Hindus had been demolished and Jagannath's teashop was set on fire.

We ran home. It was my first close brush with a direct Hindu Muslim conflict. The event happening on our side of the village was a direct challenge to the authority of Chandra Kishore. Our extended family elders and elders of other Hindu families were summoned to the community hall for urgent consultations.

We kids peeped in curiously and with apprehensive looks on our faces. Were we going to be divided into two countries? I was conscious of India or Hindustan being our country. The creation of another country, a Pakistan out of India puzzled me. 'We've been living together in India for so many years. What is the need for a new country for Muslims?' I asked Jasim.

'Don't know. Lutfa knows better. Should we ask my baba?' Rahman was busy pruning the croton hedges. He looked worried. 'Don't really know. I presume Jinnah wants to rule over one part and Gandhi on the other. It's a fight between two kings.'

'So, it's a war between two kings? What about the present king, the king of England, who owns us?'

'He wants to go home. We want independence. Gandhi wants his and Jinnah his own. You and I are trapped between two giant rocks.'

Rahman's reply did not satisfy me. I stood outside the chandimandap and heard the elders debating the burning issues. Chandra Kishore, suffering from chronic unrealistic glory, filibustered the meeting by proposing to lead a deputation to the district magistrate and superintendent of police, submitting wired messages to Fazlul Haq, Kiran Shankar Roy and other leaders. He favoured summoning the local police chief and directing him to arrest Dudu and Dhala.

Subhan Ali and Matanga Roy, the local Congress leader spoke about the great national divide and total withdrawal of British initiative in maintaining law and order.

'Karta,' Subhan spoke in a mild voice, 'the British have abandoned us. They have now left India to the mercies of Congress and League leaders. Partition is inevitable. I'd request you to tread cautiously.'

'I agree,' said Matanga. 'Let us convene a peace committee and maintain local peace. The madness of our leaders should not affect us. We have to live together, be it in Hindustan or Pakistan.'

'I'm a respected mahashay. The Lt Governor would listen to me.' Grandpa tried to assert his aristocratic superiority.

'No karta,' said Rashid Sarkar, a schoolteacher, 'we can't maintain peace for long. Bihari and upcountry UP Muslims have started migrating here. They speak Urdu. They don't understand our Bengali culture and unity. Let's form a peace committee with important Muslim and Hindu leaders like Madhu mian, Chhoban Khondakar, the sub-registrar, government doctor, the headmaster of the high school and a few leading businessmen. Why don't you head this committee?'

'We *namahsudras* would support the League. Big landlords have not done anything for us.' Panchanan Mandal said in a forceful voice on behalf of the low caste Hindus.

'Pachu,' grandpa roared. 'How dare you speak like this? I'm still the zamindar and you till my land.'

'Karta, forget these old things. We're getting Independence. We won't be your serfs anymore.'

Chandra Kishore stormed out of the meeting, entered his private chambers and asked Katia to prepare his opium. Nonetheless, Uncle Birendra agreed to chair a peace committee. He had a big business at Bhairab market and he was in no position to antagonize the majority opinion.

On 20 July, my father returned from Calcutta. Dejected, his gait betrayed his state of mind. 'What's happening?' mother asked him after an early dinner.

'Bad times are ahead. Jinnah is adamant in his demand for a Muslim homeland and Congress is yet to decide the ultimate fate of India. The British officers like Sixsmith and Walker are very unhappy with the Hindus and pro-Netaji forces. They have not liked the observance of INA and Captain Rashid Day. They're determined to divide the country. I fear the worst. Jinnah has given a call for Direct Action Day on 27 July. I fear huge bloodshed. Suhrawardy is determined to swing the entire Muslim League towards Jinnah.'

'What about Fazlul Haq?'

'He's in a minority. He would be forced to follow other provincial leaders. Abul Hashim, the Muslim League general secretary is opposed to Partition.'

'What do we do?'

'Stay put, and watch the situation. Sharat Bose and others are trying for a united independent Bengal. Suhrawardy is not averse to the idea.'

'I think you should plan on shifting to a safer place.'

'Can't. They're talking about a merger of Sylhet with Pakistan. Jinnah wants the whole of Assam. Nehru is not averse to the idea of giving Assam away. We cannot allow that to happen. I must go over to Sylhet to campaign for a united independent Bengal and Assam's inclusion in India.'

'Stop dreaming, dear. Try to see reason. Neither the Congress nor the Muslim League is ready for a compromise. The British wants to break up the country as they did in 1906. We should plan to move up to Calcutta.'

My curiosity got the better of me. I jumped out of the bed and blurted out. 'Do we have to leave the village?'

Father was stunned. I had never asked any questions so far, not on such serious issues. He had no time for us, beyond his swadeshi activities and love of music. He was almost a stranger to me.

'I am not sure. Be careful. Don't move around aimlessly. Take care of your Ma.'

I failed to understand how I could protect my mother in the event of attacks by a hoard headed by Dudu or Dhala but the feeling that he had placed his trust in me stretched my imagination. Immediately I had visions of me standing guard over my mother with an open sword. I spun another daydream of leading my children's army with Saifi, Jasim and others by my side with bows and arrows, swords and daggers. It was not just a dream. I took out my small knife that I kept hidden under the bed, an improvised bow made out of split bamboo and arrows made out of dried jute sticks with sharp ends of bicycle spokes as arrowheads.

Our total army of six met at the bamboo grove and planned a battle order to fight Dudu and Dhala. Our idea about the enemy was confined to a gang of villains. We had no idea of larger and mightier villains of the political parties.

The perplexities of the situation were compounded by the sudden arrival of several grown up cousins from Calcutta. They were government employees and private entrepreneurs and working as trained professionals. Visitors from Calcutta always excited our imagination. Calcutta was like a distant heaven, full of surprises and fun. This time around, they did not bring gifts and candy. Calcutta, they said, was bracing for a holocaust. We had no reason to disbelieve them.

The next night presented us with the most ghastly experience. Around 9 p.m., two stout Marwari businessmen limped to our house and knocked on the main gate. Ramdeen, the Bihari guard rang the warning bell and called the elders of the family.

The visitors were bleeding profusely from stab wounds on their fat bellies. Their story was horrifying. Travelling to Chittagong from Dacca they were attacked inside their railway compartment by a gang of Bihari Muslims. They were stabbed and thrown out of the compartment after their belongings had been plundered. They walked along the dry canal bed to reach our home.

Grandpa Chandra Kishore did not come out of his room. Katia stood guard with a double barrel gun. Father Debendra helped the Marwari traders and attended to their wounds. He directed Sabur mian, one of his followers, to the police station to request the chief to rush with a force.

Mother called Father aside after the din settled down and the injured traders were shifted to a hospital. 'I'd like to go to Dacca.'

'What for? A train journey is not safe. You saw it for yourself.'

'Our elder son Vijay is in Kurmitola. I'd like to be with him.'

'Don't rush into a situation. He'll be okay. Kurmitola is an army base and he's working with an army contractor as a junior engineer. Stay here and take care of the rest of the family. I have to go to Sylhet. He will be safe in the army cantonment. It's not safe anywhere anymore. I think the Leaguers and the Bihari Muslims won't disturb Dacca so soon. Calcutta, they know, would go to India and Dacca to Pakistan. Stay calm and help the womenfolk maintain the peace.'

Father's soothing words did not remove our fears. Tension hung in the air. Suddenly the Muslims started looking at us with cynical eyes. Except Saifullah, our other school friends avoided us. Jamini, the school chowkidar was dismissed by our headmaster Abdur Razzak, a noble looking person. No one knew why. However, our language teacher Sher Ali spoke volumes about the virtues of having a Muslim chowkidar instead of a Hindu one.

Uncle Birendra was a member of the school management board. However, he declined to intervene. Next day, Ibrahim, the new chowkidar, served our tiffin of puffed rice balls sweetened with *gur*, delicious brown sugarcane molasses, and a ripe banana.

Information reached us through newspapers, radio broadcasts and people returning from Calcutta that Hindu Muslim riots had started in a big way. This fearsome news was followed by the arrival of the Chittagong Mail at Bhairab station with loads of dead bodies.

Saifullah, Jasim, Mani and I were playing our favourite game at the railway siding. We climbed the wagons and tried to jump to the next roof to prove that we had super human abilities. We jumped like monkeys but never suffered injuries. Badan Misr, the portly Bihari porter ran in and shouted at us to climb down. We obliged because we respected the authority of his red uniform and a metal medallion he flaunted around his neck. Badan was a permanent feature at the railway station.

'What's happened Badan kaka?'

'Bad things are happening. The Chittagong Mail has arrived with three compartments full of dead bodies.'

We ran towards the platform where the train was cordoned off by a few policemen. Some of the porters were being directed to offload the dead and injured people. We stood at a safe distance and counted about forty dead bodies and nearly twenty injured men and women. The outer walls of the stricken compartments bore strange chalk marks—a big circle with a crescent moon in the centre.

The ghastly scene rattled me. I stood rooted and wondered why all these Hindus travelling to the safety of their rural homes from Calcutta had to die! My first brush with mass killings generated mixed feelings—fear, anger, sadness and pain. I wondered if Jasim, Saifi and my other Muslim friends would kill me in the name of Hindustan-Pakistan. I shrugged off the idea. We were Bengali people, both Hindus and Muslims. Our village, our land of Bengal would remain united and I would have the opportunity of growing up with Jasim, Saifi and my other Muslim friends.

I returned home with a heavy heart. Jinnah's Direct Action Day in support of Pakistan was carried out with direct precision and total indifference by the British heads of administration. One story had it that Suhrawardy had recruited 1200 Bihari Muslim sepoys to Calcutta's police force to counterbalance 1200 Hindu sepoys. Calcutta witnessed a bloodbath.

The British rulers were more eager to escape from India than implementing the rule of law. They had the blood of feuding Hindus and Muslims on their hands.

∽

28 July 1946.

Rahman Sheikh and Subhan Ali rushed into our house with disturbing news. Muslim hordes had attacked the nearby villages of Kuliarchar and Sarail. They had killed over a hundred Hindus and kidnapped several women. Kuliarchar was the home of my aunt, one of the two daughters of our grandparents. Our anxieties were partly allayed when Aunt Kunti from Kuliarchar and Aunt Shanti from Baghaura in district Comilla reached our home with their extended families.

It was not a joyous reunion. Fear and uncertainty stalked our minds. However, we still had to be fed and cooks prepared our usual Bengali food to feed over 200 members of the joint family and the guests. The retainers had their own kitchens—one for the Hindus and the other for Muslims.

Neither did we stop playing football nor swimming for hours together in the family pond. We were, however, restrained from visiting Bhairab railway station, attending the junior and senior high schools and splashing in Gagan Deeghi, the vast water body.

The radio set drew all the elders as the daily seaplane flight that delivered newspapers at Bhairab port had stopped operating since 23 July.

Uncle Birendra, in his capacity as the president of the Union Board, summoned a meeting of the elders of the port town, heads of nearby villages, representatives of the traders and a few British officials of the jute mills operating in our area. About thirty people attended the meeting at the secretariat campus of the king of Muktagacha (grandpa's land granting authority). A sub-divisional police officer from Kishoreganj was a special invitee. Political leaders, conceited bureaucrats, and the elite often make speeches for public. The assembled peers of the area spoke volumes about the centuries old communal amity, social interactions and shared economic fortunes.

Rauf Sardar, Dudu mian's boss from Mymensingh, represented the Muslim League, and Subhan Ali and my father's boss from Dacca, Manilal Dutta represented the United Bengal forces. The meeting co-chaired by Birendra and Jack Smith, a jute-mill manager, administered an oath of amity, that the Hindus and Muslims of the area would maintain peace and would not allow Bihari Muslims to disturb the peace. A peace committee was formed and a volunteer force was raised. People returned home with pensive smiles on their faces.

That night Ramzan mian, the notorious river pirate and dacoit visited our home along with his sons Suraj and Chand. The Ramzan gang had some links to the swadeshi movement. He helped out with money, looted weapons, and occasionally with a work force.

Mother prepared tea and served homemade snacks. I crouched behind a huge wooden rice vat and listened.

'Things are bad Deben karta. The League people have hired the gang of Nibharsa that untrustworthy dacoit. He has about fifty men and good weapons. His gang was responsible for attacking Kuliarchar and Sarail.

'Why don't you oppose him?'

'We can't as it's not a fight over spoils but political banditry. How can I go against the general feelings of the Muslims?'

'Don't you support our United Independent Bengal movement?'

'I do but both Congress and the League is opposed to the idea. Suhrawardy might agree but on his own terms. Jinnah will not support him on this demand. This Khoja Muslim wants his own kingdom. And the other Kashmiri Brahmin wants his own turf.'

'What do you suggest?'

'After the great Calcutta killing, they are planning even more killings in Dacca, Noakhali and Sylhet. The League and Assam Congress want Sylhet to go to Pakistan.'

'It's well known. What do you want me to do?'

'Leave the village for a short period. Your peace committees and unity movements cannot stop the killers. Suhrawardy and Jinnah are exporting Muslims from Bihar and UP to this part of the country. They want to destroy the popular bases of Fazlul Haq. They don't like our peaceful coexistence.'

'Where do I go? I never thought of leaving all of you.'

'Boudi,' Ramzan addressed my mother. 'You have your parental home in Agartala. Go over there, just for a few weeks.'

'Ramzan bhai,' mother replied, 'that house at Banamalipur has been taken over by my maternal uncle. I don't think he would like the idea of my claiming that property.'

'Don't claim it. Just go over a short period. Would you like to have a pistol for self-defence?' Ramzan asked my father.

'No Ramzan,' father replied, 'I can't fight an army with a single pistol or kill poisoned hearts with bullets. Let me know when we should leave for Agartala. But I assure you that I'll be back after a few weeks.'

'Boudi, keep this,' Ramzan offered a bunch of currency notes to my mother, 'You will need it in Agartala.'

'No thanks, I don't need it.'

'Keep this Deben karta. I have been your follower all these years. I've a right to assist you.'

Ramzan and his sons disappeared in the darkness of the night. A gang of six waiting in a boat that was berthed in a small lake joined them.

∽

5 August 1946.

Rahman rushed in again at about 7 p.m. with bad news. A gang of Bihari Muslims had arrived that evening from Dacca and had summoned Dudu and Dhala for consultations. The gang had pitched tents on an open ground in front of the house of Shashi Nath, a weaver by caste. The Biharis served intoxicants and their fair looking women were enticing local Muslims by singing popular film songs.

In fact, Dudu and Dhala had ganged up with the Bihari Muslims and were planning to attack villages with a sparse Hindu population. Later when Bihari reinforcements arrived from Dacca, our Hindu majority village would face attack.

The elders of the family doubled up our security by mounting guards all around. Over 180 Hindu inmates of the village congregated at our sprawling campus with whatever arms they could lay their hands on. They had not come to defend us. They had abandoned their homes for the secure walls of the big landlord's house.

We kids of the immediate family were huddled inside huge wooden crates of about eight feet in diameter and eight feet in depth, dry vats that were used to store rice. The womenfolk were pushed inside a big room in the northern building that was guarded by about twenty able-bodied males.

Rani, our football and sports captain, who stood guard with a ramdao was the only daughter of Mukunda Majhi, our retainer fisherman. She knew no fear. Rani's assurance always carried credibility. She was the fastest swimmer, she scored the vital goal at an unexpected moment and plucked ripe mangoes from the tiniest twigs. I was an avowed fan of this thirteen-year-old playmate and friend. She had taught me several tricks of football dribbling and the art of climbing the tallest trees to steal coconuts, jackfruits and mangoes.

The night passed off peacefully though we nearly suffocated inside the wooden vats. That fateful night was also the beginning of the end of our joint family and our family's suzerainty over the village and the mahashay status at Bhairab, Sarail and nearby villages. Grandpa Chandra Kishore sank into his opium and his sons decided to go their own way, separately, to safer abodes at Brahmanbaria, Mymensingh and Agartala. Each one was on his own. We started parting company as if we were strangers in a weekly market. We were on our way to uncertain destinations. Brothers did not share their thoughts with brothers; cousins guarded their secrets, about their destination of flight to more secure places.

The subjects and royats looked helplessly at Grandma Chandrakanta. She was the only person to declare her determination to stay put in the village. 'I won't go anywhere,' she proclaimed. 'Deben please send a telegram to district magistrate Saunders and police superintendent Dutta.' (G.C. Dutta was later a senior Joint Director of the Intelligence Bureau and security in charge of Indira Gandhi). 'I'm a British grant holder and I get a yearly *nazrana*. I won't go anywhere till the maharani orders me out.' (My grandmother sometimes lived in another era—this was her reference to Queen Victoria).

Her loud proclamation could not restrain three of her sons from leaving the village. Uncle Birendra left for Brahmanbaria after temporarily shutting down his business; Uncle Upendra stayed put at Bajitpur. Uncle Harendra, in charge of the river steamer service at Narsinghdi, decided to stay out there. Our uncles, our father's cousins, boarded trains for Agartala.

Father followed his mother's request and sent a telegram to the DM and SP, and started mobilizing his supporters. SP

Dutta arrived on the third day. He marched to our house with a small police force and confabulated with grandpa and grandma. 'There's very little that I can do. It appears the British want to leave the field to Muslims and Hindus to fight it out. I don't have the manpower to control the situation. The Muslim officers don't carry out my orders. The Hindu officers are worried and don't dare challenge the Muslim hordes.'

'You represent the maharani,' Grandma insisted.

'Don't be misled by my uniform. I'm opting for India—most Hindu officers are. Most of the rajas of Mymensingh have left for Calcutta. It's better for you to go to safer places till the tension clears up.'

'Who'll worship the family deity?' Chandrakanta was referring to the life-size statues of Gauranga, Vishnupriya and Netai (worshiped by Vaishnavites as reincarnations of Vishnu, the Hindu god).

Dutta consoled the old lady, 'Entrust some employee. It's a matter of a few weeks. The gods should be able to take care of themselves. Men can't in the present circumstances.'

That clinched the issue. We prepared to leave our roots at Kamalpur in India. Father decided to go over to Agartala, the capital of Tripura, a princely state with special treaty relations with British India. (The ancient Hindu kingdom of Tripura acceded to India after Independence in 1947). But leaving the village did not mean mere physical dislocation. It was a kind of spiritual trauma. Only dislocated people know this pain. I felt that my dislocation would also dislocate the birds, butterflies, the hens and ducks, my dearest friend Tomtom, the dark brown dog, mother's favourite Chandana, the talking parrot; and my constant companion Pintu, the all-white goat. Who would take care of Sonai, the graceful mother duck?

What would happen to Rani, Jasim, Saifi and other friends? I revolted. 'I won't go.'

'Don't worry. Rahman, Jasim and the others will take care of our pets. Our maid Ranga will take care of the ducks.'

Her assurance could not assuage my apprehensions and pain at the very idea of leaving the village. 'Who'll worship the family deities?'

'Don't worry. Rani would come daily, light the lamps and burn the incense sticks.' Mother had a ready answer.

'What will you do if the Biharis attack you?' I confronted Rani.

'Don't worry. We're low caste people. They're targeting the big people like you. We're a fishing community. They'd require us to catch and supply fish for their kitchens.'

'Yes, *khoka*,' Rahman joined the chorus. 'Young boy, it's a matter of a few weeks. Such madness comes like a malarial shiver and disappears with time. We're going to stay here in this village be it in Hindustan or Pakistan.'

We were the last to leave the village and take a train for Akhaura, on the Tripura border from our dear Bhairab station. I had no idea that my father was so popular with the masses. A small crowd of about two hundred turned up to say goodbye and wish him an early return. Subhan Ali and a few other political colleagues of United Bengal Movement also boarded the train. The assembled crowd raised slogans hailing Netaji Subhas, Fazlul Haq and other leaders.

'Are you also coming to Agartala?' mother asked Subhan Ali as the steam engine started rolling.

'No boudi. We are going up to Akhaura to escort you. Some Biharis have started attacking passenger trains,' replied Subhan Ali. 'We'll come to Agartala to pick you up once the mad League people settle down. Times are bad and it's better for Deben karta to remain out of sight. The League and Congress people hate him. No one supports his ideas.'

Mother's eyes shifted towards the green fields and the horizon beyond. Father animatedly discussed the issue of a united Bengal and left instructions for Subhan and the others to go over to Dacca and Calcutta to lobby with Fazlul Haq and Suhrawardy. I was lost in my thoughts about Tomtom, Chandana and Pintu. My elder brother Benoy consoled me in his usual mild voice. He was my antithesis. A studious person he loved books and had few other interests. To divert my attention he started reading stories such as *The Selfish Giant* and *Lady of the Chalet*. My mind was not with the giant who finally overcame hatred and anger and died in love.

The distance of about sixty miles from Bhairab to Akhaura was completed in little over an hour. Subhan Ali arranged a special vehicle out of the chaotic mêlée. A few thousand Hindus scrambled for seats in a handful of motorized vehicles to take them to the safety of Agartala. They pushed each other, fought with blows and abuses. Each was on his own. Scrambling for safety had snatched away all human values.

For the first time I saw that big money could also be made out of human misery. The touts, both Hindus and Muslims, charged exorbitant rates for providing horse drawn tongas and bullock carts. Some of the scoundrels tried to tease the young girls and made obscene gestures at them. Much later, I realized that trading in human misery was the oldest trade in the world. They traded in merchandise, flesh, misery and helplessness.

My first journey out of what was then part of India to a part of a future India had begun with strange lessons in human behaviour that were never taught in schools and history books.

three
___

A Brief Escape from India

Courtesy Subhan Ali, Akram and Hassan Ali Mintu, all workers of the Bengal Volunteers, Forward Block and United Bengal Movement, we boarded a respectable looking bus. Our baggage was dumped on top of the carriage. It had a capacity of carrying thirty passengers. It was stuffed like a chicken-coop. It lurched precariously, the left side tilting nearly by a foot. The road to Agartala was a sea of humanity. Indians were escaping from their country to the safety of a princely kingdom. They walked on foot, rode in bullock carts, horse tongas and cycle rickshaws.

My eyes were riveted. The distressed and panic stricken faces did not appear to be strangers. We too were in jeopardy and running to safety and I felt an affinity with them. Tears rolled down my cheeks and I sobbed rather visibly. Mother drew me closer, wiped my eyes, and consoled me.

'Don't cry. It's a matter of a few weeks. We'll be back, be it in Hindustan or Pakistan. Let the madness pass over.'

Father was quiet. For the first time I noticed that the usual placidity and radiance had disappeared from his face. What was he planning? I was not in the habit neither were we encouraged to ask questions. In a huge joint family, we kids were left to mothers, philosophers and guides like Rahman. We grew up along with wild flora and fauna. We were almost born free. The elders did not have time for us. Especially father who was no good at practical affairs. He was busy with politics, music, composing songs and very occasionally in the science of ayurvedic medicine.

Much later in life when I tried to understand my father, I realized that he was a strange combination of a silent revolutionary, a stoic, and a chronic believer in the goodness in men. Was he a lesser version of the ancient Stoics like Persius, Thrasea Paetus and Seneca, the famous teacher of Emperor Nero? For a son it's not unusual to dissect the character of a father who was so distant when alive and such a vague figure when he left me when I was just nine years old.

On that early afternoon of 9 August I was worried about my father. Suddenly he drew me close to his chest.

'Don't be afraid of life. When you grow up you'll know there are peaks to climb, seas to cross, and deserts to negotiate. Steel your mind and resolve when you face danger, so said Netaji. This is your first encounter with danger.'

He patted the back of my older brother. 'I've been a poor father; never looked into your problems. Sorry for that. Be a good father when you grow up. You're the older one. Remain steadfast in your studies and take care of your ma and brother.'

'You're not going to war, Baba,' he replied in a low voice, 'you're with us.'

'I'd be with you even when I'm not there. The war has started. We don't know what's going to happen but I have to fight.'

His words, the first intimate expressions of love and affection, soared my sagging spirit. I realized I wasn't afraid of an unknown Agartala. Knowing the unknown was my father's forte. Why should I be afraid of the unknown ahead?

∼

The bus dumped us at Gole Market, a cute round-shaped area with plenty of greenery and tin and thatched homes around. It was not as impressive as our sprawling and thriving Bhairab Bazaar, an important river port on the Meghna and a flourishing export centre for fish, chilli, jute and rice. British trading agents dominated the market helped by their traditional allies—the descendants of Jagat Seth, the most important facilitator—for the establishment of the British Empire.

The market area looked chaotic with the flood of people from India overwhelming the tiny capital town. Makeshift thatched structures had sprung up to cater to the needs of the refugees. The human butchers took advantage of the old market cliché: create scarcity, soar up demand, and hike up prices. A lozenge, sold at our favourite railway station, Bhairab, for one paisa was being sold at four annas.

Father managed to haggle with two rickshaw pullers to transport us and our baggage to Banamalipur, a respectable locality in a corner of the capital. The Banamalipur home was supposed to be my mother's inheritance from her late mother. However, it was occupied by one of her maternal uncles and he followed the golden policy: physical possession is de jure possession. We were supposed to be his guests.

Back in 1946 Banamalipur was a rural habitat of about 250 Bengali Hindus who either worked for the Tripura Durbar or pursued other professional vocations. The Bengali speaking Tripuris like the Deb Barmas and Dev Barmans, mostly related by blood to the royal family or descendants of the royal class lived in separate quarters. The Bengali gentry maintained a respectful distance from them. Most of them were addressed as kartas, like a Sachin Dev Barman (S.D. Burman of Bollywood) would be addressed as Sachin karta. That signified the dignified distance between ordinary Bengali gentry and the blue-blooded Tripuri community.

Most of the tribal people lived beyond the town limits, on the far banks of the Gomti, beyond forested Bishalgarh, Takarjala, Chandrasadhubari, Kasba and Gobindapuar or in the Jampui foothills. They were different from the Tripuris and Bengalis. Most of them belonged to the Reang, Jamatia, Chakma, Halam and assorted Kuki, Garo and Mizo branches of tribes. Even in 1946 there were Santhal, Munda, Oraon Bhutia and other tribal groups in the kingdom of Tripura.

. On a later occasion in 1948, on my first visit to India from Pakistan, I was amazed to see the kaleidoscope of Tripura's tribes when the groups came down to Agartala on Garia Puja, Vijaya Dashami, Kharchipuja (the fourteen gods' festival in July) and other festivals. Though generically described as Hindus, the tribal groups like the Halam, Chakma etc. maintained their Buddhist identity, and most other groups practised a different form of Hinduism which embraced plenty of tribal cultural characteristics and the worship of distinct local deities. What bonded them together was the Habugra kings of Tripura who had gradually taken on a Hindu Bengali identity and culture and the honorific title of Manikya Bahadur. The Ujjayanta palace and the institution of kingship had built up a bridge of trust between the tribal communities and the state of Tripura. In 1946, Bengali culture and religious practices were confined to the Bengali speaking community and those Tripuris who had come in touch with Bengal and Bengalis in the course of intermarriages, business transactions and administrative interactions. Tripura was not beyond the cultural pale of Bengal, yet it was a unique parabola of tribal diversities.

Banamalipur was a rectangular shaped locality, its size and contour following the banks of the sprawling water body. My mother's maternal uncle Brajmohan Dutta (Braj dadu), an employee in some office of the royal government of Tripura, lived on the northern bank of the water body. On the south bank lived a more affluent brother of my eldest aunt. He was known as Dinesh Nandy, supposedly a high official in the king's court. We were allowed to live in a big tin-roofed house amidst green vegetation. Mother, like a magician, had set up her kitchen. Father, I think for the first time, started practising his ayurvedic skills and my elder brother Benoy was immersed in his books. I did not think I carried mine. But mother sprang a surprise when she took out my book from a tin portmanteau and started teaching me arithmetic, English, geography and history.

I thought the flight out of India offered me an extended holiday. It did not. I had to study at least four hours a day. I used the rest of the time to survey all that I could in the company of a few cousins who had also migrated to Agartala. My skills in manipulating the catapult, making bows out of bamboo sticks, arrows from jute straw and cycle spokes, my ability to climb the tallest coconut tree and swim past the huge water body in record time had also earned me the admiration of a few tribal boys. I had made friends with Dayal Reang and Mantu Jamatia. Much later in life, Dayal told me about his son becoming a communist leader and later a minister in the government of Tripura.

Dayal and Mantu helped me explore the small town, its market places, the Ujjayanta palace, two ornate towers flanking the abode of the king and other wonders. The Maharaja Bir Bikram Manikya Bahadur College and the Malancha Bhawan impressed me immensely. Malancha was the place where Rabindranath Tagore had spent some time and wrote some of his pre-Nobel Prize compositions. The Maharaja of Tripura had contributed liberally to Tagore's pre-Nobel journey to England. They were great patrons of Bengali art and culture.

The cottage was well maintained and had become a tourist spot. I was fascinated by a line of Tagore's song written on a polished bamboo plate: 'Jakhan aamar payer chinha parbe na aar aei bate.' (When my footprints won't be treading this road).

Much later in life I realized the deep philosophical meaning of the song derived from Baul (a mix of the Muslim Sufi and the Hindu Bhakti cult) metaphysical philosophy. On a later visit to Malancha with my wife in 1969, on a sort of pilgrimage, I could not find that polished bamboo strip and the invaluable line. Perhaps the burgeoning palace of the governor, and the heavy urbanization in the vicinity had removed any signs of Tagore from the historic house. Similarly, the disappearance of Tagore's imprints from his homes in Shillong and in Mongpu, Darjeeling did not surprise me. Succeeding generations deify a persona like Tagore but they forget to preserve the ambience that goes into the making of a genius.

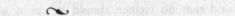

Dayal Reang was a genius. He knew the secret abodes of wild elephants in the forests beyond Joynagar, an upcoming habitat of the migrant Bengali community. In late August, he and Mantu Jamatia called me out for a fishing expedition to a pond near Joynagar, a distance of about three kilometres. Mother was opposed to the idea. My maternal grandfather objected on the grounds of my abhorrently close association with the Reang and Jamatia boys. He alleged that my parents had spoiled me by allowing me to keep the company of Muslim boys and girls and of the lowly tribals. How could a blue-blooded Bengali fraternize with half civilized 'jungli' Reang and Jamatia boys?

These social considerations were anathema to my mother. Perhaps to register her disapproval she allowed me to accompany the tribal boys and stuffed our bag with some *chida*, puffed rice and lumps of *gur* for our lunch.

A journey of three kilometres, at the age of seven, was just like the Concorde flight from Paris to New York. It finished no sooner than it started. Our fishing expedition did not yield a huge catch. My share was a small bagful of over ten small carp. However, wild sprints along the banks and plucking fruit from a nearby orchard compensated for the paucity of fish that refused to bite our bait.

The wretched fish were uncooperative, but the wild elephants were not. Our wild sounds had probably annoyed a small herd, a bull and cow accompanied by a toddling calf. The parents stood erect on the high ground behind us and delivered two loud warnings. Dayal dragged Mantu and me and said, 'Run. These are wild elephants. They are new parents and are very protective of their calf.'

We ran and did not look back until we hit the dirt road to Joynagar, two kilometres away. Dayal sat under a blackberry tree and dragged me to his side. After a brief breather, he said that no chance should be taken with a charging wild elephant herd. Normally they did not attack humans. But they rampaged into human habitat, tea plantations and even plundered rice, paddy and other food.

'Why?' I asked.

'We are encroaching into their habitat. Until five years ago the forest stretched to the borders of Banamalipur and Joynagar. People from India and the neighbouring regions are pouring in and the elephants are getting angrier,' Mantu replied.

'It's like exacting taxes from us for intruding into their territory,' added Dayal.

'It would be better to go to Bishalgarh near the Gomti river for fishing,' Dayal suggested.

The idea sounded good. But who could ensure the absence of wild elephant herds in the forest tracts of Bishalgarh? I did not have a second occasion to walk into the abodes of the giant mammoths. They visited us early one morning, at about 3 a.m.

We were woken up by Braj dadu. 'Get up. Take the empty tin cans and beat them as loud as you can. Deben,' he said to father, 'you take this flaming torch. Light up the forecourt by burning wood, dry creepers and hay to frighten the elephants. A herd has invaded our village. Can't you hear drum and tin-can beatings? They come to loot food and they damage our homes, gardens and even kill people who come in their way.'

It was a fearful but exciting morning. We lit torches made of twigs, created loud sounds and shouted war cries as loudly as we could. A good hour later, the small crowd ventured out with flaming torches, drums and tin cans. The raiders of the wild had wrecked two houses, looted a few quintals of rice and some bunches of bananas before lazily walking back to their endangered habitat. I remembered Dayal's tax-realization simile. It was some kind of nature's revenge.

On my last visit to Agartala in 1990, a professional one, I got the impression that the elephants and nature had accepted defeat in the hands of the millions of Bengali refugees encroaching into their habitats. They had simply disappeared. My visit, however, reminded me that the descendants of the Dayals and Mantus had not accepted defeat gracefully. They were fighting back for their rights on the land that belonged to them. The invaders and occupiers failed to recognise the rights and privileges of the aboriginals. To the Dayals and Mantus the Bengali invaders had become devils.

In 1946, Tripura belonged to the Tripuris and other aboriginals. Now it is more of an occupied Bengali territory. Anyway, I could not record my real thoughts and feelings in my reports to the government. I was on a tour to study the 'Problems of Terrorism in Tripura'. I wished I could meet my friends Dayal and Mantu.

Another funny but crucial event highlighted our brief stay in Tripura. I had gone over to the far banks of Banamalipur's waters to the bamboo ramp in front of the house of Dinesh Nandy. Those days fishing was not treated as poaching. It was a sport.

Busy as I was focused on even a slight nibbling at the bait by any fish, small or big, I did not notice a toddler, not more than three years, walking up the ramp and proceeding towards me. He was probably fascinated by the rod and line that I was holding. Whatever it was, his feet slipped on wet bamboo strands and he fell into the pond. I dropped my rod and managed to hold his legs. His head was still in the water but I did not grasp the gravity of the situation. I should have pulled his head up and put his feet down in water. However, my shouts for help drew the attention of the Nandy household. I also managed to reverse the order of my rescue operation. The drowning child belched out water and I managed to bring him up to the bamboo ramp. The situation was then taken over by the elders.

That noon I was welcomed as a hero by the Nandy household, my eldest aunt's paternal abode. I was given a royal treat—sumptuous food with luchi, fried aubergine, fish and meat followed by mishti doi, delicious sweetened yogurt, and sweets. I was told I had saved a precious life, one of the youngest kids of the elder Nandy. The heroic incident was well publicized in the locality and I basked in its glory for a few days.

Later, I was told that the child had become a renowned doctor in Delhi. However, I did not get the opportunity to meet him again.

～

Our short escape from India was disrupted by the sudden appearance of Subhan and Akram, my father's political colleagues. Braj dadu did not welcome Muslim guests at his home so they stayed in a pice-hotel (pice was a unit of the old rupee), where one night's lodging and boarding cost less than sixteen annas, a full rupee. It was big money. Those were the days when rice used to sell for twelve annas a maund (approximately 37 kilos). They left after two nights.

Both Akram and Subhan were staunch political activists and opposed to the partition of Bengal. They and my father owed allegiance to Sharat Bose and Abul Hashim, all protagonists of a United Bengal.

Their visit lit up my curiosity. I pretended to be fast asleep when father began his political talks with mother. 'I think we've to get back. I've been summoned by Fazlul Haq. He wants to meet me and a few other Unity workers. I may have to go to Assam as well. The Assam Pradesh Congress Committee and Bordoloi are opposed to Assam joining Pakistan and the merger with India of the Sylhet district of Bengal and the Cachar areas of Assam.'

'Why?' asked mother.

'Don't you remember the Assam PCC resolution of 1945 which decried Bengali migration to Assam? They fear Bengalis gaining demographic majority in the event of Sylhet and Cachar merging with India.'

'What does Nehru say?'

'We don't understand him. He says Assam can remain outside the Indian dominion for a period and later decide whether to join India or Pakistan.'

'How can he say that? Assam is an integral part of Bharat.'

'Only Netaji could silence that egoist Nehru. Even Gandhiji has lost control of his creation.'

'You can't fight alone.'

'In a war like this the last soldier has to fight. Don't worry. You know me. You married a vain soldier. I'm sorry.'

'You don't have to be sorry after all these years. When did I complain? Have I not supported you? What do you propose to do? Is it safe to go back? The children can't remain idle for long. They must attend school.'

'I know dear. I think the Direct Action madness has cooled down. Suhrawardy is now clearly with Jinnah. He no longer supports a United Bengal. We can go back to a United Bengal or to Pakistan.'

'When do you want us to go?'

'After another week. Akram will arrange for our safe return. Our volunteers will guard the home. Don't worry. It is a critical time. Let's face the situation with courage. Tell the boys it's time to go home.'

I did not sleep for the rest of the night. I pretended to but it was the excitement of going back to our village. However, I was going to miss Dayal and Mantu. Would I be able to meet them again and go on fishing expeditions and face herds of wild elephants?

Akram and Subhan accompanied by Jatin Bhuinyan, another Bengal Volunteer activist were at the Akhaura station. We said goodbye to Agartala.

A small crowd waited for us with Rahman at its head to welcome us at Bhairab railway station. There were Muslims and Hindus, men and women. Jasim, Saifi and Haripada, the son of our village chemist, accompanied them.

We took the narrow village road past Gagan Deeghi, towards the betel nut tree and bottle palm-lined silhouette of our house. I was back where I belonged. Tomtom greeted me first, followed by Ramdin, the chowkidar. Pintu, happily munching on tufts of grass and flaunting his own tuft of beard showed up behind a thin crowd of family retainers. Chandana greeted us: *namoskar, asun, basun* (greetings, come and sit down).

～

On the face of it nothing had changed. The grayish black and sandy soil of my village contrasted starkly against the red earth of the Agartala hills and dales. The vegetation looked greener, the ducks shinier and the birds and flowers almost fairylike. This was heaven if ever there was one.

Our sprawling quarters and the neighbouring homes of our extended family hummed with activity. I was reunited with Saifi, Jasim, Mani, Haripada and other friends. Rani didi joined our football club. I resumed the three kilometre walk past the railway station to Kader Bux School. I was relieved to see that my world was intact.

Behind the apparent placid ambience, serious fissures were showing up brazenly. Mehboob Alam, my classmate broke the news first. 'Are you going to stay put in Pakistan or escaping to India?'

'We are living in India.'

'No my friend. This part of India will be Pakistan and things will change very fast. Father says we Muslims will get back our full rights on land and wealth.'

'That does not mean we have to escape.' Would we be forced to escape to India?

∾

The thought was suppressed by new developments. It was early October and Durga Puja was approaching. We were excited when on an auspicious day Dhiru Acharya, our primary teacher and village sculptor was summoned and asked to start building and sculpting the images of goddess Durga and other deities worshipped by Bengali Hindus so fervently. Five Brahmins were invited to perform special purification rituals. Special offerings were made to sanctify the raised earthen platform behind the chandimandap before the installation of the clay image. A grand festivity preceded the welcome of the Mother goddess to our home once again from her Himalayan abode. The women sang traditional *agamani* songs invoking daughter Uma (Durga) to come on her yearly short visit to her parental home. On the tenth day, she would return to her husband's home at Mount Kailash.

Dhiru Acharya applied layers of clay on the bamboo and hay structure of the images. Drapers, tailors, jewellers and vendors of cosmetics started visiting our homes from far-flung places like Calcutta, Dacca, Benares and Amritsar. They were followed by Kashmiri shawl and carpet sellers and Kabuli dry fruit vendors. In those days, we waited a year for these vendors to flock to our homes with their dazzling wares.

Sabbir Pathan came with the sweetest dry fruit, Afzal Ansari came with glass bangles, bindis and semi-precious stone ornaments. Sardar Kirpal came all the way from Amritsar with gold jewellery. Barqat Dar and Mehr Hangoo came with stoles and carpets.

Durga Puja was not just a religious festival. It was a big marketing event for traders from almost all over India. We all joined in the celebrations, some of us in new clothes. Ladies dazzled in newly acquired gold and silver ornaments, glittering saris, bangles and bindis.

It was a time of celebration and home coming. All family members were required by an unwritten covenant to reach the village home well ahead of the puja. Our city cousins were a hit with us kids. They smoked nonchalantly, spoke English, and exchanged tall stories about distant cities like Calcutta, Delhi, Bombay and Simla. Their stories often sounded stranger than the folk tales we were told by our mothers and aunts.

That year Adhir dada, our cousin pursuing some course in Calcutta was the star attraction. He brought what we thought of as a magic box. With his camera he clicked photographs of all our family members. He was an avid angler. His stories about fishing in the turbulent waters of the Ganga really scarced us. He came up with all kinds of stories to establish the superiority of the Ganga over the Meghna. We did not have the courage to contradict him. For us no other river could be wilder than our Meghna and Brahmaputra.

Our household help, the evil Dhiru was selected by Adhir to be his batman and cook cum housekeeper in Calcutta.

Mukund Majhi, a fisherman, and Rani, his daughter were allowed to live around a large water body, Satmukhi Beel, a lake with seven inlets and outlets. The water receded in the winters, but the cold wind brought in its wake flocks of strange birds from different parts of the world. With its rich paddy fields, fruit orchards and monsoon forests, our village was no less rich than the fabled niches in heaven.

Rani was not a show-off, but her story had become an inalienable part of our folklore, a story of courage and fortitude. Rani was more beautiful than a sea-fairy. I loved her charming beauty but I was not attracted to her physical charms. At seven, I was too young to appreciate feminine beauty. Her leadership and wild qualities made her different from our shy and quiet sisters. She was more of a tomboy and could do the wildest things that we boys dared not try. Given an opportunity, I would visit their humble thatched home. Having lost her mother at a tender age, Rani grew up as a companion and friend to Mukund.

My last visit to the fisherman's home was an accidental one. A group of cousins and assorted relatives had planned a bird shooting expedition to Satmukhi Beel. Cousin Adhir by his own admission was a great hunter, with many trophies to his credit. We were chilled to the bone by the stories of his daring forays against the Royal Bengal tigers of the Sundarbans and the grizzly bears of Darjeeling Terai. One of his stories about his encounters with a Kaziranga rhino had almost sent some of the women swooning. He was indeed a great hunter and a greater storyteller.

Soon after his arrival, he insisted on visiting Satmukhi Beel to hunt for birds. This could be fun, I thought, as there were no tigers, rhinos or grizzly bears around. And one of the cousins might even allow me to handle their double barrel Manchester gun.

Rani was another attraction for tagging along with the shikar party. She had made a name for herself by nabbing an armed robber all by herself. The low caste girl had earned her way into the inner precincts of our upper caste homes by her loveable nature and daring actions.

We reached the banks of the lake around 6 a.m. Cousin Adhir, the cleverest of the lot, carried the gun and a bandolier of pellet cartridges. Dhiru carried his Players cigarette box and a basket containing his spare shoes.

'Mukund,' Adhir shouted, 'are you home?'

Mukund, our family fisherman trudged out of the shack covered from head to foot in a woollen rug. 'Master, I'm here.' He spoke in a feeble and shaky voice.

'Where is your boat? We're ready for bird shooting.'

'Master, I can't go today. I'm down with malaria. Please seek out my brother Kundan.' Mukund pleaded with folded hands.

'You bloody swine.' Adhir fired abuses and slapped Mukund on his face.

The malarial attack had weakened the elderly fisherman. He slumped on the ground with a loud cry. A few others of the party joined Adhir in heaping abuses on the sick man. I made a feeble attempt to help Mukund to his feet. I was shouted at by Anil, another celebrity cousin.

A shrill feminine voice shouted. 'Why the hell are you assaulting my father?'

A young girl of considerable beauty wrapped up in a simple cotton sari came out and helped Mukund stand up.

'Who the hell are you?' Adhir shouted back. I tried to intervene in a feeble voice.

'Rani. I'm Rani, Mukund Majhi's daughter. Get lost. He can't ply the boat today.' She helped her father limp back inside the shack.

Santosh, one of the saner cousins, intervened. 'We're sorry but we've come all the way for bird shooting and we need the boat.'

Rani ignored him. She entered an adjoining room, emerged with a glass of water and administered some medicine to her father.

'You better take the boat out,' Mukund pleaded with Rani. 'The masters have come all the way. Please go. We must obey our masters.'

Rani looked up at Adhir and once again at Santosh. She called me aside and asked about Adhir. I briefed her about him. Rani eyed me with an impish look and said, 'Fine, I'll take the boat out. But only for an hour.'

She fastened her sari around her waist, which she wore without any blouse or chemise, picked up a wooden paddle, and asked us to follow.

Satmukhi Beel presented a magnificent sight. Small islets and sand banks dotted its vast expanse. At some places, the lake was unbelievably deep and others were shallow. Green hyacinth, watercress and other weeds had clogged parts of the lake. Only an expert boatman could navigate the tricky water body. Migratory birds—ducks, cranes, teals, painted storks and many others—occupied the vast watery expanse and the shrubby islets.

Our destination was Deotar Char, the god's island, a green patch where the delectable ducks nestled in comparative safety. The nearest human habitat was about two kilometres away. Only determined and skilled hunters could venture beyond the shallow marsh, pushing boats through packed carpets of hyacinth and innumerable aquiline weeds.

'Take us to Deotar Char,' Adhir ordered. 'The big and juicy ducks are there.'

'I can't,' Rani replied. 'I can't push the boat through hyacinth and weed. This stretch is shallow. Only father knows the safe channel.'

'You must.' Adhir insisted.

Rani stopped paddling the oars and stood defiantly, her arms on her waist. 'When I say I can't, I can't.'

'Hey you low caste lout,' Adhir shouted back, 'take us to Deotar Char.'

'I can't.'

Santosh intervened with a conciliatory note. 'Please try. We'll help you.'

Rani glared and at the same time displayed a mysterious smile. 'Hey Krishna,' she shouted, 'help me.'

I was too young to navigate the boat. Nonetheless I walked up to her.

'Must teach this animal a lesson or two. Hold the oar steady.' Rani muttered inaudibly and started pushing the boat with a long bamboo pole. The loaded boat moved grudgingly through the hyacinth packed shallow waters.

Adhir lost patience. He snatched the bamboo pole from Rani and lunged heavily against the soft mud. The boat lost balance and tilted dangerously to its left. We scrambled for safety and the narrow fishing boat capsized.

Rani stood waist deep in muddy water and giggled at our plight. Adhir, dressed in cotton trousers, full-sleeve shirt, a pith hat, and the mighty gun in his hand stood like a scarecrow and reeled out abuses.

'You bloody fisherwoman! Why did you bring us this way? Why didn't you take us the other way around?'

'This is the only route to Deotar Char that I know.' Rani replied and plunged into the muddy water.

A non-poisonous water serpent climbed up Adhir's fancy pith hat. Some other cousins cried out and asked Adhir not to move. The scarecrow frame stood frozen with his mouth wide open.

Rani swam past us and stood in front of Adhir. She surprised us with her swift move. Her right hand moved like lightening and firmly clasped the hooded head of the snake. She opened the reptile's mouth, looked at its teeth, and threw it back with a powerful swing of her hand.

'Why did you let go the serpent?' Santosh asked.

'It's a harmless creature. Why should I kill it?'

Rani took another dip in the muddy water and stood before Adhir. The fear of death had disappeared from his eyes. It was replaced by a different look. The wet clothes clung to Rani's body revealing all her feminine assets. Adhir's nasty abuses suddenly stopped. His eyes were riveted on Rani's upper torso and went past the wet flimsy cotton sari that covered her breasts.

'Um,' Adhir managed to gurgle out some guttural sounds, 'not bad! What do you say Santosh?'

'Stop it. Let's help her in straightening the boat. It's your fault. And you made such a big fuss over that snake!'

'Oh forget that. I live in Calcutta and you don't get to see cobras there. Well! No luck with the ducks today. But she should be good to bed.'

'Stop it.' Santosh hissed out in disgust.

'Hey Rani,' Adhir shouted with a nasty look in his eyes, 'come and help us.'

'Help yourself master. The mud is soft. You won't drown. You can't push the boat through these waters. No one can. The weeds are too thick. I'd forewarned you. Now help me straighten the boat.'

'This girl is a spoilsport. She's done it deliberately.' Adhir shouted back.

'I'll swim back, if you're not interested in helping me.' Rani started wading towards the banks.

'Wait Rani.' Santosh lunged forward and we helped him to straighten the boat and drain out the muddy water out from its hold. Rani rowed the boat back to the banks, tied the ropes with a wooden pole, and disappeared behind bamboo curtains.

Adhir continued abusing Mukund and his daughter. Dhiru tried in vain to comfort his would be master by offering a dry towel and helping him light a cigarette. His high pitched shouts dragged Mukund out from his sick bed.

'I'm sorry master. Rani doesn't know the channels to the best spots for a shoot. Come back after a few days. I should be on my feet by then.'

'That's fine.' Santosh replied.

'Your daughter is mischievous. I'll tell grandpa to evict you from your home and to deny you fishing rights.' Adhir fortified his anger by throwing the burning cigarette at Mukund.

'Sorry master. Don't do that. I'll bring you lots of fish before you return to Calcutta.' Mukund managed to croak out the words.

Adhir did not talk to us. He produced another packet of Players and kept on smoking and conversing with Dhiru, 'You know her well?' Adhir whispered.

'Yes master. She's an all rounder, an expert in climbing trees, swimming, and playing kabaddi.'

'You must get her. I want her. Here's twenty bucks. Expect more once you deliver her to my bed.'

'Yes master.' Dhiru hummed a tune from the latest movie and pocketed the money.

The village was preparing for a junior football match against a team from Raipura the neighbouring village. The outing to Raipura brought out the ugly truth Mehboob had spoken about. When our team reached Raipura, a village elder stood up and loudly declared that our team would be disqualified if Rani captained and played for us.

'Allah has banned women from taking part in manly activities. This girl cannot play and lead. How can a woman lead a boy's team?'

'What are you talking about, Shariat mian? They are mere kids. Why drag religion into an innocent game?' Our manager Tara mian protested.

'That girl is no more a kid, she is a woman. Islam does not allow this. If you want to play then drop her.'

We played a terrible game and lost for the first time in three years and returned crestfallen. I couldn't understand how Rani didi could offend Allah by playing football!

A few days later, Dhiru came up with a tempting offer. He dangled a shiny toy pistol that could fire real lead pellets and kill small birds.

'Want this?'

'Would like to. Why are you so generous?'

'Adhir dada will gift it to you if you do a job for him.'

'What's that?'

'He wants to meet Rani in private and apologize for the boating event.'

'Is that all?'

'By God.'

I caught up with Rani at a private corner of Satmukhi Beel which was normally used by the lower caste women folk for bathing and washing. She was bathing in the shallow water with her sari on. She rebuked me. 'What're you doing here? Don't you know this bathing spot is reserved for the ladies?'

'Yes, I know. But you're not a lady.'

'What do you mean by that?'

'Only moms and aunts are ladies. You're our friend, my friend. What's the problem with you? Why have you stopped talking to me? What's my fault?'

Rani smiled and wrapped herself up with the sari, filled the water pitcher and silently walked towards her shack. I followed.

'Why are you following me?'

'Following you? I'm coming to your home.'

She greeted me with an indulgent smile. I felt relieved. The ice had finally melted. I chatted with Mukund. He was repairing a large fishing net and talking to himself about the state of the economy and the high price of rice. Rani emerged with a glass of tea for her father.

'Would you like some tea?' Mukund asked and hastened to add. 'But how can you? We're low caste people. You're not supposed to eat and drink from our hands.'

'I don't care. I'd like to have some tea.'

Rani obliged with a broad grin. 'You're sure to go to hell for eating out of our kitchen.'

'I don't mind that. At least you'd be there with me.'

She laughed aloud. That was a welcome signal. Here was the Rani I knew and adored.

Mukund left with his net for the lake. Rani got busy collecting matured seeds and roots of the lotus plants that were made into exotic snacks. Mother used these ingredients to make wonderful curries as well.

'Hey Krishna, come and help me. We need lots of seeds and roots,' Rani called out.

I was game. I plunged into the shallow and slightly chilly waters and started plucking the mature lotus pods.

'School is reopening and I'm scared of the exams.'

'Don't worry, you'll get through. Just cut down on games and sports for a few weeks,' she suggested.

'Rani didi,' I wanted to broach the suggestion hinted at by Dhiru but words failed me.

I decided to forgo the shotgun, that blighted piece of allurement that was standing between me, the greedy Krishna and Krishna, the faithful admirer of Rani. I narrated the offer made by Dhiru, including the offer of the shotgun.

'You want that gun?'

'No.'

'Well, listen . . . ' Rani came up with a plot which she felt was sure to work. The shotgun would be mine, she assured me.

The rendezvous for a meeting between Adhir and Rani was fixed at a far corner of the lake.

One such spot was covered with a thick growth of bamboo cane that was used to make furniture. Ripe cane fruits were as luscious as litchis but a few pieces often found their way into the merciless hands of our teachers. They used the dried canes on our palms and buttocks to punish errant students.

Rani instructed me to guide Adhir to the northern edge of the cane forest and disappear behind the bushes only after taking physical delivery of the shotgun and pellets. Dhiru, she advised, shouldn't be told about the meeting which should be an exclusive and private one. I nodded in agreement and hoped things would work out according to the plan, and no harm would come to Rani.

Adhir joined me exactly at 6 p.m. soon after the sun slipped below the tree-lined horizon. He carried a small torchlight and the shotgun in his left hand. We crossed a sandbank and climbed a few high grounds covered with lush green growth and finally reached the northern edge of the cane forest.

'Where's she?' Adhir asked in a lustful voice.

'Should be here. Rani didi . . . ' I called out.

Adhir flashed his torch. There Rani stood, about twenty metres away under a huge mango tree. The torch flashed again and focused on Rani's face.

'Okay. You go.' Adhir ordered me.

'The shotgun!' I extended my right hand. My cousin grimaced and handed over the gun and asked me to scoot. I turned back and waited behind a bush.

Adhir started walking down a slope that led towards the mango tree. He had barely taken five steps when his lanky body started sinking in the hidden slush and mud covered by the thick growth of watercress and hyacinth.

'Hey, what's happening? Krishna, where are you? Help, I'm sinking!' he cried out in panic.

The plan worked. I cried out for help and Rani disappeared. She went straight home.

The fishing community, about ten members of Rani's clan, rushed to the spot. They threw ropes and nets at Adhir. He was dragged out of the hidden slush which the villagers said had sucked up several of their cows and goats. My fashionable Calcutta cousin was covered in a thick coat of mud. His shoes and torchlight were gone. He groaned in pain and begged for a glass of water.

Rani joined the gang and offerd him some water in a metal glass from a pitcher. Adhir didn't look at her. He tried to stand up but couldn't. He had sprained his right ankle. Mukund and the other fishermen carried him home.

Rani took the shotgun from my hand and asked to me go straight home.

'He'll crack my skull.' I expressed my apprehension.

'Don't worry, nothing of the sort is going to happen,' she reassured me.

Adhir didn't crack my skull neither did Dhiru bother me. Three days after the forest incident, Adhir boarded a train for Calcutta. Uncle Raj Kishore announced that his son Adhir's engagement ceremony was indefinitely deferred because of the brilliant law student's preoccupation with his course.

Rani visited our home the next morning with a basketful of fish and pulled out the shotgun from underneath the pile of fresh fish. We exchanged merry glances.

~

The Durga Puja of 1946 was the last joint family and village event. *Probasi* family members, those living away from home, left for their work places. Our grandparents lost hope of retaining their stranglehold on their Muslim subjects. Even the Hindu royats and subjects unfurled the banner of revolt. The family barber Sachindra suddenly declared that he would charge two annas for a haircut and one anna for a shave. He defied the family by opening a shop at the Bhairab market.

The most unthinkable act of rebellion came from Halim mian. He tilled five acres of our family land. In that year of a lean monsoon, he declared he would give only a quarter of the crop to our family. Dhala and Dudu mobilized a sizeable armed crowd in support of Halim. Our familes were falling apart. Its heads were advised by the local police to accept the fact that the winds of change were real and sooner rather than later the lands would revert to the Muslims.

Some family members initiated the process of escaping to the promised safe haven for Hindus in Hindustan, be it in distant Calcutta or nearby Agartala. Father was one of those who believed in human goodness and refused to entertain the very idea of leaving his homeland. To some these new developments were a dream, to others an abominable idea. The idea of assuming a new identity of a refugee did not allure most of us. However, the pangs of fear and disorientation were briefly sweetened by a trivial incident.

Mukund rushed to my mother accompanied by two neighbours. 'Ma, I've a big problem.'

'What's happened Mukund? Do you need some money?'

'No Ma. Tarpan Majhi from village Shimulkandi is visiting us today to look up Rani and fix a date for her marriage with his son Darpan.'

'That should be fine for the motherless girl. She's already seventeen. Let me know if you require any help.' Mother offered Mukund a glass of tea.

'There is a big problem, Ma. Rani has climbed up a palash tree and refuses to come down. She doesn't want to marry, nor leave the village. What should I do? How can I keep a grown up unmarried daughter at home? My caste members will ostracize me.'

Mother, a few women of our clan and I went to Mukund's house. Rani was perched on the top branch of a flowering a palash tree. The bright red flowers partly covered her red sari.

'Come down Rani.' Mother demanded.

'No thakurain, I won't. Baba wants to marry me to a stranger and leave the village.'

'All of us women have to marry some day. Come down.'

I tried my luck. 'Come Rani. We'll request Darpan to stay in our village and you can continue to be our captain.'

'Sure? I think you're talking nonsense.'

One of the older aunts said, 'Krishna is correct Rani. We'll ask Tarpan, the groom's father to settle his son in our village. We'll grant him a piece of land.'

'We promise.' Mother assured Rani who then climbed down like a red squirrel.

'Look Rani, you're now a woman. Marry the fine boy and set up home. We're here to support you.' Mother caressed Rani tenderly.

'See how clever I am? Won't have to leave the village or you.' Rani whispered into my ear.

A week later, Rani was married off to Darpan Majhi. A separate shack was built for her on the Beel bank, a few metres away from Mukund's hut. It was a great event. Rani glowed like a lotus in full bloom. But she stopped playing football, rowing our boats and plucking our fruits.

The changes around had started destroying our lives. For me personally, Rani's marriage was equally devastating. Her courage and will to fight was manifested years later when she valiantly fought a Bihari Muslim crowd.

four

Winds of Change

The festive season was over. It was November, time to prepare for the final examinations. It was also the season for sowing mustard, lentils, tobacco and winter fruits like guava, grapefruit, passion fruit and olives. Fishing and occasional trips to Satmukhi Beel kept us busy. The football team had lost its lustre after Rani was debarred from captaining and playing for our team. Majid, an excellent right winger replaced Rani. An ugly incident also restricted our forays to neighbouring villages for soccer games.

We had a challenge cup to play at Kalipur village. The cup was instituted in the memory of Girish, the elder brother of our grandfather. Girish, besides owning landed property had diversified into private banking with the Girish Bank, river steamer operations and the export of chilli and jute. He also owned a fleet of fishing boats.

Chandra Kishore had large landed properties at Kalipur and the Muslim royats paid taxes to him. The royats worked in his fields and were paid a grand salary of eight rupees per month. Chandra Kishore was a complex and scheming person. His intrigues, manipulations and doublespeak fitted his assumed importance of a landlord. Girish was the open-minded, giving type and depended on his elder brother for managing money and property matters.

One evening he returned from a river trip to Nabinagar (the village of Ustad Alauddin Khan) after attending a musical soirée. He fell violently sick with incessant vomiting and loose motions. Father was called upon to treat him. He concluded that his uncle was about to lapse into a coma due to a severe cholera attack and dehydration. He might have eaten something at Nabinagar that proved fatal. Girish Chandra expired the next morning.

Chandra Kishore schemed to deprive his brother Girish's two sons and three daughters of their inheritance. The immediate fallout on my father was his total and complete disinheritance from his father's possessions except for a little land endowed by his mother. I overheard a strange conversation between my parents quite late while I was in bed.

'Are you asleep Su? Father is not doing the right thing with uncle's properties. I should tell my cousins Hirendra and Dhirendra. Father is cheating them. Hiru and Dhiru are still young and Mudra is yet to be married. What would happen to the family? It's wrong. I'm going to protest.'

'How many wrongs can you set right? How many people can you fight? You do know that you have very few friends in the family?'

'I've two friends, you and God. I don't know if my children will understand me or not. But if you agree I must fight for the truth.'

There was a prolonged silence.

'Say something, what should I do?'

'Do whatever you think is right. Don't worry about us. Just don't forget that we all depend on you.'

'You're there.'

'I'm not a fighter like you.'

We were not present at that historic family event. However, Rahman told me that my father fought for the right of his cousins and forced a partition on a reluctant Chandra Kishore. The annoyed and embarrassed patriarch proclaimed that he had already disinherited his third son Debendra from all his properties.

There ended, Rahman said, the relationship between my father and my grandpa. The patriarch later did everything to harm his son and was not unhappy when he was imprisoned for championing the cause of the swadeshists by mobilizing funds for Netaji Subhas. Father was in the Brahmanbaria jail for three months.

However, grandpa, the scheming person that he was, had instituted a challenge football cup in memory of his beloved brother. About ten villages participated in the junior group. Our junior team played a round-robin league and the final was played in our village in the presence of senior officers of the sub-division and important local gentry. Our match at Kalipur was the last one of the league.

That year, soon after Durga Puja, we were teamed up under Majid Khan to train and play against Kalipur. Our team played well. I kept the goals efficiently and Majid scored two goals against the Kalipur team. Some enthusiast in the crowd raised the slogan, 'Bande Mataram, Kamalpur Zindabad'.

Jalil Sarkar, the Union Board president of Kalipur objected to the Bande Mataram slogan shouting. 'Who raises the kafir slogan? Allah ho Akbar. Ladke lenge Pakistan. Hindustan Murdabad.' Jalil Sarkar shouted. 'Down with India.'

His followers joined him. The game was interrupted and a section of Jalil's followers started pelting stones at us. We took shelter behind guava, pineapple and berry bushes. Our Hindu and Muslim supporters faced the ruffians headed by Jalil with sticks and stones.

'What's wrong with Bande Mataram?' asked Rahman.

'It's a Hindu slogan. It is against Islam,' shouted Jalil.

His group responded, 'Allah ho Akbar.'

'Listen you kafir and slave Muslims,' Jalil continued. 'We're only a few months from Independence. We'll have a pure Muslim homeland under Jinnah sahib. Those who support Pakistan come to my side. Those who support Hindustan go behind the kafirs.'

'What is a kafir?' I asked Saifi.

'Don't know. What's there for Pakistan and Hindustan in our football match? Let's play.'

One of the elders went forward, literally flaunting a white handkerchief. 'Jalil bhai, forget the small incident. No one will shout Bande Mataram again. Let's proceed with the game.'

'No, chhota karta. Times have changed. We Muslims won't submit to Hindus. It's our land. You're no more our masters,' Jalil shouted.

'These matters can't be decided in a football match. We must discuss the issue. You and we are brothers. Do you think we would cease to be your brothers even if Pakistan is created tomorrow?'

Jalil was not ready to see reason. He stood firm and announced that the matter would be reported to Muslim League leaders at Dacca and Mymensingh. No one in Pakistan had the right to utter Bande Mataram.

We returned home disappointed. That year our final round at Kamalpur did not take place. The shield remained locked in an ornate mahogany almirah. The old man fumed, fretted, and sent a telegram to the subdivisional officer and the district collector. Unlike in earlier years, the high and mighty officers did not rush to our village. Only Sehzad Khan, the local station house officer called on Chandra Kishore and advised him to stay calm. Nothing could be done, under the circumstances, against Jalil Sarkar, a prominent Muslim League leader. Had not the old landlord heard of the rattling footsteps of Pakistan advancing to the heart of his domain? It was time to change. The old order must yield to the new.

Chandra Kishore was livid. His old frail body shook with anger, which was muted by his regular smoking of the hukka. He sat down on the reclining chair and closed his eyes. For the first time he conceded defeat to a mere policeman and a petty village Union Board president, who was elected under his very benign patronage. We were advised to avoid the old grouch. Only our grandma, a lady of over eighty, maintained her cool demeanour. She deputed Rasid mian, our revenue supervisor to Kalipur. He returned with Jalil Sarkar and a few other elders of that village.

'Jalil, from where have you got the courage to scuttle the annual game? Who empowered you to decide the issue? Hindustan or Pakistan, remember one thing—I am still your landlady. You live in my jagir. I do not know politics. If you defy me you will have to leave the village.' She spoke in slow and steely sentences and no one had the courage to contradict the iron lady.

'Beg mercy from our mother, you stupid Jalil,' shouted Rashid mian.

'That's fine Jalil. Next Sunday our Kamalpur team will play a final game against the Ashuganj team. You should be there to supervise the game and attend to the honoured guests.'

'Yes Ma.'

'Rahman,' grandma shouted, 'give Rs 200 to Jalil for making arrangements for the final game.' Our grandma, whom we called thandidi, stood up and made a dignified exit. Rashid mian was left to deal with the bewildered Hindu and Muslim crowd.

We played the final match that was to be the last one. Ashuganj defeated our home team by a solitary goal. Politics, violence and social change left us maimed and pained. Jalil and his ilk, including Dudu and Dhala took over the events.

～

Another ghastly event made us even more aware that changes were overtaking us. The communal devil had started driving the dagger deep into our Bengali soul. The Congress and the Muslim League's communal politics had almost succeeded in defeating our cultural nationalism. Father said the tired and hungry leaders were busy planning for their *gaddis*, their thrones, and had no time to plan for the people. He used to be very critical of Nehru and Jinnah, saying that between 1937 and 1947 the two egotists had fought for their own welfare and not for the people. We were simply thrown into a fiery situation where our only option was to take a train to India.

The story of our final flight from what was to become East Pakistan and taking trains to India was punctuated by the dramatic interlude of Nafisa alias Aparajita visiting our home on a rainy night with the dead body of her husband. It was an event that rocked our area and left a deep imprint on my young mind. Nafisa appeared to me an epitome of love, courage and fortitude. Till then, I had not encountered another woman of that dimension besides my mother.

It also brought home a sharp message that Indian politics had divided us irretrievably. It was time to escape. Many were escaping. But my father stoutly refused to believe that religion could divide Bengali hearts.

Thandidi was seated under the shade of a golden champak tree. She swirled her palm leaf fan leisurely. Our life-sustaining monsoon had failed to keep its date. The skies were tantalizingly blue with shreds of fluffy clouds traversing leisurely like solitary lambs. They did not look like they were in a hurry to kiss the earth with it with a wild storm. Famine was about to knock on the doors of the common people, and death was about to stalk the homes of the farmers like they did back in 1943 that many believed was a government-engineered famine. The impending one was to travel on the back of nature's fury and political uncertainty.

The early forenoon sky was spotlessly blue and the blazing sun was getting warmer by the minute. But the grand old lady turned down pleadings to move inside her room to rest under the ceiling pull-fan operated by a servant.

She had compelling reasons to suffer the scorching heat. She waited with bated breath to hear the welcome birth cries of the baby. Her adopted daughter Aparajita was about to deliver and was lodged in a segregated maternity shack.

Nafisa, renamed Aparajita by our grandma, gave birth to a male child. The village maid emerged and announced the good news.

Thandidi displayed a big smile on her toothless face. 'I've named the boy Nabarun, the new Sun.'

Our grandma had taken a fancy for this girl who had taken refuge at our home one stormy night a few months ago under mysterious circumstances.

The senior ladies of the family stood behind the elderly matron waiting to carry out her orders. Grandpa Chandra Kishore was closeted with Jainab Alam and his wife, Aparajita's parents and her father-in-law Amar Mukherjee, the munsif from the lower court.

Aparajita's arrival at our home and her adoption by grandma were more dramatic than a village jatra, popular open air theatre shows. But no one, not even her husband, had the guts to question her actions. Grandma prevented any questions being asked either by showering toothless smiles or contorting her wrinkled forehead and white eyebrows conveying serious displeasure.

Aparajita had knocked on our gates at about one in the morning after a seasonal rainstorm had subsided. The busy household had gone to sleep after superficially managing the havoc wrought by the cyclone. Only five night watchmen roamed about the vast expanse of our sprawling homestead and blew whistles intermittently to announce that they were on duty. One of them, Ramdin, a Bihari ex-army sepoy rang a bell to announce the hours of the night. No one was allowed to enter the premises after 8 p.m.

Ramdin shouted. 'Who comes there? Friend or foe? Halt.'

But the female figure defied his military stance and the double barrel Manchester gun and continued dragging something heavy towards our main gate. Ramdin trained his Manchester on the lurching figure and repeatedly demanded to know her identity. Aparajita refused to be scared away by the menacing gun and the even more menacing moustache of Ramdin.

'Can't you see I am dragging the injured and unconscious body of my husband?' she replied in a screaming voice. 'Are you blind? Can't you differentiate between a helpless woman and a real foe?'

Flustered by her reply, Ramdin blew his whistle repeatedly. His fellow night watchmen rushed to the spot.

'Allow me in,' Aparajita demanded, 'I want protection from the zamindar.'

'I can't.' Ramdin rang the heavy metal bell to wake up the household. He was more scared by the defiant and burning eyes of Aparajita than by the shining edges of the scimitar she carried in her left hand.

All the able-bodied men came out with whatever weapons they could lay hands on. The womenfolk followed them. The grown up girls kept us children at bay. Grandpa, forced out of his opium induced sleep, came out grudgingly. Katia, the dark Garo, and Rahman, the bonded labour and a part of our family guarded his flanks with two huge swords. Someone flashed a torch beam at the intruders at whom Ramdin's gun was still pointed in a menacing posture.

There she stood, covered with mud and blood, a young woman of about twenty-five. She carried a big scimitar in her hand and a determined look in her eyes. She was trying pitiably and miserably to drag a male figure. He was in pain and was bleeding profusely.

Grandpa ordered a chair to position himself as the self-assumed dispenser of justice and directed one of his sons to help the watchmen produce the intruders before him. They lifted the injured man and guided the woman to the open general court of the mighty mahashay.

'Who are you? Who is this man? Why have you barged into my house?' He fired the questions in a single breath.

The young woman, dressed in a flowing gown generally worn by English ladies, didn't reply. She slumped at Grandpa's feet and begged for medical assistance for her husband, Rabindra or Robin. Chandra Kishore, who boasted of ten sons and three daughters summoned one of them and ordered him to rush to the police station. He ordered Ramdin to quarantine the intruders in a room behind the cowshed.

So engrossed were we with the drama that we had forgotten the presence of Thandidi. She stepped forward, clutching her ivory walking stick and chewing a paste prepared out of areca nut, betel leaf and tobacco. 'What's going on there?'

'Some intruders, Ma,' replied uncle Birendra. 'They entered our house without permission.'

'Yes. I've seen all that. Bring the girl to my room. She needs a wash. And call Brajen Acharya, the pharmacist, to treat her husband,' she ordered.

'But,' Chandra Kishore squeaked, 'I've sent someone to the police station. It can be a complicated legal case.'

'I know all that. You don't have to teach me. I know the rules and laws of the Maharani.'

Aparajita looked intently at the grand old lady, dropped the scimitar and burst into loud sobs. 'Thank you Ma.' She fell at grandma's feet.

Brajendra Acharya arrived with his first aid box. He examined the wounded man under a petromax light and declared that the poor soul had died of severe stab and gunshot injuries to his stomach and lungs.

'You take care of the dead man,' Thandidi ordered. 'Do whatever is required, and ask Brajen to clean up the dead body,' she directed her husband.

'Yes.'

'And see that after the police examination he receives a proper Hindu cremation.'

The next morning the dead body of Rabindranath, the deceased husband of the woman, was carried with full religious rites to the western part of Kamalpur for cremation.

The village Brahmin came out with a last minute objection. 'Only the nearest male relative can light the pyre. Do you have any?'

'No.' A stunned and stricken Aparajita replied.

'In that case I cannot allow this body to be cremated.'

'Why not?' Aparajita shouted back, 'I'm his wife. I'll perform my husband's last rites.'

'Are you a Hindu?'

'No. I'm a born Muslim married to a Hindu.'

'I'm a Hindu priest. I can't preside over an unholy act.'

'Hey Madhu Pandit,' Thandidi shouted back, 'perform the last rites according to Hindu tradition or I'll evict you from my land. Is that clear?'

'Yes Mother.'

Madhu Pandit allowed the young lady standing defiantly before him to light a pile of twigs and set fire to the pyre.

Soon after the cremation, the burly station house officer Sehjad Khan and his deputy Netai Guha appeared. They were ensconced on two massive ornate chairs in our primary school building. They interrogated Rabindranath's wife Nafisa (aka Aparajita) in the presence of two lady servants. Thandidi and the other ladies sat behind a muslin purdah and listened to the heart-rending story that had rocked communal harmony in certain parts of eastern Bengal.

Nafisa, the daughter of Jainab Alam, a Sayeed aristocrat and the principal of a school at Tungi in the vicinity of Dacca was an exceptional Muslim girl. After graduation from the local co-educational school, she had taken admission in a Dacca college. A Muslim girl was not supposed to violate the purdah and study in a secular school. But Jainab Alam and his brave wife ignored the mullahs and encouraged Nafisa to keep pace with her Hindu counterparts.

She committed the great crime of falling in love with her school teacher, Rabindranath Mukherjee. The communal divide, severe Hindu–Muslim communal riots and the impending partition of the country could not deter Nafisa's love for Rabindra.

Rabindranath was keenly aware of the implications. The first salvo was fired by Maulana Sahiduddin Qurayashi, who claimed to be a descendant from the purest of the pure Qurayash tribe, the holiest tribe to which the Hazrat Mohammad, Praise be to Allah the Merciful, was born. The maulana, an Urdu teacher, and the guardian of the souls of the Muslim students fired a probing shot during the lunch break, in the male teacher's common room, by exposing the alleged love affair between a Hindu teacher and a Muslim student.

Sahiduddin used his political and religious influences to blow up the affair. He declared that Jainab could avoid hell only by marrying his young daughter to the direct descendant of the Paigambar, Peace Be unto Him, Maulana Sahidudin Qurayashi, aged fifty-two.

The maulana's machinations even generated communal disturbances in Tungi and nearby rural areas. Nafisa and Rabindra committed another so-called crime. They married in a secret ceremony and had planned to escape to Nabinagar, Rabindra's ancestral home.

Getting out of Dacca, especially after the mayhem unleashed by Sahiduddin, wasn't a cakewalk in the India of 1946. They decided to dress up in European clothes and pretend to be an Anglo-Indian couple. Rabindra had plans to escape to the princely state of Tripura. However, to reach Nabinagar one had to take a rail journey to Bhairab and then a steamer or ferry boat.

Bhairab, named after the Hindu god of cosmic destruction, was a feared name for various reasons—its notorious landlords, menacing river pirates and Marwari loan sharks. The pirates maintained a private flotilla of boats and barges. They plundered the boats and steamers and extracted a monthly commission from the chilli, rice and jute-exporting barons. The trading houses, both British and Indian, did not mind paying. The British law enforcing machinery was not geared to combat the river pirates.

Rabindranath was known in the area. His father, a munsif in the neighbouring town of Brahmanbaria was a respected citizen. The assistant stationmaster, Nabin Paul recognized Rabindranath. He advised against a night journey and invited the couple to rest at his quarters. Rabindranath smilingly declined the offer, summoned Badan Misr, the portly Bihari porter, and engaged his cycle rickshaw. Ordinary country boats normally did not draw the attention of the river pirates. With a favourable downstream current and steady tail wind, the journey to Nabinagar should not have taken more than forty minutes.

But Rabindranath didn't take into account the devil prowling next to the burial ground, just ahead of the railway station. Stretched over a vast wasteland the burial ground was a favourite haunt of Nibharsa, the most infamous river pirate. His gang of desperadoes often took shelter behind the tombstones and untrimmed bushes. They did not normally attack railway passengers, except cash carriers of the big trading houses and revenue bags, who were escorted by two gun wielding *barkandaz* to the government treasury.

That night Nibharsa was high on marijuana and locally brewed spirit. He had had a successful day and his gang members were high on opium. His group of brigands had a victorious skirmish with the gang of Ramzan just below the railway culvert which connected the Bhairab trading centre and Bhairabpur village. Both the warring groups fought well, with spears, swords and guns. At the end of the day, the Ramzan gang retreated after leaving two dead.

The rickshaw reached the main gate of the burial ground while Badan Misr narrated the blood-curdling events of the day.

'Who goes there?' a growling voice asked from behind the shadows of a tombstone.

'Master, this is your servant Badan the porter carrying a passenger.'

A torch beam lit up the interiors of the rickshaw and its occupants.

'Chief, there's a lovely woman. And the party appears to be rich.'

'Hey, Badan,' another voice shouted from behind the beam of light, 'run for your life. That girl's mine.'

Nibharsa emerged from the shadows and pulled Rabindra out of the rikshaw. The sudden attack surprised him but he fought well. He snatched a machete from one of the goons and hit Nibharsa.

Nafisa joined him. She snatched a dagger from a drunken pirate and blindly hit Nibharsa. The injured brigand pumped two bullets into Rabindra's lower abdomen. Nafisa swung her machete and hit Nibharsa's neck. The redoubtable pirate slumped on the ground and his gang members were stupefied for a few moments. They could not believe that a mere woman could vanquish the sultan of the Meghna pirates. Nafisa swirled the machete over her head like a possessed sorcerer and cried out for help. Robin was bleeding profusely, and he was in acute pain.

Badan Misr did not abandon Rabindranath and his wife to the mercy of the dacoits. He returned with two other Bihari porters and a couple of swords. He fought well with the drunken followers of Nibharsa, who picked up their unconscious leader and made a beeline for their boats.

The skirmish over, Nafisa placed Robin's head on her lap. 'Badan, where do I go with him? He requires medical help.'

'Run for the bara bari. Only the big house masters can save you from these pirates and dacoits.' Badan helped Nafisa carry Rabindranath to the outer gate of Chandra Kishore's house.

'Beti, I've got to go. The dacoits are ruthless. I don't want to be identified. I'll have to leave this station by the next train. Nibharsa doesn't know the meaning of mercy. Go and seek protection from the landlord. God will save you.'

He left Nafisa in the darkness under the areca nut-lined dirt road which led to the outer gate of the sprawling house of Chandra Kishore. Nafisa looked around, tightened her lower gown with her scarf, lifted Rabindranath and headed for the front lawns. That's where Ramdin the night guard spotted her and sounded the alarm.

～

Thandidi expired two months after the birth of Aparajita's baby, at the ripe old age of ninety. Her passing away was followed by the sudden death of grandpa after a shouting match with a group of Muslim *bargadars*. The sharecroppers had assembled under the banner of former serf Dhala mian, now a leader of the Muslim League. They claimed that under the new provisions of the Muslim League and Krishak Praja Party government in Bengal they would pay only a quarter of the crop instead of half. Chandra Kishore shouted, ordered his Garo guard to bring out a gun, and finally collapsed.

He had refused to recognize the march of time and changes in the political scenario. His death was followed by a series of communal clashes in the villages under his mandate. It was time to face up to the dark and ugly face of Indian politics. Chandra Kishore was lucky to escape the glory of being branded a 'refugee.' He died on his own turf, though a disillusioned man.

Uncle Birendra shifted his family to Brahmanbaria. Uncle Upendra, the advocate, decided to stay put at Bajitpur. Harendra, the eldest son remained well entrenched at

Narsinghdi until he migrated to Calcutta. His line of the family maintained a distance from the humdrum of village life and its intrigues.

Father Debendra decided to send Aparajita to Calcutta with another branch of the family. It was not safe to keep her in the village and invite trouble from the Qurayashi maulana from Tungi. An amount of Rs 20,000 was raised by her father and father-in-law for her initial settlement expenses. Our remaining family members assembled at Bhairab station to see off Aparajita and her son.

Many years later, in 1967, her son was to join the Indian Administrative Service, fulfilling the dream that the father he had never known had for him. Jainab Alam and his wife Ayesha were close to their daughter and grandson and quietly retired to Calcutta under the caring roof of Aparajita.

Father was a chronic dreamer. He refused to take a train to Calcutta and said he had more political roles to play to ensure communal harmony and more struggles to realize the dream of a united Independent Bengal.

I was mostly left alone. My elder brother was a serious type and busy with his studies. He did not care about the natural beauty around him. I was too young to understand his dreams for his future. I was left with Jasim, Haripada and Saifi. Gradually a couple of so-called low caste and Muslim boys joined our club. Majid continued to captain our football team, for which it often was a struggle to put together eleven players. Life was not the same. Many ugly events were overtaking us rather quickly.

five

Changes sweep Meghna Basin

2, November 1946.

Father returned from Calcutta early one morning accompanied by his young cousin, Manoranjan Dhar (later a minister in the Mujib government), Keshab Ghosh, my mother's cousin from Rajnagar, Subhan Ali and Karamat Ali. After an early breakfast, they locked themselves in the eastern court building. My curiosity got the better of me. I was aware of the drastic changes. News and rumours of the communal clashes, burning of the Hindu majority villages and the abduction of Hindu women filtered down through Rahman and other retainers of the family who had not yet shifted loyalty. Saifi shared my anxiety and hoped that we would not cross over to Hindustan. Our village was our country and Hindus and Muslims had an equal right to live there. Had he not participated in our Durga Puja and had I not partaken of roasted meat at his home on Eid?

Jasim fortified his argument. Had not Lutfa taught me the Ram mantra to drive away ghosts and jinns? Had I not taken puja prasad to his mother? Did she ever refuse? So, where did I stand? In Hindustan or Pakistan?

My curiosity drove me to cut a corner of the lattice work of a window of the eastern court building. Perching myself on the windowsill I listened carefully to a group of idealistic politicians debating.

'Deben babu,' Subhan Ali said, 'I think we've lost to Jinnah and Nehru. They are keen to partition the country.'

'I think it's a matter of weeks for the formal announcement to be made by the Viceroy.' Father added, 'What do you propose? We've been together all these years in our struggle for freedom. We've followed Netaji. Now, Suhrawardy has also gone over to Jinnah.'

'Deben karta,' Karamat spoke in a slow voice, 'let's decide our own ways. All said and done we are Muslims. The communal divide is now beyond repair. You had better plan for the future.'

'Karamat, you have disappointed me. Give me a hand with the Sylhet referendum.' Father spoke in a hurt voice.

'No karta. I think on this issue the Muslim League and the Assam Congress are unanimous. Maulana Bhasani is also supporting the League. You have heard of the young leader Mujibur Rahman. He's spearheading the League's campaign in Sylhet. I can't go against my own nephew,' Karamat added in an apologetic voice.

'Karamat is right, Deben karta,' Subhan spoke. 'Religion has replaced common sense, politics, social bondage and our traditional unity. I don't think any one of us can go against the fatwas issued by top religious leaders.'

'So, all of you are abandoning me?'

'No. We're with you. Don't leave the village. This religious frenzy will soon die down. We'll work again for our new country. Hindustan or Pakistan, our village is our country.'

'Take care, Deben karta. Suhrawardy and Jinnah have started flooding our part of Bengal with Bihari Muslims. We've no control over them. You know what the Bihari constables did in Calcutta on Direct Action days. We'll ask our loyal people to protect your village. Tell boudi that she should speak to the ladies of the neighbouring villages regarding maintaining communal amity.' Karamat stood up with a tone of finality.

～

Father emerged from the eastern court with a dejected demeanour followed by Manoranjan and Keshab. From a distance, I noticed the sadness shrouding his restlessness. His face reminded me of the face of Karna (the illegitimate son of Kunti, the mother of the Pandavas) trying to extricate the wheels of his chariot and expecting the final arrow hit from his brother Arjuna. The picture of the unsung hero of the Mahabharat that I usually read out aloud to mother came alive in my mind. Who were these Jinnah, Nehru, and Suhrawardy to divide our country? How could they decide our fate? Was religion above everything? Were a people bonded together by religion alone? I had no one to answer my questions. Lutfa was still in jail and Rani was happily married.

As if to answer my anguished questions, that evening our basin was lashed by a severe cyclonic storm. It brought wind and rain and finally hailstorm that lasted for hours. Mother braved the hail to run out and cover the shelters of our pet ducks and the shed that housed Pintu and the other goats. Father accompanied by Rahman secured the cowshed. Tomtom gave me company often scowling and growling at the swishing wind and the loud rattle of hailstorm.

Huddled under a heavy quilt I heard father talking to mother in a subdued voice. 'I think Su, I've been defeated.'

'Defeat is part of life. Don't get dejected, you've fought well. Do something to claim your mother's property. Remember you have been disinherited and you've not practiced your vocation. Now you have to stand by the family and give us more importance than your political career.'

'I know. It's time I took fresh stock of the situation.' For the first time I noticed a note of pessimism in my father's voice. 'I forgot to tell you about a new family joining us tomorrow.'

'Which family?'

'The new station master, Wilson sahib. He wants to rent a house.'

'Do you want to rent out a portion of the house, your father's home?'

'Yes. Everybody has gone. The house is empty. You'll have company and some new friends. The younger one would have a new friend to play with.'

'What's your plan?'

'I have to accompany Keshab and Manoranjan to Sylhet. I must do what I should do.'

'You're alone.'

'I should not stop fighting because I'm alone.'

I gathered courage and sprang out of bed. My move startled Tomtom who normally slept by my side.

'Baba, I want to fight.'

I think father was stunned by what I said. 'Who asked you to fight? Whom do you want to fight? It's not a kid's job.'

'I want to fight the Biharis and anyone who may attack mother.'

'I'm there. Why worry?'

'Suppose you're out. Give me a gun.'

'I don't have one.'

'I know you have plenty of guns.'

'Shh! Look son, you're too young to wield a gun.' He spoke for the first time with a grin of hope in his eyes. 'This is the time to bury weapons. The enemy is leaving the country. I don't want weapons to fight my own brothers.'

'What if the Biharis attack mother?'

'Keep this knife. This is good enough to protect your ma. Don't hurt anyone if you're not attacked.'

Father took out a switch-blade Sheffield knife that was nine inches long from under his pillow.

'Keep it carefully. Don't get hurt. Use it only in defence. Tomorrow I'll be gone for a few days. Take care of your ma.' He eyed me again with a strange look. Perhaps he was baffled by my audacious desire to fight anyone who dared to attack my mother.

He kissed my head gently and I returned to bed with a sense of satisfaction and pride. My father had spoken to me for the first time as if I was his grown up son, fit to slip into his shoes. I slept peacefully with Tomtom by my side to warm up the cold bed.

~

We woke up to a fabulous white morning. The ground was covered with thick layers of solidified hail, over two feet at places with a bright sun above. I had never seen so much ice except when ice blocks were brought home to preserve fish and to serve whisky to visiting dignitaries. Grandpa used to add a few pieces to his marble wine glass.

Jasim called me out and Saifi and our other friends soon joined us. We ran up to the fields near Gagan Deeghi and started frolicking and dancing on solid ice.

It was probably 6 November when Manorama Hubert Wilson came to stay with us briefly in our sprawling and almost abandoned homestead. Manorama, her mother Preeti, younger brother Jeremy and father Jackson Hubert Wilson walked down from Bhairab railway station along the areca nut-lined gravel road. A retinue of coolies and a few handcarts, carrying their belongings followed. Their sharp features and fairer skin colour proclaimed that they were different from us.

Manorama's family had to waddle through muddy slush and ankle-deep water puddles. The devastating southeast monsoon cyclone had been accompanied by a freak hailstorm. Little did I know that it also brought in its wake disastrous consequences for farmers. Their wheat, pulses and mustard were ruined; the potato, onion and groundnut fields were flattened out.

Patches of the gravel road were submerged. The orchards, with broken branches and uprooted trees wore a ghostly look. Branches of trees, remnants of thatched and tin roofed houses littered the surrounding fields and the scrawny mud road. Knee-deep hailstones covered the fields. We danced on the solidified ice patches, a rare opportunity for children living in the tropical and riverine Meghna basin.

We kids, upper and lower caste, rich and poor, Hindus and Muslims didn't have the worries and anxieties of the elders. Saifullah was still my best friend and Haripada was my faithful shadow. We danced and skidded on the ice and sang a folksong, inviting rain clouds to burst forth.

The procession of Manorama, her family and the retinue of coolies excited us as it was not a regular feature in our village.

'Krishna,' Jasim cried out, 'I think they are the Angrez sahibs coming to stay at your home.'

One of the coolies, a burly Bihari, announced that the stationmaster and his family were on their way to our homestead. His fat belly, fierce moustache and demonic voice made us sprint to the safety of our homes. Jasim did not run. He coolly joined the procession and guided them to our home that was flanked by bottle palm-lined ornate gardens.

My curiosity got the better of me and I surreptitiously peeped into their home to look at the strange fixtures that came with the Wilsons. I was not a very social creature and had not learnt the tricks of making friends beyond our normal circle. It was easier for me to communicate with the bats, squirrels, owls and rabbits.

I did not understand the Wilsons, especially Manorama. Why would a Christian girl have a Bengali Hindu name? Why was she not christened Marriott or Maggie?

Manorama caught me by surprise. I was peeping into their house through a slit in the thatched window. She came up from behind and startled me.

'Hey Krishna,' she grabbed my hand, 'why don't you come in?'

'How do you know my name?' I asked with a guilty look on my face.

'I know all about you.'

'Why have you come here? People are leaving.'

'Well!' Manorama winked and pushed two little chocolates into my palm, 'We're going to be your guests. Come in and be my friend. Won't you?'

The chocolates did the trick. A small kid of seven and a girl of fifteen had instantly become friends. No. The chocolates were not the only bond. Manorama had plenty of tricks in her bag.

～

Manorama's story was short and simple.

Her father, J.H. Wilson, an Anglo-Indian, neither a thoroughbred Englishman nor a pure Indian, was hurled into the uncertain chasm of no-man's land soon after the British announced the transfer of power to Hindu India and Muslim Pakistan.

Hubert didn't opt for India. An employee of the Bengal–Nagpur Railway posted at a remote tea garden in the sleepy hill station of Haflong in a forgotten corner of North East India, Hubert was suddenly dumped at Bhairab Junction.

His wife, Preeti, decided not to set up home in the assigned railway quarters situated on the western part of Kamalpur, mostly occupied by Bengali and Bihari Muslims. Though a Christian, she did not feel safe with Muslim neighbours. Stories of the great Calcutta massacre launched by the Muslim League had rattled her. She decided to rent a place at east Kamalpur, just a kilometre down the wooded lane from the bustling station. The latent Hindu within her overshadowed the thought that Christianity alone could inject religious equilibrium into a divided Indian society.

Manorama's story mesmerized me. I had not seen the world beyond the confines of my village. The only sources of knowledge to which I had access were Dhiru Acharya, our primary teacher, a few teachers at Kader Bux High School, the stories that I heard from my mother, and the bustling railway station.

Manorama helped open up the closed doors to the world of knowledge and learning. I was transfixed by her dreamy eyes when she narrated the Wilson's family history and spoke about her dream of becoming a doctor.

Manorama was good at storytelling. We would sit for hours on end on the cemented stairs which tapered down to the exclusive family pond, especially excavated for the women to bathe. Her eyes would glance up to the unfathomable blues above and the shoal of fish in the waters below.

She brought life and laughter back to our desolate habitat. Her family settled into one of the empty buildings at the northern edge of the campus, next to our family temple. She was, as I recall, more beautiful than many of the glossy British beauties whose pictures decorated the walls of the kacheri revenue building and the rooms of my hallowed ancestors and elders. I often peeped through her windows.

'Hey Krishna, come on in. Don't peep. Good boys don't do that.' Manorama would admonish me mockingly in her lilting sweet voice. She would come out and often grabbed my hands before I could manage to jump out from her window ledge. 'So! You've been spying on me!'

'Not exactly . . . ' I often tried to protest feebly. Words always failed me in her presence. Most of the time I stared at her beauty and her strange apparel—a skirt and blouse, very uncommon and unimaginable in my rural Bengali environ.

She was a real English woman, to me at least. My poor English was chiselled and refined by her. She told me many strange stories in English. She often drew me closer and planted an affectionate kiss on my forehead and read over the *Statesman* that carried the most important political news and analysis. I did not quite follow the main stories of the day. The stories she narrated sounded grim and sad. The

Congress and the Muslim League had virtually agreed on the partition of India; two separate homelands for Hindus and Muslims.

There were killings everywhere, in Bengal, Bihar and Punjab. Mahatma Gandhi was again on an indefinite hunger strike, this time to force the Hindu and Muslim leaders to agree to maintain the unity of the subcontinent. There was a news story on the alleged assassination of Netaji Subhas Chandra Bose by British secret agents.

'Where would you go? India or Pakistan? You are a Christian and an Englishwoman.' I looked up at her agonized face.

'We don't count. It doesn't matter, I think. They wouldn't kill us Christians. I'd like to go over to England, the ancestral place of my great-great grandpa.'

'Is it very far?'

'Oh yes, very very far. It takes more than a month by ship. I'd like to join a college and become a doctor.' Her eyes became moist with shadows of her dream.

'I hope our house remains in India and we won't have to go over to Pakistan,' I said with great trepidation.

'Pray with me before Lord Jesus. He will save you. Don't worry. I'll take you to England with me.' She pulled me gently into an adjoining room, the Wilson's family chapel. She bent down on her knees and uttered some prayer in English.

'Saifullah says that his Allah is the mightiest. He can defeat all other gods.'

'All gods are equally good and benign.' Manorama laughed loudly and pushed another candy into my mouth.

The next night Jackson Hubert Wilson shared some astounding news. Mahatma Gandhi, he said, was due to pass through Bhairab station the next day, on his way from Calcutta to Noakhali, a southern district that had witnessed the most savage communal holocaust. Important leaders like Fazlul Haq and Suhrawardy might accompany him.

Father and Mother, both committed to the Independence movement, but not exactly of the Gandhian type, called an emergency meeting of the Hindu community leaders, rather the upper caste leaders. They sat through the night below hurricane lanterns, smoked hukkas and finally decided to take a delegation to Mahatma Gandhi and other leaders demanding security for the lives and properties of the minorities. Mano didi was called upon to draft two memorandums, one in English and the other in Bengali. We watched the proceedings silently from the wings.

Next morning, around eleven, we followed the sizeable delegation, headed by Subhan Ali, another freedom fighter of a different kind.

The Chittagong Mail chugged slowly into the platform. A posse of policemen cordoned off the special bogey in which the leaders were travelling. We stood on the overbridge hoping to get glimpses of the legendary leader.

Mahatma Gandhi stepped out of the compartment, escorted by the District Collector and the Superintendent of Police. Other leaders formed a security ring around him.

Mano didi dragged me down the stairs and rushed to the crowd that had gathered around the thin and scantily clothed person. She dodged the police and managed to put a garland around the great man's neck. He gave a toothless smile, patted Mano didi's head and turned to our elders who were busy explaining the tense communal situation. Someone offered him a glass of juice which he accepted with a disarming grin.

I did not know much about Gandhi. But the frail person in a half-dhoti and bare chest with a stick in his hand impressed me. Father, who did not subscribe to the Gandhian way of struggle, also touched his feet. The weary smile on the old man's face was imprinted on my mind as the face of a tired and disillusioned man who was still determined to fight.

Mano was full of surprises.

I was busy negotiating a thin branch of a mango tree which yielded fruits only in the winter. My great-grand father, I was told, had imported the rare variety from the then remote island of Singapora.

Manorama came running through the raspberry bushes. 'Come down quickly,' she ordered.

'What's the big deal? Let me pluck the mango. It's ripe.' I pointed at the ripe yellow fruit dangling just a few twigs away.

'Come down fast. We're going to the station to pick up the Christmas tree.'

'What's that?'

'I'll explain later. It's something to do with the birthday of Jesus Christ. We're getting cakes from Calcutta and many more surprises.'

My knowledge of cakes was limited to the stone-hard muffins pedalled by the railway station hawkers, some stale and sweet and some rotten and sour. Calcutta cakes should be big and juicy. The name itself sounded magical.

'Is it a big cake? Must be big. Otherwise, why should it come by train? How will we carry it home?' I asked impatiently as we sat on the overbridge expecting the arrival of the train from the Dacca end of the mysterious tracks that vanished behind the horizon. Manorama looked over Jeremy's shoulders towards a distant column of smoke.

'Mano didi,' my excited chatter continued, 'how can they bring a whole tree in a train? Was Jesus born under that tree? Why get trees from Calcutta? We've plenty of trees in our orchard.'

'Ah Krishna!' she moaned, 'would you please shut up? It's a Christmas tree, coming all the way from the Happy Valley tea garden in Darjeeling, my grandpa's tea garden. It's a pine tree.'

'Does tea grow in gardens, like flowers? Why can't we grow tea here, in our orchards?'

'Oh Krishna!' This time she grimaced in mock anger, 'You're impossible.'

She stood up and dragged Jeremy and me towards the five o'clock Chittagong mail that clambered in slowly into the platform. Jackson Hubert Wilson, the stationmaster, surrounded by a sizeable crowd of coolies and onlookers took out a green pine sapling from the brake van. Mano, Jeremy and I trooped around the tree singing a catchy tune—Jingle something . . . Bell something.

Mr Wilson led the procession. Mrs Wilson ordered us to take off our shoes before the tree was taken into the family chapel. She washed the sapling with pond water and sprinkled holy Ganga water before it was ceremonially installed.

The next forty-eight hours were like a dream, in preparation for what Bengalis called the *bada din*, the big Christmas day. We gathered flowers, prepared and hung colourful buntings and Manorama fished out a red outfit from an iron chest, complete with a white wig and moustache. It was for Santa Claus, she explained, who brought gifts from his factory in the North Pole.

'That's a far off place. How does he manage to come all the way?'

'Krishna!' Manorama chided me, 'He goes everywhere in his reindeer sleigh.'

'But that's a long distance to cover!'

'He flies and brings gifts for the kids.'

'For me too? I'm not a Christian.'

'Yes, he brings gift for everybody. Now shut up and put on the Santa Claus costume.'

I was too small to wear that impressive outfit. The choice finally fell on Rahman. He slipped into it without any prejudice to his mighty Allah. Manorama tied the white moustache and wig on him, and taught him to laugh in a loud and deep voice—ho ho ho!

We danced around the pine sapling, well decorated with shining stars and coloured glass balls. We danced to the tune of an English number played over a gramophone, a dog monogrammed on its discoloured body. We called it *kaler gaan*—music from the machine.

Christmas, Santa Claus and nativity were new to me. The events convinced me about the humble origin, heavenly piety and cosmic compassion, if not supreme might of the son of a carpenter and a virgin mother. My happiness knew no bounds, because Mano didi was happy. Her radiant beauty had assumed an ethereal glow.

Just as the grandfather clock chimed twelve, she guided us to the tree and recited a prayer. We, including Rahman, repeated after her. Her Jesus, my Krishna, and Rahman's Allah, I felt, had transferred their energy fields to the small pine sapling. It came to life as we sang for the man who had lived and died for his fellow men.

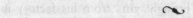

I suffered two successive shocks.

The devastating hailstorm had ruined our vegetable garden patches and the nearest market was at Bhairab, three kilometres away. Some family guests suddenly arrived from Dacca and mother had very little fresh fish and vegetables at home. She sent Jasim and me to rush to the *malopada*, the fishermen's and the Baliachar hamlet of low caste Hindus and Muslims. Baliachar was perhaps the only belt that had not suffered the hail and still had supplies of some fresh winter vegetables.

The malopada was my favourite place on the banks of the Satmukhi. It was the home of Mukund Majhi and my hero Rani. Mukund filled our bags with fish and Rani delighted us with red sherbet and coconut cookies.

'Where are you going?' Rani asked.

'Baliachar, to collect some vegetables,' I replied.

'Take care. A lot of Biharis have set up camps near Baliachar. They keep on threatening us.'

'Why are they here?'

'They say it's going to be Pakistan and we Bengalis have no place here. They speak in a tongue that we don't understand.'

'They speak Urdu,' Jasim commented.

'What's Urdu?' I asked.

'Our madrasa teacher speaks this language.' Jasim enriched my pool of knowledge and I resolved to discuss the issue with Mano didi.

'Ma sent me, Paran kaka. There are some guests at home and she wants some cauliflower, cabbage and other fresh vegetables.'

'You need not have come all the way. You could have sent Jasim,' replied Paran, one of our sharecroppers.

'It's a pleasure to meet you, Kaka. Should we wait?'

'Go in. Your Kaki has prepared payas with khajur gur. Have some. I'll be back in a few minutes.'

The payas (a sweet prepared with thickened milk and rice) was as heavenly as nectar, as was the molasses made out of date palm juice. I had two bowls.

'Like it?' asked Paran kaki.

'Excellent. Just like my Ma prepares.'

'Take some for mejo thakurain.'

Our conversation was suddenly disrupted by loud cries from a distressed female voice. We rushed towards the source of the cries. Paran led us and a few more villagers followed.

It was a ghostly and ghastly scene. Three Bihari Muslims were dragging a young Muslim girl by her sari. She had no other upper garment on her body. She looked almost naked and was screaming for help. Paran intervened.

'Hey, you Biharis. Why are you molesting one of our girls?'

'Shut up you Bengali rat. We want this girl,' shouted back a burly middle-aged man.

'No, you can't. She is our village's daughter. We will not allow it,' shouted another Muslim villager.

'Shut up you jahil kafir, you ignorant non-believer Bengali. You're not even a Muslim like we are. Allah has given this land to us. We will take whomever we want.'

His comments excited the Bihari group. They shouted for help and their compatriots rushed in from a nearby camping site with swords and knives. They attacked the mixed Hindu and Muslim crowd of Baliachar. I took out my Sheffield and tried to charge. Jasim pulled me back.

'Hide your knife. This is a Bengali-Bihari war. Let's get out.'

'Why? We should defend our people.'

'Get out. You can't fight them. Let's take a short cut to the malopada and get back home.' We ran through mustard, sugarcane and lentil fields and reached home with our supplies.

Panting and puffing we sat on the stairs of the western court and cried loudly. Rahman followed by Manorama and mother rushed in. Tomtom tried to assuage my fearful anguish by licking my feet. Pintu came from somewhere and started chewing my hair. Even Sonai, my favourite duck, rushed in.

Jasim narrated the ghastly incident of the clash between Bengalis and Biharis at Baliachar. Rahman summoned the few remaining family retainers and directed them to mount guard and sent someone to inform Subhan Ali, father's political colleague.

As we shared our anguish and apprehension Lalu, a son of Jagannath Jola rushed in. 'Kartama, save my father.'

He narrated a bizarre story. Jagannath had climbed up one of his areca nut trees to harvest the ripe nuts. The tree overlooked the private compound of Sayeed Ashfaq Khan, believed to be a blue-blooded Pathan from Rohtas in Bihar and the new sub-registrar of the land revenue department. His begum took serious exception to a lowly Hindu looking down upon her private premises and raised a hue and cry.

Jagannath was forced down from the tree and was punished with fifty shoe beatings by a Muslim employee of the Pathan officer. The sub-registrar had summoned the police chief to arrest Jagannath and register a case for violating the modesty of an aristocrat Muslim lady.

Mother thought for a while with her lips drawn in and asked Rahman to follow her to the sub-registrar's office. Other elders of our extended clan followed her. Some Muslim ladies of neighbouring villages joined in. The burly Pathan was not prepared to meet a frail Hindu lady confronting him, the senior most officer in our small town. The new police station chief was not acquainted with our family's bygone glory.

'Why are you torturing Jagannath?' She charged the hallowed Pathan.

'He outraged the modesty of my wife.'

'How? In what manner?'

'He looked into my house from the top of the areca nut tree.'

'That tree has been there for the last fifteen years. He has been harvesting it for the last ten years. How does he violate the modesty of a woman by simply looking at her?'

The sub-registrar was trapped. The assembled crowd got over their awe of a wheatish Pathan who claimed to be a descendant of the Paigambar, Peace Be Unto Him. They lined up behind my mother. The police chief retreated to a corner.

Subhan Ali appeared with a group of Muslim villagers. He took over from mother. 'Khan sahib, we respect you. But this is not the way to treat a Bengali. We have known Jagannath for the last forty years. Please do not spread a communal virus in our town. We have been living like brothers for ages. You're from Bihar and you don't know the meaning of Bengali brotherhood.'

The sub-registrar retreated. The police chief apologized to my mother uttering something which we did not hear.

No one clapped for Ma and Subhan Ali. He escorted mother to our home and promised to post four additional guards till my father returned from Sylhet.

∽

Father did not return even after a week. On the eighth day a stranger accompanied by Subhan Ali dropped in and informed mother that my father along with twenty others had been arrested at Shrimangal (Sylhet) while campaigning for the merger of the district with India. Manoranjan Dhar and surprisingly Karamat Ali were also arrested. They were detained at Brahmanbaria.

'What are the charges?'

'No charge is necessary. The League government and Assam Congress want Sylhet to go to Pakistan. It may be a preventive arrest. Don't worry. It's not new for him. I'll go to Brahmanbaria today and get him home. You stay calm.'

'Will they torture him?'

'Possibly. The British have tortured him. Now it's time for Suhrawardy to repeat the British game. Don't worry. I'll be back soon.'

Mother accompanied Subhan and returned after three days with heartening news. On Fazlul Haq's intervention and pleadings from Kiran Shankar Roy (a Congress leader in favour of United Bengal), father and the other detained persons were released on condition that they would not enter Sylhet until the referendum was completed in July 1947. Father came home with signs of torture on his body. However, I could not even imagine the wounds he suffered to his psyche. My efforts to bring up the subject were ignored. He looked downcast and meaninglessly puffed at his hukka and chatted with Subhan Ali and the others. Only Rahman was allowed to enter the room with glowing charcoal for the hukka, tea and homemade eats. Jasim and I hid behind some croton bushes and heard the elders talking in hushed tones.

'Karta,' Subhan spoke, 'now rest. Congress has sacrificed our cause. Let's join hands with Fazlul Haq. His Krishak Praja Party is still intact in our area.'

'He may join the Suhrawardy government after Partition,' father said in a gloomy voice.

'Jinnah won't trust Haq or Suhrawardy. He wants a pliable leader. His choice is likely to fall on Nazimuddin of the Dacca Nawab family or Nurul Amin, a staunch Jinnah follower. Suhrawardy identifies himself as a Bengali.'

'Are you sure?' Father asked.

'This is my opinion, Deben karta. Let's side with Fazlul Haq. He is a son of the soil,' averred Subhan Ali.

'Fine. Let's go to Calcutta and meet him.'

'I think he should be in Bhairab in another couple of days. Let's confirm his itinerary.'

'Do you think it's safe to leave my family here?' Father asked in a hesitant voice.

'Karta,' Subhan said in a hurt voice, 'we're here. You're one of us. Don't leave us. This is our land.'

'Fine. But the Baliachar incident has shaken our confidence.'

'I suggest you send a message to Ramzan. His gang could provide some security. Our men would be camping in one of your orchards. I don't think the Biharis or the gangs of Dhala and Dudu would dare attack your home.'

The meeting dispersed. After dinner father called my elder brother and me to sit by his side. This was a rare moment of togetherness. We had never seen him sitting idle. He roamed all over the province on political errands, revolutionary assignments and to create committed cadres. To the larger family he was a good for nothing nomad, to mother he was a trusted husband but he never gave us the impression that he was a caring father.

Growing up in a mammoth joint family did not require strict parental supervision and guidance. We, especially I, grew up like wild weed. We learnt from each other. We had a few dozen mothers and aunts to learn from and dozens of uncles and other elders to spank our buttocks at the slightest pretext.

I was overwhelmed by father's gesture. 'Look boys, I have not been a good father. I never earned for you. I think I lived for my ideals. But changes are taking place. The family has broken up. We're on our own. Our predominant position has virtually gone. Take care of your mother and yourselves.'

'Are we going to Hindustan?' I asked.

'No. But we're on our own. I don't know if the bargadars will give us our share of grains or whether our subjects will obey us anymore. I'll try to earn some money for you two and your mother.'

'We don't want much Baba,' my elder brother said, 'I will require a private tutor for maths and some money to pay for the examination fees.'

'Don't worry. I want you to know that I love you boys. Do take care of your mother and the properties if something happens to me.'

Father did not display any emotion. Perhaps he was not capable of it or perhaps he just wanted to hide his swelling emotions. I saw a defeated general limping on his wounded soul. A cloud of sympathy enveloped my tiny conscience. A sense of helplessness shattered me from within.

∽

I had only two philosopher guides to show me some light through dark tunnels of confusion—Rahman and Manorama. As I walked slowly towards Mano didi's room, a fat Bihari coolie entered our complex.

'Well, little master,' he talked in his Bhojpuri mixed Bengali, 'I am off to my place in Munghyr. Can't stay here after Wilson sahib's transfer.'

'Whose transfer?'

'Wilson sahib is going to Calcutta. A new Mussalman stationmaster is coming to replace him.'

'Is he going away? How soon?' I managed to ask.

'A telegram arrived this morning. The new stationmaster is coming in another three to four months.'

'I'm going over to Calcutta. There'll be better opportunities there.'

'Has Pakistan been created?'

'It will be soon.' The Bihari porter left after delivering some groceries.

'Is that correct?' I asked Mano didi.

'I really don't know. Let's talk to papa tonight.'

Mr Wilson confirmed the Bihari coolie's story. He had pleaded with the Lt Governor, an acquaintance of his father, to be transferred to a safer place. The British Lord had concurred that Bhairab wasn't the best place for young children of English descent to grow up.

My world suddenly exploded and scattered into a debris of disillusionment and depression. My brief meeting with father, one of the rare times of togetherness had shaken me. The news of Mano didi's departure for Calcutta sucked me into a whirling void. My life and my laughter were suddenly threatened by shadows of gloom and isolation. My highway to the universe suddenly disappeared. I shuddered at the thought of a world without newspapers, radio or books. I started turning myself away from life, from Mano didi and myself.

Mano too, I liked to believe, was sad to leave Kamalpur and me. But she did not betray her emotions. Her nimble feet danced around, her golden voice hummed my favourite tunes and she continued to share the mysteries of the world. Her talk, stories, her analyses of newspaper and radio broadcasts continued to interest me.

I knew that sad days were around the corner but I could not help feeling happy for Manorama and her family. They were bound for the legendary city of Calcutta and better openings to the highway of education and information. Manorama would be sailing for London, the place of her ancestors. She was a part of the Empire, a kind of associate member of the white community. She was not emotionally attached to the soil as I was.

Or was I wrong?

six

The Other World Collapses

They say Time is a ceaseless and remorseless traveller that cannot be segmented. At the young age of seven, I could not understand such grave characteristics of Time. But I was reminded by Saifi that time was not going to wait for my existential pellets rebounding inside an uncertain cavity of confusion. He woke me up to the reality that our annual examinations would commence from 12 December. Father's disillusionment with his political journey, Mano didi's impending departure and the Baliachar incident had not frozen the march of Time.

It is not that I was a reluctant student. Except the horrible subject of arithmetic, I enjoyed all the other books and subjects. I was most interested in books that were prohibited. Some of the books of Tagore, Sharat Chandra and Bankim Chandra fascinated me. Mano didi had initiated me into the world of English and I had started reading condensed versions of *Robin Hood* and *Treasure Island*.

I was ready for the exams and my class teacher expected that Mehboob Alam and I would be the main contenders for the first position. Mehboob and I competed for the annual award but that December we could not complete our annual examinations.

On 14 December when we were writing our paper on Bengali literature and grammar a sudden commotion gripped the market next to our school. Before we could figure out what the commotion was about, one of the school employees huddled us into a room and closed the door. The only window that opened to the front road was pried open by a fellow student. We saw a large procession armed with deadly weapons rushing past the school building towards the area that housed big business firms owned by Marwari traders. Uncle Birendra's chemist shop and other shops owned by extended family members were also located in the same area.

My anxiety was heightened when my brother Benoy rushed in and asked me to follow him home. We took a shortcut through cultivated fields, ran past the railway station and reached home. The story narrated by him was horrible, worse than a horror film. An armed crowd of about 200 had attacked the building that housed the richest trader, Budhai Shah. They ransacked the warehouse and plundered his treasury. In the process, three Bihari employees of Budhai were killed and a few others injured. From the many different versions that we heard, we gleaned the facts.

Budhai was a loan shark. He advanced money to needy cultivators and petty fishermen. He charged thirty per cent interest and took sole right to the merchandise produced by the cultivators and the fishing community. That particular day Budhai had imprisoned a peasant for failing to repay the accumulated interest amounting to Rs 300. A Bihari employee was directed to punish the offender with ten whiplashes.

The incident had not taken on communal tones—other Hindu-owned shops were not attacked but the organized raid rattled the thriving business community. They shut down the market and notified Jameson sahib, the chief of a jute mill, that they would not operate their trading houses until the culprits were arrested and punished. A Britisher, Jameson was supposed to have direct access to authorities in Dacca and Mymensingh. Closure of trade meant tremendous loss to the entire economy of the region. Bhairab was an important centre for fish, chilli, jute, rice, ginger and turmeric exports.

Amongst others, Uncle Birendra and my father attended a reconciliation meeting convened by Jameson. But Sayeed

Ashfaq Khan, the sub-registrar, hijacked the tone and tenor of the meeting. He spoke in Urdu mixed with Bengali and sent shivers down the spines of the Hindu traders. The birth of Pakistan, he said, was around the corner. Pakistan would be the god-gifted land of the Muslims where, according to Mohammedan laws the Hindus would have to live as *jimmis*, a protected people. As they would forfeit all rights and all loans would be written off, the Hindus would have to pay extra taxes.

Jameson's intervention did not help. Subhan Ali, Karamat Ali and Madhu mian, all seasoned political leaders were shouted down by the excited Muslim mob. Dhala mian also pitched in with an inflammatory speech against the Hindus and especially against our family for treating the Muslims as serfs. He demanded the surrender of landed properties by our family and the distribution of the same among the Muslim cultivators. Father's efforts to restrain Dhala were booed down by his supporters.

'Karta, you are a friend of the poor. Is it just that your family would have everything and we poor Muslims would starve?' Dhala charged father.

'You have a point Dhala. But these things have to be sorted out through legal means. Why bring in violence and communal elements?'

'We can't wait for the law to take its course,' Dhala shouted back. He flaunted a sword in front of Uncle Birendra and said that Hindus had no place in his Pakistan.

The meeting ended with maddening slogans: Ladke lenge Pakistan and Allah ho Akbar. The Hindus panicked and shut down their business houses. I could tell from my father's face that he was expecting much worse. The crazed followers of a new nation on the anvil blunted his acceptance as a selfless political leader, a revolutionary and a friend of the poor. Father returned home a dejected person.

The panic was further heightened the next night when the last of the chowkidars, Gulab Misr, a Bihari Brahmin, rushed in to inform us that two men with stab injuries were approaching our home from the mango grove. An alarm was raised and all available hands rushed to the forecourt. I followed Rahman and Jasim. Under bright torch light, we could see two men trying to clamber in. They were bleeding profusely and were taken to the eastern court building. Brajen Acharya was summoned to dress the wounds and treat them. We peeped in from behind the elders and could see the gaping wounds on their bellies. Some parts of their intestines were hanging out.

Hubert Wilson narrated the whole story. The Muslim League had given a call for the ouster of the Hindu exploiters—the landlords, the Marwari trading community and moneylenders. A local leader of Kishoreganj had urged the Muslims to forcibly seize Hindu properties. According to him, the affluent Hindus had established a stranglehold on the people of East Bengal. Their advancement in every walk of life was attributed as a Hindu conspiracy against Muslims.

Assimilation at the societal and cultural levels had taken place over centuries, and emotionally the two communities shared each other's pleasures and pain. However, the politics of religion had shattered old bondages. The exploited were told that total annihilation of the exploiters would alone give them political as well as spiritual emancipation. Barring a few old loyalists like Rahman and a handful of secular politicians like Subhan Ali, the rest of the Muslim bargadars had started refusing to pay land revenue and a share of the crops. The loan burdened peasantry had taken to plundering and evicting Hindu traders. Wilson's narration of the new social and political dynamics flew over my head but I understood that vast changes were about to shake us up.

∾

The tragedy of the day was repeated at night and was even more terrible. Jaynagar, a predominantly Hindu village about fifteen kilometres south-west of Bhairab witnessed a ghastly incident. The Dacca–Chittagong mail was stopped near Joynagar and a mixed group of Bihari Muslims, Kuttis and Ansar marauders alighted from the train shouting bloodcurdling slogans and attacked the sleepy village. Resistance by local Bengali Muslims was subdued on the intervention of a district functionary of the pro-Nurul Amin Muslim League. The marauders burned homes, killed about twenty Hindu males and carried away twelve women. They dumped the dead bodies in the stationary trains and directed the driver to speed off. The Hindu passengers alighted at Bhairab and forced Hubert Wilson to send a telephonic message to Dacca and Mymensingh.

On their demand the dead bodies were taken out of the compartment and covered with a tarpaulin. Some Hindu passengers including two Chakma families ran into our house for shelter. They suffered from the illusion that the old landlord's imposing structures alone were enough to secure their lives. The Buddhist Chakma's mostly inhabiting the Chittagong Hill Tracts had not sided with the Muslim League's movement. They identified with the Congress and the Subhasist groups and hoped for a merger with India. One Rupen Chakma often visited our home for discussions with father and his political colleagues.

I had no exposure to the Chakmas, but I was moved by the cries of the panicky passengers. Three of them bled profusely from stab injuries. Father applied some herbal concoction and called for Brajen Acharya who arrived with his medical kit. The news had spread like wild fire and a sizeable crowd gathered at our outer gate. Father asked a Muslim employee to rush to the police station with a hurriedly written note. The police arrived after about two hours. They questioned some of our family employees and asked some villagers to help shift the wounded persons to the primary health centre that stood on a flank of our school premises.

Hubert Wilson announced that a special train was likely to arrive from Kishoreganj with an additional police force and the afflicted train would leave for its destination under police guard. His assurances assuaged the panicky shelter seekers and they were escorted back to the station by local police officers.

Robbed of my sleep I walked down to Mano didi's room and knocked on the door.

'Who's there?'

'Krishna.'

'What are you doing up so late? Go to sleep.'

'Can't sleep. Tell me something.'

She opened the door, hustled me in and comforted me with a piece of cake. 'Don't enter a lady's room at night.' Mano laughed in the dim lantern light.

'You're not a lady yet. Only married girls become ladies.'

'Who told you that?'

'I know. Rani didi became a lady after she was married. Before that she was our football captain.'

'Stop babbling, you idiot. Tell me what's eating you.'

'What's happening around? Why are we are fighting? Why are Hindus and Muslims being killed?'

'Look, Krishna,' she sat by my side, 'it's a time for change. India is being divided into Hindustan and Pakistan. Pakistan, they say, is the land of Muslims. No Hindu can stay here.'

'Even we have to go? Where would we go?'

'Despite your dad's aversion to the idea obviously you'd go to India.'

'Which India? Where would the new India be?'

'Krishna, don't ask silly questions. India is a big place. The storm may dump you anywhere, from Calcutta to Calicut.'

Mano stuffed my palm with two Morton chocolates and closed the door. I did not feel like going to bed. I lay prostrate, face up to the dark starry sky and tried to weave the events of that past one year with my emotional stirrings. Father said I was a Cancerian. Cancerians, he said, have a retentive memory, particularly for emotionally laden events that they can recall in detail for years afterwards. I realized how correct he was. All the events flashed past my mind and it dawned upon me that my India would not remain the same after the impending political tsunami hit us. I did not go back to bed but instead went straight to Rahman's shack and slept under Jasim's quilt.

Next evening we assembled at Wilson's parlour around the radio. The 7 p.m. Bengali news bulletin announced that the British government had decided to transfer power on 15 August 1947 to India and Pakistan, a new homeland of the Muslims of India. East Bengal would be incorporated into the new country called Pakistan. The bulletin was followed by a radio broadcast by Hassan Shaheed Suhrawardy, who appealed to the people of East Bengal to maintain communal harmony and assured equal rights and opportunities to all sections of the people.

The significance of the broadcast was elaborated upon by Manorama, and the assembled ladies and children nodded their heads as if they understood the summum bonum of the historic announcement. They did not realize that the senior political leaders had actually pronounced a death sentence on them. Mano and Ma discussed the developments and tried to speculate on the exact implications. As I listened to them, I realized that Hindus from East Bengal had started migrating to areas likely to be included in India. Some Muslims were also migrating to East Bengal. It was not yet an avalanche of human migration.

'When are you expected to leave for Calcutta?' Mother asked.

'Sometime in August-September this year. It's good for me aunty. I'll be able to rejoin school and prepare for my medical course in London. At Haflong I used to study in a missionary school. There is no school for girls in Bhairab.'

'That's a big problem. My late father-in-law was opposed to a girl's school. The Muslims also don't like to send their girls to school. Now it's too late to try. I have to wait for at least two years, because Benoy is in class eight. He should complete his matriculation in 1949. Till then I will try to stay put.' Mother shared her thoughts with Mano and her mother Preeti.

'Uncle should plan an early migration, aunty. It's better to move early before the avalanche of migration starts.'

'It's difficult, Mano. He has identified himself with the soil and people of this area. He is not a practical person. I'll try. Talk to him if you can.'

I followed mother with a heavy heart. She entered the kitchen and offered our parrot Chandana her favourite food of ripe red chillies. As she pecked at the hot food, she asked a startling question. '*Mukhe hansi nai keno*? Why is there no smile on your face?'

'Shut up,' I replied rudely.

'Shut up,' Chandana retorted and started cackling some more slang. Chandana was a naughty bird but she understood our mood perfectly. As I sat down for dinner with our pet dog Tomtom by my side, I had some burning questions. 'Ma, would we have to leave the village? Where would we go? Where in India?'

'Don't worry. Your elder brother Bijoy will look for a safe place near Calcutta. Maybe we'll have to finally quit this place. Let Benoy finish his matriculation. Maybe sometime in 1949. In the meantime we have to arrange to sell some of our properties. Don't worry. I'm there and your Baba knows a lot of political people. They'll protect us.'

After dinner she gave me ten rupees to give to my class teacher Moinul Khan to get me textbooks for class six to which we were promoted en masse though we failed to write two papers owing to civil disturbances. Ma sat by my bedside along with Tomtom and started humming one of her favourite songs. The melodious tune in the midst of our anxieties had a calming effect. I slept well until Jasim woke me up early in the morning.

'There's a big problem. Papa has been summoned by the *qazi* Sharif Mullah to explain his absence from the mosque.'

'Does Rahman kaka attend mosque regularly?'

'No, he prays at home.'

'Why should the qazi summon him now?'

'Don't know. Tell Kaki to help Papa.'

Mother listened to Jasim patiently. The western wing of our village had a small mosque where qazi-cum-imam-cum-alem Sharif Mullah used to rule over a small band of the faithful who preferred to visit the shrine to offer ritual prayers. He also imparted Urdu and Arabic lessons to boys whose parents preferred to send their children to the *maqtab*, the school attached to the mosque. The main attraction was the dargah of the holy mendicant, the Pir Ashraf Jalali, and not the mosque.

The qazi was summoned to conduct marriages and other religious rituals. As the custodian of the dargah he received an annual grant of Rs 100 from Grandfather Chandra Kishore. Later a piece of land was granted in perpetuity for the maintenance of the dargah and the school.

In our part of Bengal, mosque attendance was not compulsory and the Muslims assembled at the holy site once a year on the occasion of the *urs* of Pir Ashraf. Both Hindus and Muslims attended the death anniversary and various cultural programmes were staged on the grand occasion. I remember father rendering a couple of folk songs each year on the festive urs day. We also enjoyed riding the wheel, witnessing acrobatic performances and ferries, and looking into a viewmaster which presented images of famous places like the Taj Mahal and the Red Fort. The poor qazi had very little say in the daily religious and spiritual lives of the Bengali Muslims whose first names were as common as Hindu names like Madhu, Kala, Dhala and Gora, names denoting skin colour or the nature of the child. They had not yet adopted Arabic names.

'Krishna, accompany Jasim to the mosque and report back,' said Ma.

We had a hurried breakfast of *panta bhat* and fried potato. It was a wonderful delicacy and a nutritious meal. (The parboiled rice developed a unique flavour—it was cooked the previous night, soaked in water, partially drained and served with a pinch of salt and green chillies).

To our surprise the small mosque compound was full. Dudu and Dhala sat beside Qazi Sharif Mullah. A stout man with flowing reddish hair and beard occupied the high seat.

Dhala spoke first, introducing the honoured guest as Mufti Salahuddin Qureshi, a great teacher of Arabic and the Holy Quran. He had taken the trouble to come down to this part of Bengal from Rohtas in Bihar to rescue the jahil Muslims from the 'polluted' influence of the Hindu religion and idol worship. He was a great leader of the Tablighi Jammat.

Dudu's speech started with a Muslim prayer and then he added that the Muslims in this part of Bengal had forgotten the religion of Allah and had taken to the corrupt practices of the Jalali Sufis and Bengali Hindus. He welcomed the great teacher Salahuddin and requested him to help those who had strayed to return to the path of true Islam.

The honoured guest delivered a long lecture in Urdu which we did not understand. Qazi Sharif Mullah conveyed the gist. He said that now onwards all believers must attend Friday prayers at the designated mosque, observe *roza,* the Ramadan fast scrupulously and boycott all Hindu celebrations. Worshipping a pir and glorifying a dargah was against the Shariat and Hadith. People like Rahman were taken to task for taking part in Hindu celebrations and were warned that the Qazi was empowered by the Shariat to impose a penalty on the deviants. He appointed Dhala mian as the *daroga*, the person in charge of the mosque and invested him with the power to ensure full attendance at the mosque by the faithful.

This was new to us. How could we observe Durga Puja and the worship of goddesses like Mansa, the snake goddess, Mangal Chandi, the dispeller of evil spirits, Shitla the goddess of small pox, and Olai Chandi, the goddess of cholera, without the participation of our Muslim neighbours and friends? These were community deities worshipped by all, irrespective of religion and caste.

We returned home a disheartened lot. Rahman was lost in thought.

'What's happening?' I asked in anguish, 'Won't you take part in our puja? Next month is the Shitla puja festival. Who would arrange things?'

'Don't know, khoka. I never knew Allah had said so many things against Hindus. Let me ask your mother.'

Mother had no ready reply to Rahman's puzzling questions. She stood silently against a bamboo pole and looked up at the clouded sky, as if searching for some message from above. 'Look Rahman. You must follow the dictates of the Holy Quran.'

'Never read the Quran, Shariat or Hadith. I know only Bismillah ur Rehman e Rahim. That's what my father taught me.'

'Just keep attending the mosque prayers and don't hate others. God can never teach hatred.'

Rahman was not impressed by the answers and muttered that he would find out more when father returned from Dacca.

～

Father was a much-harassed man by July 1947. The joint family had fallen apart. His own brothers had betrayed him in property matters and as a disinherited son he could not claim any income from some of the family owned business ventures. He had never cared about money. But money had become scarce after the Second World War. The science of ayurveda which he had studied had started yielding ground to allopathic medicines. Our Bhairab market already had a Licensed Medical Practitioner.

The main reason for his discomfiture was his disillusionment with the political developments. The days for revolution were over. His political icon Subhas Chandra Bose had been declared dead, believed to have died in a plane crash. His political party, the nascent Forward Block was yet to cut its ties with the Congress. He was an irritation for both the Congress and Muslim League.

It was around 8 July. Father was huddled with his close political colleagues. Besides Subhan and Karamat Ali one Guha and another Acharya from Mymensingh joined the discussions. I had not seen them earlier. Much later, I came to know that Guha was a Calcutta-based leader of the Forward Block wing of the Congress and Acharya was a titled big zamindar and our family's overlord. He owed allegiance to left wing politics. Mother and a maid served tea and snacks while Jasim and I filled the hukkas and served coconut water.

'I'm surprised at the jubilation amongst the Assamese people. The merger of Sylhet with Pakistan has been celebrated all over Assam.' Acharya commented on a sad note.

'Can't help it,' added father. 'Congress has abandoned us. Nehru has no time for Bengal. His father detested C. R.

Das and he hates Netaji. He does not trust Bengalis. No idea how much blood would flow after the real Partition of the country. Your left party has also not protested against Congress machinations.'

'That's not correct Deben. We protested and we really don't accept this Partition and sham Independence. I think I'll have to shift to Calcutta till things cool down. Jinnah is talking in terms of promulgation of the property acquisition act. Perhaps our properties will be confiscated. What are your plans?'

'I'll try to stay put. I'm a disinherited son. My brothers have cheated me. I'll stay here and serve the people.'

'Come over to Calcutta. We'll try to accommodate you at the Grey Street Ayurvedic College. You can teach there and earn a decent living and help the party,' Guha pleaded in a sincere voice.

'Let me think it over dada. My friends Subhan and Karamat would like me to stay on and help the people.'

'Yes raja sahib,' Subhan spoke. 'We're surrounded by rabid Leaguers. Fazlul Haq is directionless and confused. Suhrawardy is not sure of his standing with Jinnah. They don't like his pro-Bengali sympathies.'

'I'm sure Jinnah will ditch him. Anyway Deben,' Acharya spoke with a tone of finality, 'if you like I can still grant you a few hectares of land to support your family from its produce.'

'No karta. My father has denied me my rights. I'll strive for the rest of my life like a soldier who did not complete his journey back home. Even if you sanction a grant now the League government may annul that. Thanks for the offer.'

'How do we celebrate the independence of a divided country? Do we join with the Leaguers?' Finally, Subhan spoke in an agitated voice.

'Yes, join them. Partition is a reality. In about thirty days, our land will be in Pakistan. We'll have to welcome the new wave if we want to survive.' Guha spoke as he stood up to leave.

'Okay Deben,' Acharya stood up. 'Hopefully we'll meet again. Think of the Grey Street college offer. You can still be in the mainstream.'

'I'd let you know karta. Good luck to you all.'

Time had not stood still despite the hopes of many. Mother India was going through the pangs and pains of delivering twins from the womb that had assimilated innumerable civilizational diversities. This time around the birth spasm was more bloody and horrific. There were no signs of assimilation. Perhaps that was the beginning of another ceaseless conflict.

That night I had another opportunity to eavesdrop on the anguished conversation of my parents.

'What have you decided? Most people are leaving.' Mother spoke in a worried voice.

'Where do we go? How do we go? Violence is around us but we are still respected. We are somebody here. We would just be refugees in Calcutta.'

'I hear the government is arranging some population exchange and property exchange scheme.'

'No. These schemes are meant for West Pakistan. No formula has been worked out for East Bengal. We are left at the League's mercy.' Father spoke in a dispirited voice. 'Start planning. We have to dispose off whatever land we can sell. We'll need money when we migrate. Let's see what Partition brings in its wake.'

∽

The situation developing around me, the transformation of father from a roaring fighting tiger and dreamy singer-composer to a helpless observer of a tsunami that was about to sweep away his and our world had anguished me. Mother and Rahman could not answer my questions. Jasim was not as knowledgeable as Lutfa was. I had to fall back on Mano. Her radio and English newspapers still gave me a news update, and she herself analysed the events succinctly.

That evening I entered her room after about six days. I was trying to raise a wall between Mano didi and myself. With a wall of physical distance, her final departure from the village in another few weeks would perhaps be less painful.

I was wrong. We saw a different side of Manorama on 14 August 1947, the fateful day India was sliced into three pieces. My part of the country, my soil, and I were packaged in a wrapper of fundamentalism, sealed and waxed with rotten human flesh and blood and gifted to the destitute people of East Bengal. They called it East Pakistan.

That day Manorama hoisted a tricolour, the symbol of Independent India on a bamboo pole and lined us up to sing the national song Bande Mataram.

I did not hear the distant thunder of rolling disaster approaching our home in the form of an armed crowd headed by Dudu and Dhala. A docile cultivator, Dhala was transformed overnight into a hardened activist of the Razakar Bahini, a band of armed irregulars created by the Muslim League.

'Get up, quick.' Mano rushed to our corner of the large estate and banged on the door.

'What's happening Mano? Any problem?' Mother asked.

We were all by ourselves. Father had gone over to Brahmanbaria to attend a meeting of his party and explore the possibility of starting a practice there.

'Yes auntie. There's a big problem. Rush and come into our building.' Mano virtually dragged us past several buildings and courtyards. Rahman followed us. A shining ramdao and a hurricane lantern dangled from his hands.

'Don't be afraid, Ma,' Rahman kept on repeating. 'Nobody can touch you before killing me.' His band of faithful serfs, mostly Muslims, guarded our flanks. Mother collapsed mid-stairs, Rahman's assurance apart. He carried her unconscious body to the first floor of the Wilson's house.

'What's happening Mano didi?' I managed to ask as my chest pounded heavily in anxiety.

'An armed gang of Razakar is about to attack us.' Mano shared the frightening news.

'Are we safe here? Can't we take shelter in the jungles?' My mother, who had in the meantime gained composure, asked.

'Stay put auntie. We're Christians. They won't attack us.' Mano didi spoke in a confident voice. 'Father has spoken to the police chief over the railway phone. Help should be coming any time.'

Now I could hear the remote slogans: Allah ho Akbar, Hindustan murdabad, kill the Hindus . . .

The motley crowd of about a hundred Razakar marched towards our compound. Two petromax lights illuminated their way and Dhala marched in front, a crescent flag in his left hand and a sword in the right. His goons entered our front garden, pulled down the huge wrought iron gate and marched towards the eastern building.

Someone climbed up the stairs and flashed a powerful torch at the Congress tricolour fluttering from a bamboo pole. 'Bring down that dirty rag,' Dhala ordered his howling and scowling minions.

Rahman rushed out, his ramdao swirling over his head. 'Stop, Dhala. You ungrateful cow thief, you can't defile the house of my great masters. You can't destroy the flag of Gandhi.'

The portly leader was taken aback by the unexpected charge from the lone legionary. Two of his minions charged back with bamboo sticks. 'Thrash this bloody jahil slave of the Hindus,' Dhala commanded in a fierce voice.

Rahman's feeble resistance was blunted by the marauding mob. Wild fists and blows rained on him while Dhala pulled down the tricolour and unfurled a blue-white crescent flag.

Someone from the mob started singing Allama Iqbal's composition: Sare jahan se achcha Hindustan hamara . . . . Our India is the best in the world . . .

'Silence, silence you fools,' shouted Dhala. 'Hang Hindustan. Sing in the glory of Pakistan, father of the nation Jinnah. Recite after me: *La Illaha Illa Lah Mohammadur Rasulullah.*'

The crowd prayed in a growling intoxicated and uncertain voice. Most of them were not sure if they were doing the right thing by invading our respected home. But the brand new Pakistani flag fluttering over the enemy fortress had emboldened their otherwise timid guts. A vanquished Rahman at their feet left no doubt that the fortress had been conquered. One of them raised a machete to hit Rahman's head. Manorama darted out like a tigress. She kneeled over Rahman's body and tried to drag him in.

'Escape Mano, escape, these are hungry jackals!' Rahman shouted in a feeble voice. Manorama partially lifted his nimble body and started heaving him in towards the inner courtyard. I could see the silhouettes of the bloodthirsty gnomes dancing around Mano and crying out obscenities.

'You Christian whore,' shouted one of the standard bearers of Pakistan, 'clear out before we fuck you to death.'

Manorama placed Rahman's body back on the grassy lawn, stood erect, her hands firmly placed on her hips and shouted back. 'Are you animals? For the sake of Jesus, leave this man alone. He's half dead.'

'Memsahib,' shouted Dhala, 'this is Pakistan. You Christians have no place here.' He slapped Manorama and ripped open her blouse. She stood half-naked, hands drawn to her bosom.

'Allah ho Akbar,' shouted another gnome, 'you Christian *magi*, I'll teach you the correct way of behaving with the faithful of Allah.' (He used the slang form of Maggie—used in Bengali to insult a woman). Aided by four other goons, he dragged Manorama behind a croton bush.

'Mano didi I'm coming.' I did not know who shouted from inside me. I sprinted out in a blind rage and jumped on the gnomes feasting on the body of Manorama. The short and stout gnome fended off my attack by hurling a blow to my head. Blood splattered out of my nose.

'Run Krishna, run,' Mano didi shouted from beneath the body of three stout young Muslims, 'they'll kill you.'

I jumped again on the man squatting on her naked body and buried my nails and teeth on his back. I took out the Sheffield knife to hit the wretched fellow. Blood gushed out. It tasted salty on my tongue. The gnome looked back, picked me up by my hair and thrashed me. I blacked out.

～

I woke up, my world woke up the next evening in great pain and shame. The pain was physical, but the shame hurt me deep inside. I was too small to fight the demons who had assaulted Rahman and Mano didi. I wished I had not woken up.

My world changed. The dark gnomes kept on haunting my dreams and disturbing my sleep. Why did they assault Mano? She was not a Hindu.

Was the same going to happen to us in Pakistan? How would we fight back? I lived in a tunnel of darkness for about three days. My elder brother Benoy called me aside and said that I should not react so strongly. He was a calm and composed person and hardly expressed his inner anguish.

Manorama had in the meantime stopped venturing out of her room. Her laughter had just evaporated. Jeremy stopped shooting pellets and hurling arrows at the birds and butterflies. Mr Hubert Wilson, I was told by Rahman, had gone over to Dacca to see his seniors.

Father returned immediately after the incident. He caught me sitting under the shades of a kanchan flower tree. 'What are you doing here? Attend to your studies.'

'Why has this happened to Mano didi?'

'Look son. Sometimes liberation comes with violence. You won't understand now. We all are victims of a violent change. Go over to Mano and comfort her.'

Subhan kaka called a joint meeting of the Muslim and Hindu elders at our community centre. They all looked gloomy, serious and scared. Rab mian from Bhairabpur delivered a small speech deploring Dhala's action and assured those gathered that the headmen of all the nearby villages would approach the district administration and League leaders to punish Dhala and his goons. At his insistence two minor followers of Dhala's Razakar Bahini were arrested by the police. Father was satisfied with the assurances and told the gathering that he would remain a loyal citizen of Pakistan and would work with his team for the betterment of the area.

However, I had no reason to believe that they would in anyway be able to punish Dhala. He was the new political master of our area. He was the main instigator of hatred along with the Qureshi maulana and the Sayeed sub-registrar. Later I learnt that a three-member delegation headed by Rab mian, Subhan Ali and father would visit Kishoreganj to request the sub-divisional officer for extra police deployment.

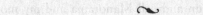

Shorn of laughter and music, stories and idle gossip, newspapers and radio bulletins, school and friends and my favourite railway overbridge I turned to the orchards, flowering trees and bushes. The monsoon flood had inundated the green paddy fields with the greens of paddy and jute crops breaking the monotony of the swirling gurgling infinite sheet of water.

I picked up my improvised fishing rods and went on solitary fishing expeditions by the side of the gurgling canal. I often chased the ducks and once in a while picked up odd eggs, which they laid absent-mindedly on the submerged steps of the ponds.

A week after the ghastly incident, I decided to go on a fishing expedition to Gagan deeghi and asked Jasim to accompany me. We started digging the wet soil in search of earthworm, the best available bait for the elusive fish.

Jasim heard the sounds first—some sort of gurgling and crunching sounds. We stopped digging. The sounds did not stop. It came from the direction of the eastern court building, a part of which was used as a primary school by Dhiru Acharya, our much loved and hated moustached teacher. I tiptoed towards the source of the noise, climbed a window ledge and peeped in.

Preeti Hubert Wilson stood on a wooden stool, a thick noose tied around her neck. She sobbed loudly. Her palms were folded in prayer. My response was fast. I knew what she was up to. I'd seen some pictures of the martyrs Khudiram Bose and Bhagat Singh. The mighty British Empire had hanged them. Rahman had painted unforgettable pictures of those national heroes on my mind. He used to sing a popular tune while narrating the exploits of Khudiram beseeching his mother to say adieu before he walked up to the gallows for the sake of the motherland.

I jumped into the room, caught hold of Preeti Wilson's legs and asked Jasim to run and call Manorama and my mother. They rushed in. Mano didi jumped on a table and untied the knot. The mother and daughter hugged each other and cried loudly. I stood in shock by the side of my mother. Rahman broke my trance. He called Jasim and me out and guided us to Gagan deeghi for a fishing mission.

'Was she trying to die? What for? The British wanted her killed?' I asked.

'Well!' Rahman shrugged, 'You can say so. It's the British, it's that devil. We have been hanged by them, forever.'

'We haven't been hanged have we?'

'Yes little master, they have condemned us to eternal damnation. They have made animals out of us.' I did not understand the weighty statement that day. He had repeated the sentence again, three years later, while escorting my family to the Pakistan–India border at Akhaura. I understood its meaning years later. We were indeed doomed eternally—we were divided from the middle of our souls.

That night, after an early supper Manorama called me into her prayer room. All of us kneeled below the Holy Cross and a photograph of Jesus. She sang a song. We accompanied her in subdued and solemn voices. She said a prayer. Her ashen face looked sad. That was our last prayer together.

On the morning of 15 September a retinue of coolies carried the Wilson luggage to the railway station. They left our house at 5 p.m. Jeremy ran down to our quarters. 'Hey Krishna,' he shouted, 'Mano didi is calling you. Keep this air gun, a gift from me. I'll get a new one in Calcutta.'

'Thanks.' I threw the coveted gun back at his feet and ran out of the house straight to the railway station, the first time after the 14 August incident, and hid behind a pier of the overbridge.

The Wilsons boarded the train for Dacca. From behind the pier, I looked down at the first class compartment. Mano didi was looking for me. Her eyes searched for me in all conceivable directions. She closed the door only after the train started rolling out of the platform.

I returned home well after dusk and walked under the shadows of Dhala's crescent flag. Sleep eluded me that night. My anxious mother did all she could to soothe my feelings.

'Don't cry. God wills it all. They'll be happy in Calcutta.'

'Can't we go over to Calcutta? Can Rahman, Lutfa and Jasim come with us?'

'Sure they can. Now sleep and pray for the Wilsons.' She opened up the Mahabharata and started reciting a chapter. Lord Krishna delivering an impassioned speech to Arjuna on the dynamics of war and death. I slipped out and quietly slept in between Jasim and Rahman.

Our Kamalpur was swept ferociously by another storm of independence.

In early November, a frenzied Bihari Muslim mob attacked the fishermen's colony and killed two. They abducted two young daughters of Ananda majhi. Some local Muslim villagers of Chandiber chased the Biharis and rescued the girls.

The event shook our cluster of villages. Neither Hindus nor Muslims had a protector. Our family authority had collapsed and the new Pakistan administration had still not decided if they had any obligation to save the lives and properties of its citizens of Hindu and other faiths. We were yet to learn that Hindus would be treated as enemies and their properties as enemy properties to be vested with the government.

Rahman came with the grim news and stood before my mother. 'Ma, it is better you leave the village.'

'No Rahman,' my father reacted sharply, 'I can't surrender to bullies like Dhala. I am as much a Pakistani as he is.'

'No karta, it's not Dhala alone. The League people and the Razakars may attack your house. They want the property and all the lands you own. Better leave. They will take away everything.'

'No Rahman. I'll stay put till I can. This land is mine. This is my home. I have nothing Rahman. I'm as poor a man as you are. If you wish you can leave our services. You are free.'

'Don't say that karta. I was never a slave. I am a part of your family and life. Don't worry, we will live and die together.'

seven

The New World Strikes

Kamalpur was swept ferociously by the cyclonic storm of Independence. In early December, Dhala and Duda mian escorted a group of Bihari Muslims to the banks of Satmukhi Beel. They pitched tents just opposite the settlements of the Hindu fishing and weaving communities. This was in flagrant violation of the settlement practices in our area. Anyone intending to settle down in the area had to approach the appointed officers of our family and obtain a *patta,* a settlement document against payment as well as a tenancy agreement.

Rahman accompanied by the revenue clerk Dinanath, nicknamed Dinu, and a *paik,* a kind of sepoy, accosted the Biharis for circumventing the revenue and administrative rules. Dhala mian threatened Dinu with dire consequences and declared that with the birth of Pakistan all rights of the Hindu landowners now vested with the people. The Biharis had the right to settle anywhere they liked as they were the victims of the Hindu killers of India. The Hindus had lost all rights on their lands in the land of the Muslims.

Dinu decided against picking up a fight. Discretion propelled him to rush back to father to consult him on this very complicated matter of the estate. Father advised him to meet his younger brother Birendra who no longer lived at our village home. He looked after his trading company and lived in a separate house near the Bhairab market.

'But you're the elder son. You are in charge.' Dinu stated the legal position.

'No Dinu. I cannot interfere. Father disinherited me. You had better go to Biren and my cousin Hirendra. He looks after the affairs of Girish Bank. He has equal say in matters of the estate.'

The new Bihari encroachers had no time to wait for Dinu, Birendra and Hirendra. They appeared to be more aggressive than the earlier lot who had pitched tents near the Baliachar hamlet. They started with grabbing ducks and goats of the fishing community and gradually poached into the chicken coops of the Muslim villagers. They appeared to be formidable and irresistible grabbers. Never tired of exhibiting utter contempt for the dark skinned Muslims and infidel Hindus they gradually started grabbing and skinning young calves for dinner and dragging young maidens to bed.

The Biharis looked different, spoke a different language and practised social rituals and habits that were alien to the Bengalis. They flaunted long and complicated Arabic names while our Bengali neighbours used traditional names. A new and strange culture had invaded us. The fair-skinned Bihari women dressed in revealing and provocative clothes that attracted the young Bengali Muslims. People with fair skin and knowledge of the language of the Muslim rulers demanded social superiority. The dark skinned Bengali Muslims, they said, were half-Hindus and were inferior to the direct inheritors of the Mughals and Pathans.

Catchy Hindi and Urdu songs played by them on the gramophone enchanted the rural folk. Their brazen behaviour, open defiance of authority of the officials of the landlord and assumed air of superiority overawed the usually simple Bengali Muslims. The leader of the group, Sayeed Mustaqin Fakhruzzaman Itrasi proclaimed that his family tree could be traced back to the desert sands of Arabia and his ancestors were companions of the Prophet. They had fought their way to kafir India and had established the reign of Deen. They had the inherent right to enjoy all the fruits of Bengal which was won by Islam hundreds of years ago.

Indeed, they had no patience or inclination to adapt to their new environment. The first incident of indecent assault on a village girl involved the daughter of Dalim Ali, a primary school teacher. His daughter Putul failed to return one evening from the family field after harvesting green vegetables and collecting cow dung that was used for making sun-baked cakes for oven fuel. Under the fading light, a search team was sent out and they returned after several hours with the unconscious body of Putul. The fourteen-year-old girl was covered with blood. Some people asked father to lodge a complaint with the police. Two police officers marched to Satmukhi Beel, interrogated scores of people and finally left after a sumptuous dinner of fish and chicken.

Harun, son of a sharecropper claimed to have seen two Bihari men dragging Putul to a desolate corner of the Beel. The village elders interrogated Harun. He guided them to a desolate spot surrounded by bamboo. Cigarette butts and some leftover eatables confirmed the suspicion that the Biharis had assaulted Putul.

A meeting of the village elders decided to accost the leaders of the Bihari group. But the fire of vengeance ignited a desolate Dalim Ali. He rushed to the Bihari settlement with his ramdao and attacked a burly person. Other armed villagers followed Dalim and the Biharis retaliated with swords and spears. In a free fight, about five villagers were injured and two Biharis were killed.

Sub-inspector Shazad Khan trooped in with a small force, arrested Dalim Ali, two Bengali Muslim villagers and three Bihari goons, including the two alleged rapists. They left without giving any assurance that Dalim would be released.

Demonstrative action by the police was not a common feature. The last such stern action was when the British forces and Indian police officers raided the dilapidated mosque at

Chandiber and arrested Lutfa after an exchange of fire with the revolutionaries.

The rape of a village girl, Hindu or Muslim, was an unheard of crime in our riverine area. The river pirates and organized brigand groups were known for acts of wanton atrocities. The lusty brigands kidnapped women from the unfortunate boats they managed to plunder but such crimes were rare and raised social turmoil.

Putul was a favourite of our cluster of villages. Daughter of a poor Muslim teacher she was a permanent fixture in the Mansa and Shitla puja festivals. Her voice was enchantingly sweet and she had mastered most of the poetic compositions rendered in song by the village maestros. The shameful violation of Putul, therefore, was an act of total denigration of our rural value system. She was not just the daughter of Dalim, she had become an icon of our community festivals. Who could think of worshipping Mother Mansa without Putul rendering songs in praise of the snake goddess?

The small but influential Bihari community had underestimated the uniqueness of a simple village belle. They were supported by the upper caste sub-registrar and the new stationmaster Zahirul Pathan who claimed lineage from Sher Shah Suri, the Afghan interlude in between the Great Mughals.

The violation of Putul's modesty was taken as a violation of the purity of the soul of all the villagers, irrespective of their religious beliefs. Two separate congregations punctuated the cultural divide and the emerging reality of power centres between the Bengalis and the Urdu-speaking newcomers. The Bengalis congregated at our eastern courthouse lawn and demanded the eviction of Biharis from the village. Despite being seated on the high chair, father never gave the appearance of a landlord. To me he appeared to be ill at ease with the status conferred upon him by the villagers.

Father Debendra spoke wisely. He shared the pains of the villagers and advised them to accompany him to Kishoreganj, the seat of the sub-divisional officer and deputy superintendent of police to lodge complaints against the Biharis.

The other meeting took place in an open ground adjacent to the sub-registrar's office. Sayeed Ashfaq Khan chaired the meeting and Zahirul Pathan spoke loudly on behalf of the Bihari community. Curiosity had drawn Jasim, Saifi and me to the Bihari meeting. Zahirul Pathan spoke in broken Bengali with plenty of unintelligible words thrown in. He declared that the Qaid-e-Azam Muhammad Ali Jinnah had declared Urdu the official language of Pakistan. The Urdu speaking Muslims formed the Muslim League and all Pakistanis would have to follow the Urdu speaking aristocratic Biharis and central Indian Muslims. Bengalis had no right to assert their identity.

Mufti Salahuddin Qureshi, the self-proclaimed direct inheritor of the Paigambar, announced that under Islamic law the girl was required to produce proof that pure-blooded Biharis had raped her. Failure to comply with the provisions of the Shariat would result in punishment—death by stoning.

We were shocked. We rushed back and narrated the speeches of the stationmaster and the mufti. Our village elders were dismayed. Father, accompanied by five villagers, took a train to Kishoreganj and returned after three days. The sub-divisional officer assured them of a full investigation and justice.

The village community however did not wait for justice to flow down from a senior officer. People in the Meghna–Brahmaputra basin believed more in the fury of nature and natural justice. That night Jasim and I overheard a thrilling conversation between father and Chand mian, the son of Ramzan the river pirate. Along with three other Muslim village elders, they were seated in the community centre.

Subhan Ali spoke in an agitated voice. 'Pakistan is our homeland. No problem. But Bangla is our mother tongue. We cannot accept these Biharis imposing Urdu on us. We don't want any Bihari amongst us.'

'I agree Subhan,' father added, 'but Biharis have a right to be in our part of Pakistan. We may oppose Urdu but our problem is their social behaviour. How do we get them off our private property?'

'Deben karta,' Chand mian spoke in a gruff voice, 'leave this to us. We'll take care of the Biharis. Abbajan has ordered me to drive the Biharis out from our area.'

'I don't want bloodshed, Chandu.'

'Blood is our business, kaka. You take care of the village folk through legal means.'

'What will happen?' Jasim asked me.

'I think there could be a Bengali-Bihari war. We'll fight the Biharis,' I replied placing my hand on the Sheffield steel in my pocket.

'Can we fight the Biharis?'

'Why not? My father and others have fought the British.'

'But they say that we're no longer Bengalis, we're Pakistanis.' Jasim spoke with a tinge of pain.

We couldn't think of a solution to the serious matter of ethnic and linguistic incompatibility. 'Let me ask my class teacher, Mainul sir. He knows everything.'

Mainul Khan was jolly by nature. A young person of about thirty he was a fanatic Bengali. He explained that Pakistan was the name of the new nation and the linguistic and cultural groups were its citizen—the Sindhis, Punjabis, Balochis and Bengalis. The Biharis, he said, were *mohajirs*, refugees—who were trying to occupy the lands of the Bengali speaking people. A Bengali did not cease to be a Bengali just because his land had been annexed to Pakistan.

❧

Saifi ran in from the direction of the railway station. He panted like an engine at full steam. 'Huge problem Krishna.

Last night dacoits attacked the village of the Biharis and killed two. The Biharis are escaping towards the station ground.' He drank a scoop of pond water and described the plight of the war-torn Biharis with a flourish. It was big news, but not the only frightening event of the day.

Rahman advised us not to venture towards Bhairab railway station. About 200 Biharis had taken shelter on a vacant piece of land at the southernmost tip of Kamalpur, far removed from where the Bengali Muslims lived.

The police again descended on our part of the village. The homes of several Muslims and fishermen were searched. Finally, they dropped in to enquire from my father if he had any suspicions about any known miscreants of the area. As usual, they were served coconut water and home made sweets. They left with full stomachs but little enlightenment about the problem at hand. The very word Bihari had become an object of hate to us rural Bengalis.

I learnt more in my usual way, eavesdropping on the nightly conversation between my parents. A slight drizzle and strong winds had brought down the early April temperature. Mother, as all mothers do, covered me up with a light kantha. There could be a *kalbaishakhi*, a spring cyclone, later in the night.

A kalbaishakhi was raging inside me. I think that night a number of storms rattled my small world. India, Pakistan, Hindus, Muslims, the migration of people and an unsurveyed and unchartered future haunted my thoughts.

Mother spoke first. 'Don't you think the Biharis will retaliate?'

'I presume they would.'

'Why don't we migrate to Agartala or Calcutta?'

'We have not prepared for this contingency. Never thought of leaving the village and our heritage. Can you cut all ties in one go? Should we not try the new nation? Our Bengali Muslim brothers are with us.'

'I think you're not taking into account the facts of life. The separation between India and Pakistan is complete. It's a separation of the mind. Our Muslim brothers would be forced to hate us, despise us and even kill us.'

'I don't think Fazlul or Suhrawardy would do that.'

'Jinnah has not chosen them as the premier of East Bengal. Nurul Amin, the staunch Leaguer is his choice. Why don't you understand that Jinnah does not trust Bengalis?'

'Well Su, let Benoy clear his matriculation. Only one more year and we'll take a final decision. Ask Krishna to avoid the railway colony route to school. That's Bihari dominated. He should take the main station road.'

I realized that the storm outside was gathering strength and rattling our home. I realized that the storms inside me were going to churn out more twisters in the coming days. I felt tormented.

∼

April 1948 presented another shock.

Headmaster Abdur Razzaq, a tall, handsome and suave man convened a meeting of teachers and students. Members of the school committee, including Uncle Birendra and Father Debendra flanked him. A large Pakistani flag fluttered over our heads.

He started with reading from a printed order from the district education officer that carried two devastating items: we were required to sing the national anthem of Pakistan in our morning assembly, and Urdu would become a compulsory subject, it being the state language.

He read out the song to us:

'*Pak sarzameen shad bad Kishwar-e-Haseen shad bad*
Tou Nishaan-e-Azm-e-aali shan Arz-e-Pakistan
Markaz-e-yaqeen Shad bad
Pak sarzameen ka nizaam Qouwat-e-Akhouwat-e-Awam

Qaum mulk saltanat Painda tabinda bad
Shad bad Manzil-e-murad
Parcham-e-Sitara-o-Hilal Rahbar-e-Tarakkeey-o-Kamal
Tarjumaan-e-mazee-shaan-e-Hal Jan-e-Istaqbal
Saaya-e-Khuda-e-zuljalal.'

We blinked with awe. The language was alien and the style of delivery beyond our comprehension.

Asgar, a student of class ten said audaciously, 'We don't know the tune and the words are not known to us.'

'Don't worry. I'll give you the Urdu version written in the Bengali script along with an English rendering.'

He read out the English version:

'*Blessed be the sacred land, Happy be the bounteous realm Symbol of high resolve Land of Pakistan.*

Blessed be thou of faith

The Order of this sacred land is the might of the brotherhood of the people

May the nation, the country, and the state shine in glory everlasting.

Blessed be the goal of our ambition

This flag of Crescent and Star leads the way to progress and perfection,

Interpreter of our past glory of our present inspiration of our future,

Symbol of Almighty's protection.'

The Headmaster announced that each student would be supplied with a printed copy of the national anthem and they should memorize it by heart.

The other shock was the order regarding the study of Urdu as a compulsory third language. Maulana Wahidullah, assisted by Mufti Hanifuddin would teach Urdu and the first textbook with Bengali translations would be distributed free. 'I hope you all understand the government orders. Any doubts?'

'Yes sir,' Asgar spoke loudly. 'How can we final year students take Urdu as a subject?'

'A good question. Urdu will be introduced from class five to seven. Gradually, over three years it would be taught to higher classes also. I'd advise you to study Urdu at home. If you want good jobs in the government, you must learn Urdu. It is our national language and will soon be the official language. You must have heard and read about the pronouncements made by the Qaid-e-Azam. It is his order.' Abdur Razzak was greeted with stony silence.

'We Bengalis don't want Urdu.' Khalil, another senior student, joined Asgar.

'We're Pakistanis first, Bengalis second,' Abdur Razzaq shouted as a faithful soldier of the nation. 'Listen you boys. Soon Arabic would be introduced as a subject.'

The Headmaster gauged the mood of the gathering and ordered its dispersal. We were asked to line up and collect a new Urdu textbook. Our class was the first to form a queue. Our teacher Mainul Khan distributed the new book. The alphabets looked like spider webs and we were advised to read from right to left and not from left to right.

That night I approached Rahman to teach me the Urdu alphabet. Rahman threw up his hands. 'Don't shame me little master. I do not even know the Bangla alphabet. You had better approach Saifi's father.'

I could not go to Saifi's home at Jagannathpur just two kilometres away. A new unwritten and rarely spoken about law had restricted our free movement from village to village. No one spoke against fraternizing with Muslim friends. I could feel a transparent wall gradually coming up. But signals from my mother's eyes told me that it would soon become a stone barrier.

Mufti Hanifuddin looked quite old, though he could not have been more than forty-five. Head of the mosque at Kalipur he was known for his devotion to the Hadith. He started the class with Bismillah ur Rehman ar Rahim. We were made to recite the verse several times before he started teaching us the Urdu alphabet. His tenacity and our fear of landing in hell in the event of refusing to learn the language prompted us to pick up the basic alphabet faster than we thought we would take.

After an absence of seven days, Hanifuddin resumed teaching Urdu. He was dressed in a shiny sherwani and a gold embroidered fez. His hair was brownish orange, his face bearded, and heavy kajal highlighted his eyes. Saifullah, my friend Saifi, stood up and asked the silliest question.

'Sir, you look nice. Any auspicious occasion?'

'Yes, yes. There are some sweets for you boys. I have taken the fourth wife.'

'Fourth?' My audacious friend Saifi asked.

'Yes. The Shariat prescribes four wives and forty-four children if a true Muslim is to cross the bar to the inner court of heaven.' He stroked his long beard and coyly took out a packet of sweets. Who cared if four wives and forty-four children were the best props to reach the doors of heaven! We scrambled for the sweets and the Urdu class was forgotten for the day.

The Urdu issue did not die out with Abdur Razzaq, Hanifuddin and Wahidullah. We had no idea who Jinnah was but young as we were, the consensus was that no one, not even Jinnah had any right to ask us to forget our mother tongue. How could a Mymensinghia Bengali dialect speaker imagine forgetting his uniquely flavoured language? Could anyone compose *Mymensingha Geetika* and *Bhatiali* songs in Urdu or English? Could any other language capture the pathos of Chand-Sundari folktale songs and the lilting songs composed by my father or the ballads of Mymensingh and local boat songs?

Asgar and his friends probably agreed with my silent thoughts. They had different ideas from the father of our new nation.

That was an eventful day. The narrow road in front of our school was jammed and students joined by members of the public stopped all traffic. They raised slogans against Urdu, Nurul Amin (the premier of East Pakistan) and Jinnah. Sahzad Khan, the police chief and a sizeable crowd headed by Mufti Salahuddin Qureshi and Dhala mian and Dudu mian, occupied the other end of the road. They raised slogans in favour of Urdu, Nurul Amin and the Muslim League, and abused the students as the fifth columns of the Hindu zamindars.

My brother Benoy never liked to take risks. He turned back and asked me to follow him. Curiosity dragged me to the core of the protesters. Saifi followed me. All hell broke loose with stones, wooden and metal missiles flying in all directions. Sahzad Khan charged at the students with rifle-wielding police men and Dhala joined him with his armed goons. Asgar and a few other students squatted on the ground and loudly sang: *Moder garab moder asha, Aa mari bangla bhasha* (My beautiful Bengali language, you are our pride and hope).

Perhaps this was the last straw on the camel's back for Shazad, Dhala and Qureshi. They charged like rhinos and clashed with the senior students. Caught in the whirlwind I had no idea what to do. I had not realized that I was the only Hindu kid to join the protesters.

Mehboob Alam came to my rescue. The very fair and noble looking Mehboob lived just across the main gate of our school in a government quarter occupied by his family. 'What the hell are you doing here? Come in.' Mehboob dragged Saifi and me in.

'We have not done anything,' I protested.

'Shut up. You're a Hindu and from the mahashay family. Soon they will start blaming the Hindus and your family for the language movement.'

'Why should they? We all speak Bengali.'

'Correct, but the new masters want us to speak Urdu. This is no time to argue. Hide for a while and go home when the dust settles down.'

The dust did not settle down until 4 p.m. Mehboob accompanied Saifi and me in a cycle rickshaw to the railway station and advised us not to turn up for classes for the next two days. A large-hearted boy, Mehboob purchased three lozenges and shared one each with us. I never forgot his kindness even after I accompanied my family on an uncertain journey to an unknown India. Much later in life, I learnt that Mehboob had joined the civil services and retired as a Secretary to the government of independent Bangladesh.

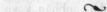

Mehboob was a prudent boy. But prudence was not the order of the day. Most people were swayed either by bloodcurdling slogans or the compulsive urge to rewrite the history of the Bengalis. To them, religion had become the only yardstick to measure human values. However, some people were still around to carry the torch of sanity and argue that streams of blood never added to the birth of civilization or renewal of a people. Much later in life, I read what Lord Mountbatten had written about Mahatma Gandhi. 'In the Punjab we have 55,000 soldiers and large-scale rioting on our hands. In Bengal, our forces consist of one man, and there is no rioting. As a serving officer, as well as an administrator, may I be allowed to pay my tribute to the one-man boundary force?'[1]

We did not have a Gandhi in Bhairab. But we had people like Subhan Ali, Karamat Ali and Father Debendra on the one hand, and Dudu and Dhala at the other end of the spectrum. Qazi Sharif Mullah, Mufti Salahuddin and sub-registrar Sayeed Ashfaq Khan reinforced the latter.

[1] As quoted in D.G. Tendulkar's *Mahatama*, Vol.viii, p.iii

A group headed by Subhan Ali and Father Debendra sat on satyagraha in protest against the police attack on the students. Their alleged sacrilegious action of following Gandhi's policy of passive political resistance led to sporadic attacks on isolated Hindu homes in nearby villages. A senior administrative officer from Kishoreganj persuaded the satyagrahi group to withdraw their mass action against the imposition of Urdu. He explained that Pakistan had decided to adopt Urdu as the state and official language. Token opposition would serve no purpose. This would only invite retaliation from the rabid Muslim Leaguers. In Pakistan, one had to live by the rules of the State. Opposing Urdu would be treated as an act of sedition. The word 'sedition' was well known to my father, as he had been a guest of the British jails on several occasions. They withdrew the satyagraha. Subhan kaka told me that Bhairab in Pakistan could not be an experimental ground for Gandhian principles. Jinnahbhai Kathiawari was not ready to toy with the pranks of Gandhibhai Kathiawari.

Jinnah was a Kathiawari and so was Gandhi—both belonging to the trading community. Jinnah's Khoja community was neo-converts. In fact, his grandfather was a Hindu and he himself was not a practising Muslim. What an irony of fate—one Kathiawari trying to keep India united and the other trying to break it up on religious lines.

After a few days, our school reopened with a strong contingent of police guarding it. Headmaster Abdur Razzaq lined us up and delivered a speech highlighting the principles of language that were intended to unite Pakistan.

With these earth-shattering events behind us, we settled down with Maulana Wahidullah and Mufti Hanifuddin, our Urdu teachers. We hated the alphabet and our prejudiced minds failed to grasp the tender beauty of the language that had added a distinct flavour to our cultural heritage. The finest of beauty appears to be the ugliest apparition when imposed on a people by the rulers. That was what happened to us

Bengalis. The Biharis who had migrated to East Pakistan, and the fathers of our new nation, were in a hurry to proselytize us to new cultural values before we could understand what had really happened to us.

Did we really get freedom or did we sign another lease of bondage?

∼

Our young minds had many questions but few answers were forthcoming. More questions rained on us from remote places called Kashmir and Karachi. India and Pakistan were at war over Kashmir. The Bengali news dailies from Dacca brought in vivid descriptions of the ding-dong battle on the Kashmir front. No one wrote about the prisoners of war taken by either side. But in our small place, we were treated virtually as war criminals.

All the prominent Hindus of our area were summoned to a meeting convened by the sub-divisional officer, Kishoreganj, at the police station grounds. These included Madhu, Chhoban Khondakar, Rauf of Mymensingh, all Muslim League leaders and Panchanan Mondal, a prominent leader of the scheduled caste community. No member from the landlord's family was asked to share the dais, as they represented the suspect section of the Hindu community.

About sixty Hindu landholders and traders were directed to line up and sign a pledge to support Pakistan in its war against Hindustan. Chhoban Khondakar stood before a table and directed people to sign on the dotted line.

'Why are we being singled out to sign a pledge? Are we not Pakistanis?' Father stood up and asked the most politically incorrect question.

'We're fighting a war against a Hindu country. All Pakistani Hindus must sign this pledge. This is the command of the Qaid-e-Azam. Any problem?' The young Bihari officer glared at father.

Someone made him calm down. He was perhaps the only prominent Hindu of the area who had refused to flee to Indian safety. He silently signed the paper and vanished behind the crowd. I followed him to the only music shop in the market owned by Nazar Ali. A noted instrumentalist, he sold musical instruments and was considered an exponent of Bhatiali music.

'What are you doing here?' Nazar uncle asked.

'I've come to call Baba. Ma wants him home.'

'There's a musical soirée this evening at your home. Tell your mother to make some nice sweets for us.'

I followed father silently. 'You look sad Baba.'

'Yes. It's sad that we're suspected by the government. What a pity. The British suspected me and now Pakistan refuses to trust me,' he replied in a contemplative mood.

'Are we going to India?'

'No. We'll fight for our rights. This is our land. Has not Jinnah said that both Hindus and Muslims have equal rights in Pakistan? Don't worry. Pay attention to your studies. Have you memorized the tune I taught you?'

'Yes Baba.'

'Are you keeping notes of daily events as I taught you?'

'Not always.'

'Make it a habit. You're going to grow up through a period of historical changes. Wherever you are, keep a record of events. I know you will be able to present today's events as tomorrow's history.'

'That's a big task Baba.'

'Be prepared for life. I'll teach you a new tune, my own Bhatiali tune. It's about our land and rivers. Don't get upset about these small incidents.' Father tried to console me.

I thought I would console him after the humiliating pledge-signing incident. I was yet to discover the complete man that he was. His easy attitude never betrayed the depth of his mind and the strength of his character. We walked in silence. I felt sorry that he did not open his heart and share his pain. He never did, until he accepted death silently.

eight

Turmoil In and Around

1947. A year that ended like a burning home crashing down on us. The beginning of 1948 was a disaster. Expectations, apprehensions, acts of felony and counting the footsteps of fear and death pervaded the atmosphere. The cluster of villages around Kamalpur was spared fire, death and dishonour. This pocket of sanity, though very near Shabazpur, the birthplace of Nurul Amin, the second chief minister of East Pakistan, had not yielded to the provocative actions of the immigrant Biharis and rabid communalists like Dudu and Dhala. The core group of Subhasists, followers of Fazlul Haq and United Bengal protagonists, of which my father was an activist, had been able to strike a balance between the expectations of the deprived Muslim tenants and affluent Hindu landowners and the business community. The language dispute helped forge better bonds between the Muslims and Hindus. For a while, it appeared that the Bengali-speaking people of East Pakistan had rediscovered the soul of their nationalism.

However, sometime in March 1948 our school was again embroiled in turmoil. Asgar and some other senior students urged the community to observe a strike to oppose the arrest of Sheikh Mujibur Rahman. We knew very little about him. He had probably campaigned feverishly for the merger of Sylhet with Pakistan. What was the strike for? Asgar enlightened us by distributing a Bengali pamphlet that contained a brief bio-sketch of Mujibur Rahman, his links with Suhrawardy and Fazlul Haq and his opposition to the imposition of Urdu.

Our school along with several other schools in the neighbouring areas remained closed for three days. This time around, the government did not try to force open the school. We were too young to be interested in what Mujibur Rahman stood for. All that mattered was that school was closed.

Jasim, Saifi, Majid, Haripada and Mani and I enjoyed stealing the juiciest fruit from our neighbour's orchards. One of those ecstatic afternoons, we expected Haripada to return early from his father's chemist shop at Bhairab. He was to join us on our journey to Jagannathpur to witness a jatra play. The Royal Saraswati Drama Company from Mymensingh was touring our area and staging open air dramas like *Siraj ud Daula* (based on the life of the last independent nawab of Bengal), and *Kankabatir Ghat* (a Bengali folk story). I coaxed mother to spare four annas, two annas for the ticket and the other two grand annas for hot jalebis and lozenges.

We waited anxiously for Haripada to turn up. Saifi was keen to occupy front seats. Jasim wanted to peep into the tented greenroom to see how the cute dancing girls were dressed. We were told that in the Siraj drama a few winged fairies flew down to the stage. We had never seen a live fairy least of all flying through the air.

My excitement knew no bounds as Father Debendra and Uncle Nazar Ali were supposed to render Bhatiali songs before the play was enacted. But the sudden rushing of two human figures towards our front garden stunned us. They panted and screamed loudly. One of them was Barqat mian, a royat and the other was Sachin, the barber.

'What's happened Barqat,' Father asked.

'Something terrible sir. Haripada, Brajen Acharya's son has been killed.' Barqat wailed as if he had lost his own son.

'Who did it? Why?' asked Uncle Nazar.

The story narrated by Sachin boiled down to a detailed account of what appeared to be the first Hindu blood drawn by communal Muslim miscreants in our village. Haripada was moving fast ahead of Barqat and Sachin with fish and other vegetables in his shopping bags. They too had been looking forward to the jatra show. Suddenly, as they reached the east bank of Gagan Deeghi, three young men wearing black masks appeared in the approaching dusk. They grabbed Haripada and stabbed him thrice. Barqat tried to intervene. He was ordered to cease acting as a lackey of the Hindus. Sachin ducked behind a hedge to save his life.

'Didn't you check if Haripada was still alive?' Father asked.

'*Aapne banchle baaper naam* (I can take father's name only if I remain alive).' Sachin replied in the typical local dialect.

Uncle Nazar and Father assembled a small force of six, collected a torch and a few lathis before proceeding to the eastern bank of the big water body. Rahman was rushed to Bhairab market to inform Brajen and the police station. Despite my mother's pleading, Jasim and I followed the small rescue team. Mother sent a housemaid to Brajen's home to inform his family.

We reached the spot marked by mango, jackfruit and blackberry groves. The nearest home was of Sadhu mian, a cultivator who tended our land. He and his two sons joined us with hurricane lanterns. Haripada's body was lying in a pool of blood. Father stooped over the still body, checked his pulse, jugular and heart and stood up with his palms folded in prayer.

'What happened karta? Is he still alive?' asked Sadhu mian.

'No Sadhu. The poor boy is dead. Let Brajen and the police arrive. This is a matter of crime and law. We need to guard the body from wild animals.'

Father squatted on the ground followed by his rescue team. We waited at a respectable distance. My eyes filled with tears and my heart cried out for a dear friend. Haripada was older to us by about five years but his mental retardation had forced him to study in a junior class with us. He was not good at studies but was gifted with a sweet voice and a talent for playing the tabla. He was a popular figure at all the village functions and often entertained us with haunting bhatiali, keertan and *murshedi*, Muslim devotional songs. He was invited to both Hindu and Muslim religious functions to sing in his intense melodious voice.

'What's going to happen Jasim?' I asked as I clutched the Sheffield knife in my pocket. 'Do you think the Nibharsa gang is responsible?'

'I think it is the Dhala gang.'

Brajen Acharya accompanied by three police officers arrived first. They examined the body and found it stiff. After a brief consultation, Brajen was made to write down a complaint and get it signed by five people. The police searched Haripada's body and found two ten rupee notes, a few lozenges and a ticket for the jatra show.

The elders carried Haripada's body to his home in a hurriedly made bamboo stretcher.

I returned home with Jasim and abandoned the idea of visiting Jagannathpur. We sat by the side of a slow burning wood fired oven over which a pot of rice was gurgling. Tomtom sat by my side and looked up questioningly at my sad face. Our parrot Chandana was as naughty as she always was.

'*Kee holo, kee holo?* (What happened?)' she asked.

'Shut up Chandana. Haripada is no more. Someone has killed him.'

I don't know what she understood but she whistled a keertan tune dear to Haripada: *Shyam bina kee kare Rai* (What would Radha do without Shyam–Krishna). Did I imagine it? In the dim light it appeared as though Chandana too was shedding tears. I placed a fat red chilli in her tray. She did not bite into it and moved the chilli pod to a corner of the cage.

Haripada's murder had not divided the communities. A large number of Muslim and Hindu villagers turned up at the cremation ground.

Dhala was not to be seen anywhere near the cremation ground. I had never forgiven him for what he did to Mano didi, for hurting Rahman and thrashing me. Haripada's death strengthened my resolve that Dhala deserved severe punishment.

Jasim, Saifi and I sat under the banyan tree and watched the blazing cremation fire consume Haripada's body. The silence was louder than words and connected our thoughts.

Uncle Nazar approached us. 'What are you boys doing?'

'It's Dhala, uncle. Dhala has killed Hari.' Jasim blurted out.

'How do you know? Who has seen Dhala killing Hari?'

'We haven't. But Dhala is stalking Hindus to kill them and create trouble.'

'Not a word,' said Uncle Nazar and joined the procession that carried Haripada's ashes to his grieving home.

Haripada's last rites assumed unique importance. Head Master Abdur Razzaq accompanied by a couple of teachers and village elders of eight neighbouring villages turned up to console Brajen Acharya. Subhan Ali and Nazar delivered speeches stressing on harmony between the communities and the preservation of traditional family ties. My father, Uncle Nazar and their troupe rendered joint performances of keertan and murshedi songs.

The vacuum of losing Haripada was partially filled in by the reassurance of camaraderie, brotherhood and amity between the communities. We returned with a surging feeling of brotherhood that was synonymous with our rural Bengali culture.

September 1948 snapped the rhythm of unity and brotherhood. Fear reappeared in the form of false propaganda calling upon the *ghazis*, the living martyrs, to wage a holy war against the kafir Hindus. The pamphlets contained news about the demolition of mosques, the dishonour of Muslim women and killing of thousands of Muslims in Bihar, Punjab and Delhi.

One inflammatory pamphlet in Bengali declared that all of India was a Muslim homeland. Hindus were required to surrender to Islam if they wanted to escape the wrath of the ghazis. The pamphlet did not leave anything to the imagination. It depicted a sketch of a Muslim severing a Hindu neck in the *halal* style.

Some miscreants circulated a pictorial depiction of dishonoured Muslim women: female figures with cut noses and breasts, burning homes and piles of Muslim dead bodies. The pamphlets distributed at the railway station and Bhairab market generated communal heat. These were supplemented by newspapers like *Ittefaq* which carried vivid stories of ongoing atrocities on Muslims in India. The Calcutta newspapers were banned by the Pakistani administration. We had no way of knowing the real picture.

In addition to these inflammatory materials there were more false vivid details of Hindu atrocities on the Muslims of Kashmir where a war was in progress, exciting the rural Muslim masses.

Maulana Qureshi summoned the Muslim leaders of the area and delivered provocative speeches. Jasim, who was present at the meeting, brought back grim news. The maulana had inspired the Muslim leaders to take an oath that they would avenge the death and dishonour of Muslims in Hindustan. He urged the leaders to collect funds for the Kashmir war and organize prayer meetings in support of the Pakistani troops.

Kishan Shah and Magan Shah, two affluent general merchants were the first victims. Their palatial buildings and sprawling warehouses were set on fire and stocks of jute, chilli and rice were looted by the rioters. Kishan and family rushed into the neighbouring bungalow of Robert sahib, a prominent British trader. Magan was not so lucky. One of his three sons was stabbed to death. Panic and chaos pervaded the port town and most business houses closed down. The remaining British managers of jute mills and export houses also locked themselves in fearing attacks from marauding fanatics.

The police refused to treat it as a case of communal attack and registered a case of dacoity, arson and murder. The gang of Chattar Ali, a famous river pirate and an affluent trader, was accused of the charges. Chattar Ali, a fugitive, was not available to refute the charges.

Saner people like Nazar, Subhan Ali and Karamat Ali took out a peace procession in which some of the older students headed by Asgar took part. They went around the market and encouraged the Hindu traders to open their shops. Gradually a façade of normalcy was restored but the people were not convinced.

Jasim and I sneaked into a meeting that took place at our community hall after four days of the ghastly incident. Besides father's usual political colleagues, a few traders and village chiefs were there to take stock of the situation and the grim developments.

Qaid-e-Azam had died and Nazimuddin, the chief minister of East Pakistan and a scion of the nawab family of Dacca was sworn in as the Governor General of Pakistan. Nurul Amin from our neighbourhood village Shabazpur, a prominent Muslim League leader, was sworn in as the new chief minister. He was an antithesis to the political and social values pursued by Suhrawardy and Fazlul Haq. Still a member of the League, Suhrawardy had fallen foul of the top leaders of Pakistan. Fazlul Haq was identified with old agrarian Bengali values and was not communally biased enough to carry the torch of the Muslim League.

With Nurul Amin at the helm of affairs, the Punjabi and Bihari bureaucracy occupied most top slots in the governing machine of the province. The Bengali officers were relegated to lower slots and were not considered competent enough to steer East Pakistan and its Bengali people to the orbit of the real Pakistan, the west wing of the country. Someone, probably Jabbar Shikdar from Bhairab Bazaar, an affluent fish exporter, said that the Bengalis were straddled with two imperial tethers: Punjabi and Bihari.

'Let's go to Fazlul Haq sahib. He's our grassroots leader. You lead us karta.' Jabbar Shikdar pleaded with folded hands.

'Jabbar, I'd like to but there's a problem. We've received a notice under the East Bengal Emergency Requisition of Property Act that has been promulgated this year. My advocacy against the Muslim League might prompt Nurul Amin to confiscate whatever legal rights we have on our lands, bank, steamers and other properties. I suggest that Subhan should lead you,' father replied, I think for the first time in a pragmatic manner.

'How can they take away your family properties? You are as good a Pakistani as any of us are. We'll stand by you. Let's go to Dacca and see Fazlul Haq.' Subhan Ali pleaded and convinced father.

The five of them left for Dacca the next day.

Partition had changed the mood of most of the elders who looked grim and worried. After Haripada's murder mother put a stop to my venturing into the Muslim areas. The sizeable Bihari community on the other side of the railway bund was a prohibited area for the Bengali kids. Our grown up girls were strictly forbidden from venturing anywhere near the Bihari camps.

Jasim, Saifi, Majid, Mani and I, and two new friends Kartik Jola and Kali Malo assembled near the spice orchard below fragrant cardamom and bay leaf plants.

'It's difficult to come to your place Krishna,' said Majid, our football captain. 'A few days back Qazi Sharif Mullah and Mufti Salahuddin Qureshi visited our village mosque. They assembled all the Muslim inhabitants and rebuked them for angering Allah by attending the funeral of a Hindu boy. The village elders argued that Hari was a good murshedi singer. He sang in praise of Allah. Mufti Qureshi warned the villagers that no Muslim hereafter should mix with Hindus. Bengali Muslims, he said, had been contaminated by Hindu social customs. Any Muslim following Hindu customs would be ostracized and fatwas would be issued by the Imam of Makka.'

'Where is Makka?' I asked.

'Makka is the holiest place of the Mussalmans. My uncle had gone to Makka on the Haj pilgrimage. That's why he's called Haji Irfanullah,' Saifi replied.

'Not only that Krishna,' Majid continued in a saddened voice, 'the mad Mufti made all Mussalmans take an oath that they would only follow the Shariat and Hadith and no Hindu customs.'

The unthinkable happened the very next day when Majid asked our Urdu teacher Mufti Hanifuddin, to explain what Mufti Qureshi had pronounced.

Master Hanifuddin chewed his aromatic betel leaf, and finally answered with his eyes closed. 'The Bihari Mufti is in a way correct. We Mussalmans are required to follow the Shariat and Hadith scrupulously. A Mussalman cannot be part of Hindu social practices.'

'But sir,' Majid stood up, 'we've been living together for so many years. Hindus join our festivals and we join theirs.'

'What's Shariat and Hadith sir?' Saifi asked in a curious voice.

'You great fool,' Hanifuddin rushed at his errant pupil with an oiled cane in hand. 'Are you a Mussalman or a kafir?

Haven't your parents taught you the rules of the Hadith and Shariat?' Hanifuddin's harsh words were accompanied by a few cane strokes.

The great commotion inside the classroom and Saifi's loud cries drew the attention of Moinul sir, our class teacher. He rushed in. 'What's happened Hanif sahib?'

'These Hindus have polluted our great religion. A Mussalman boy has the temerity of asking me the meaning of Shariat and Hadith! Next time he will ask who Allah is. This is the result of Hindu pollution.' Mufti Hanifuddin blurted out without caring about the presence of five Hindu boys in his class.

'These are young kids. They'll learn the essence of Islam as they grow up.'

'I don't care. I would suggest special classes to teach the Quran, Shariat and Hadith to the Mussalman boys. Pakistan without Islam is a mockery.' Master Hanifuddin stormed out of the class.

We were dumbfounded. It struck me that along with the country our minds were also divided. Would every aspect of life be evaluated by religion and not our bonds that had transcended our faiths and certain social customs? Would they stop me from joining their Id festivities? Should we stop them from joining our Durga, Mansa, Shitla and Olai Chandi pujas? Could not I invite Saifi to our Saraswati puja, our worship of the goddess of learning? My heart throbbed as loudly as Saifi screamed in pain.

I escorted him out of the classroom after taking leave of Moinul sir. He came towards us and patted my head. 'Don't mind the language of the Mufti. Religion is only a way of life. People like the Mufti can't divide us. Go home and don't skip classes.'

His words comforted me. I liked to believe that people like Moinul sir would always be there to balance the precariously tilted and jolted psyche of the people. Our Pakistan would be as sweet a home as it was before they divided it.

How could I comfort Saifi? I took Saifi to the nearest shop and bought us two pink ice cones with one precious anna. We sucked on them with great delight and walked home.

'Don't mind the Mufti.' I consoled Saifi.

'He's a liar. Amma says all gods are equal. It's the way of worshipping that's different.'

'I never questioned the greatness of the Allah. You never questioned the beauty of Ma Kali. We'll be together as we have always been.'

But bigger forces were at work beyond harsh words and oiled canes.

Haripada's ashes were collected and scattered. Saifi's wounds healed. The September heat had ripened the late mangoes, litchis, grapefruits and jackfruits. The floodwaters still filled the canal that separated my village from that of Saifi's. Satmukhi Beel had started brimming to the top. The gardens had started flowering and the fields were partly yellowish with ripening paddy. It was about time to separate the jute fibre from the twigs. In the fishermen's settlement, strings of fish were hung out on ropes to dry under the intense heat of the sun. The air was filled with familiar aromas. It was time for us to enjoy a few holidays, rod-fishing, trap-fishing and swimming with the swirling floodwaters.

Father was away to Dacca with his political colleagues to meet Fazlul Haq and some other leaders. They wanted to plead against settling the Biharis in the Bhairab area where the Hindu and Muslim communities lived in perfect harmony and where the economy flourished in spite of the nasty attacks on Kishan and Magan Shah's farms. They hoped that Urdu would not be forced on the Bengali people.

They returned three days later with grim news. After Jinnah's death all the hopes of Suhrawardy and Fazlul Haq were dashed to the ground. The fanatic League loyalist Nurul Amin was being guided by his Punjabi masters in West Pakistan. He was in no mood to accommodate Hindus.

I overheard my parents' conversation that night. 'How was your Dacca visit? Did you meet Suhrawardy and Fazlul Haq?'

'Suhrawardy had no time for us. You know what kind of a playboy he is, and how unscrupulous. He's thinking of forming a new party. Fazlul Haq is disillusioned. He has the welfare of Hindus in mind but I feel that he may soon revive his KPP (Krishak Praja Party).'

'You know Nurul Amin. Why don't you approach him? He can protect the Hindus. His father was your patient,' said mother.

'Nurul has forgotten that I saved his father from cholera. He is blindly committed to the Muslim League and trusted by Nazimuddin and Liaquat. He won't stop the Bihari and upcountry rush to our areas. I suspect he would encourage communal riots to consolidate his position. That is the only weapon he has against Fazlul Haq.

'We'll have to flee Pakistan as soon as Benoy completes his matriculation. I feel terrible about the land and my colleagues. Once we leave, outsiders will swamp the poor villagers. But that's how it's shaping up.'

'Try to sell some land and other assets. We'll need money in India,' mother replied.

'I think Karachi is piloting a bill to freeze all Hindu properties. I'll try to dispose off some before they put a ban and declare us enemies. I think that's what they're planning, to treat our properties as enemy properties. Anyway, I regret that I would have to leave my land as a defeated soldier. We did not fight for this India,' said father.

'Geography keeps on changing with history. Nehru and Jinnah have defeated Gandhi and written a new history. We don't fit into the new redrawn borders. I foresee a long and uncertain journey. We need to put away some money for the bad days ahead,' replied mother.

A sudden distant noise brought me back to where I was, on my bed with Tomtom snoring unmindful of the grim scenario. The noise became louder with distressed cries of men and women running towards our home. I jumped out of my bed, shook my father and mother and clutched the handle of my Sheffield knife.

In the pale morning light, father searched for his *gupti*, a sword hidden inside a wooden stick. He cried out for Rahman and the other employees, Ramdin and Ramphal, the two Bihari guards who refused to leave us. They all lined up with double-barreled guns and a couple of swords.

I noticed from a distance the anguished face of Rani and her husband Tarpan. Over twenty members of the fishing community followed them. The panic-stricken crowd ran past the barber Sachindra's house and stormed into the courtyard of our eastern court lawn.

'The unthinkable has happened karta. Three boatloads of Biharis guided by Dudu landed on our side of the beel and started setting fire to our huts. We resisted for a while but they kidnapped two young daughters of Jiban Mallah. They were about fifty, well armed with guns and swords. Most of them were drunk.' Mukunda slumped on the lawn grass and started sobbing inconsolably.

'Come in Rani. What happened?' Mother asked the girl so dear to our hearts.

'It's terrible kaki. Tarpan and I tried to fight but they started torching our huts and hunting our women. How could we fight against fifty armed people?' Rani, sobbed loudly. I noticed her torn clothes and the back of her blouse. There was a bleeding wound on her left arm. Perhaps the Biharis had attacked her as well.

The distressed villagers milled around my parents and the extended members of the household. They expected some deterrent action against Dudu and his Bihari cohorts. On the records, the land still belonged to our family and only we had the right to evict our tenants either through a legal process or by force. Father did not consider himself the rightful shareholder of his parental property because of his father disinheriting him. His helpless looks and pained face tormented me. Here was the man who had not hesitated to keep the company of the gun wielders to fight foreign rulers.

Mother diffused the situation. 'Come on Ramdin. Open the gate of the eastern court building. Let them rest. Rahman, you go to Bhairab and inform Subhan bhai, Nazar bhai and the others. Also summon Dinu and Rashid.'

Ramdin opened the front gate of the building and helped the distressed villagers settle down. The pall of gloom and fear had tainted the sky gray. Clouds flew in from all directions accompanied by strong winds. In our wild Meghna basin freak gales and cyclones were not uncommon. We were pushed indoors by our elders. Our newly married aunt, the wife of father's cousin Hirendra, served us puffed rice and date palm jaggery. This was followed by glasses of milk. I did not feel like eating as the pale face of my father disturbed and agitated me. I shared the milk with Tomtom and Pintu and offered Chandana some puffed rice.

I sneaked out of the room with Jasim and Tomtom. 'Where are you going?' asked Jasim.

'Let's go to Majid. Let's call the others. We should attack the Biharis.' I fished out the precious Sheffield knife.

'Stop Krishna. This is not the time for games. These people are bloodsuckers and there are people like Dhala. Don't you recall the thrashing he gave you?'

'We should do something Jasim.'

'Let's serve the distressed Mallahs. Let's comfort Rani didi. She is now a mother and her young baby requires milk. Let's arrange some food for them.' Jasim spoke as if he was a disaster management expert.

Rani was visibly shaken and was bleeding from her left arm. From below her sari, I could see a gaping wound. I tried to remove the cloth that covered her hand.

'Don't do that Krishna. Don't touch a woman's sari.' She pushed my hand aside.

'Why not? I have touched your sari several times while playing football.'

'Stupid! I am now a woman and a mother.'

Her blush confused me. What difference did it make. We brought her into our room and mother took over and bandaged the wound. The young kid was given a glass of milk. Gobinda, the grandson of Mukunda, took a fascination for Pintu, the goat with the fluffy beard. Pintu too took a liking for the tiny manikin.

Rahman returned with a posse of friends and three policemen. They looked unhappy. Subhan kaka, Matanga Roy, Shorab Ali, Abani Guha and Manilal Dutta, all political and stage colleagues of my father's followed Nazar kaka. Roy, Guha and Dutta represented the Pakistan wing of the Congress party. Subhan and the others were silent revolutionaries who had lost direction in the din of Partition.

They looked at each other, sipped tea and puffed on hukkas. 'We should go to Dacca and meet the chief minister,' Manilal Dutta opined through his white moustache.

'What purpose would be served? Amin is a slave of Jinnah and the Bihari-Punjabi mafia. He cares little for us Bengalis. Our friend Deben is in double jeopardy. He has given shelter to the fishermen. That itself might provoke Amin to invoke the East Bengal (Emergency) Requisition of Property Act. Let's meet Fazlul Haq sahib. He may be able to help.' Nazar kaka spoke with all the gravity the singer in him could muster.

A police constable interrupted.

'This big house has gone to the dogs, no tea and no lavish food.'

'We've lodged a complaint of an organized attack on the fishermen's colony. They have forcibly evicted the fishermen, burnt their homes and seriously injured several of them. What does your law say?' Subhan Ali retorted.

'Sir, we hear that there were about fifty attackers. We'll go to the police station and come back with a larger force. But we have no instructions to intervene in such incidents. You'd better talk to the district magistrate.'

The police sepoys turned their backs in disappointment. Their earlier visits to the house were usually rewarded with a feast and entertainment. They were no longer interested in showing any respect for the laws they served and a fallen giant lurching towards extinction.

The directionless speculation was terminated by mother's words, which she spoke from behind her covered face. 'Why don't you go to the spot and see the situation. Perhaps the *jalias* can be resettled on land granted by this very house.'

Her words propelled the gathering and some able-bodied fishermen. They ambled along the narrow pathway lined by betel nut trees. We young enthusiasts followed at a respectable distance. I had my Sheffield in my pocket. Jasim, Mani and Saifi picked up bamboo rods and cousin Chuni carried a gorgeous stringed bamboo bow and a few arrows, iron tips mounted on jute twigs. We were proud of our armoury but not sure if it was sufficient to deter the Bihari mob.

Our arrival was greeted by the Bihari trespassers with slogans like Allah ho Akbar, Pakistan zindabad, and Kafir Hindu murdabad. They were busy constructing bamboo and thatch homes, pitching tents and removing the debris of the burnt shacks of the fishermen. Their hostile posture did not deter Nazar and Subhan. They approached the mob headed by Dudu and his Bihari supporters.

'You're a blot on our entire area Dudu,' shouted Subhan Ali. 'Why have you brought Biharis to our area? Why have you forcibly occupied the zamindar's land?'

'Hindus have no right to rule over us. In free Pakistan we own every inch of land,' Dudu shouted back.

'You're not the owner of Pakistan to decide these issues. Take the Biharis back to where they came from.'

'The Hindus killed the Biharis in India. It's our turn to kill the Hindus. Blood would be avenged by blood. Traitors like you are enemies of Islam. Turn back before we kill all the Hindus.' Dudu, now joined by Dhala mian, Chhoban Khondokar and Jalil Sarkar, all prominent Muslim League leaders advanced menacingly with swords and sticks.

The unarmed group headed by Subhan Ali and my father did not retreat. Their stubborn defiance halted the patriotic Pakistanis, behind whom the burly Bihari men had lined up with flags of Pakistan and lethal weapons.

'Come and kill us.' Nazar advanced a few steps. He was well known in the area as a great devotional and bhatiali song exponent. Not a politician, but a popular cult figure, with both devout Muslims and Hindus. The man who played the harmonium, percussion instruments and flute with ease did not hesitate to face the brandished swords and bamboo rods. People shouting Allah ho Akbar suddenly stopped. Perhaps they realised that this frail singer and poet was as fanatic in his faith in peace and brotherhood as they were fanatically thirsty for human blood.

'Look Dudu. We've been living here peacefully for centuries. Your politics cannot divide us. Take the Biharis back. Take them to the Bihari colony set up on the other side of the railway embankment.' Nazar kaka spoke in a soft but resolute voice.

'No. The Bihari brothers will stay here,' Dhala shouted back. 'We've orders from Dacca to evict all the Hindus.'

'Don't disturb Deben karta and his people. That's a warning, Dudu and Dhala. This embankment of the beel is your limit.

Any infringement beyond this would invite retaliation from the other villages. We won't allow you to destroy our brotherhood,' Subhan Ali shouted back.

Then something wonderful happened. Father walked towards the armed group of Dudu and Dhala and spoke to them in his usual unassuming voice. 'Look Dudu. I treated your father and saved him from sure death. And Dhala, don't forget the day I saved you from a flogging by my father's slaves. Just remember that I am one of you. My home has been a sanctuary for all of you. Why disturb us in the name of politics? Your uncle and I fought together for Independence. What difference does it make if we Hindus live in a free Pakistan? We all struggled for the independence of this very land. The Biharis did not fight for it.'

Dudu and Dhala did not reply. Their eyes were riveted to the ground perhaps with shame and old memories.

'Well karta,' Dudu finally replied, 'we promise not to disturb you.'

'I advise you to take these Biharis back to their colony. Let us Bengalis live together as we have been living for centuries.'

'Yes karta.'

'Come back one day. I'll explain how you people can get your land back peacefully. Come, we have not had a meal together for months now.' Father's last words perhaps melted Dudu and Dhala. They kneeled and touched father's feet and turned back with their supporters.

'Look Dudu. I've no problem if you people want to settle some of our own poor on the Satmukhi tract. They can pitch their homes next to those of the fishermen. They can learn fishing. I've no problem.'

'That's great karta. We're sorry. Allow fifty of our landless Bengali families to settle on the Satmukhi tract.'

'No problem. Come to my place tomorrow. Request and assure the fishermen that they can return to their homes. Help them to rebuild their shacks. I'll provide free bamboo and bush-cane for all of them and to your people. Let's live together like we have been.'

We turned back after witnessing this miracle. I never expected the events to take such a dramatic turn. I had war and blood in mind. Nazar and father's attitude frustrated me. But it was an eye opener. I had not heard much about Gandhi who travelled alone, though he led millions. Had I known that, I would have bowed my head to these minor Gandhis, Subhan, Nazar kakas and my father.

My regard for my father filled my heart with pride and faith. Perhaps the small and big Gandhis are equal in their basic approach. The difference in the magnitude of their struggle made them different. It is a pity that we all expect a big Gandhi to come and ignore the existence of the small Gandhis amongst us. We do not believe that a congregation of sincere small Gandhis can transform us radically.

nine

The Flame Closes In

We had unexpected house guests in February 1949. Kamal Ghosh, my mother's cousin from her paternal village Rajnagar, and her great-uncle Shirish Shome, a deputy manager at Ashuganj jute mill dropped in. Kamal worked in Jamshedpur in Bihar and was visiting home to take his family back to India. Shirish dropped in to consult father about migration to a safer place in India. A Muslim tycoon, Ispahani, was in the process of acquiring the jute mill owned by a British company. He was likely to retrench Hindu managers and hire Muslims who migrated from India to Pakistan.

Rajnagar could be negotiated by boat from Bhairab. That forced Kamal to break journey for the night at our home. He also wanted father to consider migrating to Jamshedpur, set up a shop and avail of better education facilities for us. Shirish wanted us to migrate to Agartala, reclaim my mother's inheritance and start a new life.

By now, I understood the importance of words like Hindustan, Pakistan, migration and riots. I think I started maturing faster than after the Mono didi incident and later developments.

I was not surprised by the accounts Kamal narrated about the mass killing of Muslims in Bihar by organized Hindu mobs. These were in retaliation to the mass killing of Hindus in Calcutta at the behest of Jinnah and Suhrawardy, he said. For the first time, Kamal added, the Hindus displayed their fighting prowess. He wondered how the Hindu fighting arms could lose to the Muslims and British when they served the

Mughals and the British Crown so creditably! Perhaps because of political disunity and societal disharmony, commented Shirish. I wondered what bravery had to do with Dudu and Dhala attacking the unarmed fishermen's colony and the Hindus attacking poorly armed Biharis in Jamshedpur and other Muslims in India!

I was not supposed to be privy to such serious adult discussions. But my elders had not noticed that I had mentally grown during the last two years. I did well in studies and I developed a habit of reading the newspapers. Mono didi had left a treasure trove of books on geography, history, astronomy, biblical studies and general books on science. A few precious books by Chaucer, Shakespeare, collections of romantic poems and short stories were locked in a steel box. These were her gifts to me. The spark lit by Mano encouraged me to try to understand what our elders were discussing on grave issues of migration, abandoning the huge properties and seeking a stable future in a new India.

'Look Deben,' Kamal Ghosh spoke in a blunt tone, 'You are a highly qualified ayurvedic doctor. You fought for the country, you dreamt of revolution, you pursued music and you antagonized your elders. You stand disinherited for supporting your cousins and poor tenants. You never claimed what you were supposed to get from your father-in-law. This is not the way of life. The realities are harsh.'

'I know Kamal. But that's me. Tell me what should I do.' Father spoke rather timidly.

'Sell your lands here. Sell the lands you are supposed to get at Sarail in the former Tipperah district and Sahjadpur. Claim your wife's house at Agartala. Claim what is yours.'

'The Agartala house is jointly owned by my wife and her sister who lives at Johor Baru in Malaysia. We must consult her. Do you really think I should abandon my people here?'

'Be realistic Deben. You owe as much duty to your wife and children as you think you have to your people and the land you inhabit,' Shishir Shome intervened. 'Human relationships change with political and geographical changes. We plan to migrate next year. You too should plan accordingly. Salvage what you can—you know your greedy brothers.'

'You're correct uncle,' mother intervened. 'His brothers have been cheating him all the time. His self-imposed righteousness is his great enemy. His brothers are stacking away our family wealth to safer places. Please advise him to be practical.'

I do not think I liked this virtual condemnation of my father. I idolized him as a person of high moral values, integrity, silent courage and humble to the extent of self-abnegation. But the realities around prompted me to ask father if he would now like to change course.

Shishir Shome invited me to his home at Ashuganj to spend a few days. Ashuganj, a small industrial town boasted of a jute mill and other small industries but Bhairab was the biggest river port of the area. The trip was immensely enjoyable, well spent in angling, football games and a rare outing to a cinema show with cousins older to me.

This indulgent trip was perhaps chalked out by destiny as it was to turn out. My memory cells had etched the topography of the area so well that on my fatal train journey in May 1950 those very memory cells popped out like a GPS map and helped me reach the safety of great-uncle's house with my distressed mother. The story of that fatal rail journey is an integral part of the final train journey to India.

∽

It was an early April afternoon in 1949.

My brother Benoy had passed his matriculation examination with good grades. Our parents were planning to send him to Calcutta for higher studies. Bhairab did not have a degree college and the ones in Brahmanbaria and Mymensingh were not known for scholastic achievements. I felt disturbed. Benoy had not been my playmate. We had not known each other intimately. He was close to a few friends of his own.

Benoy was and still is a person of integrity, immense humility and resolution. It was difficult for a bubbling boy like me to strike up a friendship with him. However, with a lot of temerity I dared ask him if he would be happy in a new India. His reply was pragmatic—the new India was a country of opportunities. He was going there with lots of dreams and plenty of aspirations. It was not easy to accept the idea.

However, the idea of exchanging mature views with my father on the grave matters raised by Kamal and Shishir were still on my mind. Father was at Nazar kaka's music shop of dispensing medicines to some clients from the kit he carried. I never knew how much he earned but there was always a free supply of medicines to the poor villagers who thronged our house and Nazar's shop. It could not have been more than ten to fifteen rupees a day, I thought. Why did he not charge his patients, I often wondered.

As I patiently waited for him to close his kit, a woman rushed in. 'Karta, please come to Rani bazaar. Akhtar Bai is very sick,' she pleaded with folded hands.

'You're going to the red light district?' asked Nazar kaka.

'I go to see a patient. It does not matter if she lives at Rani Bazaar or inside a temple. It's my profession to see a patient in distress.' Father replied in a firm voice and asked me to carry his medicine kit.

I did not know that Akhtar Bai was a beauty in her time. She had probably drifted out of some haveli in Lucknow and was spotted by a potentate at Sunang-Durgapur in Mymensingh. Like most fading beauties, she was later discarded. Later my mother would tell me the story of this legendary beauty.

Father examined her and said that she was probably infected by tuberculosis and required better medical attention in the district hospital at Mymensingh or Dacca. He gave her some fever and cough medicines and refused to accept a fee. Even at the evening of her life, Akhtar Bai glowed like a dying ember. She was doe-eyed and as beautiful as the painted picture of Shakuntala that I had seen in a Bengali translation of the great work of Kalidasa.

'You're blessed to be born of a grand person. Allah will bless you.' Lying on her deathbed she whispered in my ears and filled my palm with a few Morton chocolates.

We started walking home. I offered my father a chocolate and asked, 'Why did you visit such a bad quarter?'

'Who told you that? Good or bad, it doesn't bother me. She is a patient. When you grow up you'll understand that people are not born bad. They're made bad by society.'

'Why don't you agree to migrate? The Mussalmans will kill us. Majid says that the mullahs and the League people won't allow us to live here.'

'I know. Now that your brother has completed his schooling I'll send him to Calcutta and by next year we'll migrate. I have to dispose off some land and other assets. You require money in a new place.'

'Calcutta is not new to you. You studied there.'

'Yes I did. But I don't know the place and the people. That's a new India for us. Our India was here.'

'It's now Pakistan. My friends say that it is only for Muslims.'

'That's not correct. The moment I make a move to leave this place the entire village will flee to somewhere in the new India. We've been their anchor. I hate to leave this place but we must as soon as I can wind up financial matters. Don't panic. I love you.' Father embraced me standing in this midst of the green paddy field. I felt like weeping. I loved the much-misunderstood man.

'Can't we fight the Mussalmans?'

'No. They're your friends, my friends. The time for fighting is over. We must learn to live together. When you grow up you'll understand that people get uprooted and re-rooted. That's the history of civilization.'

Father hummed a song that he had composed: *'Tumi ni amaar bandhure Aami ni tumar bandhu?* (I am your friend, are you mine?). I joined in as we climbed the railway embankment. I felt happy to be able to speak to father almost as an equal.

A sudden commotion disturbed our rhythm. The stationmaster Zahur Pathan, a Bihari Muslim, rushed in followed by his assistant and a posse of porters.

'What happened Pathan sahib?' Father asked in a panic. 'Has there been another communal outburst in some nearby village?'

'A great disaster has struck Mr Deben. There is a raging fire in the Bihari colony and no local villagers are coming forward to help them. In our Pakistan the Bengalis don't like us upcountry Muslims. Can you help? Can you mobilize the local people?'

'Why not, Pathan sahib? Let's call for help.' Father directed me to go home with the medicine kit and directed the porters to announce in the western part of the village that he was coming to fight the raging fire and wanted their help.

I did not go home, but followed father and the others. As he rushed through the village road over a hundred villagers followed him with buckets and earthen utensils in their hands. The wailing Bihari women and children made way for their hated Bengali compatriots who, like an army of ants, carried water from ponds and tanks and doused the raging fire within an hour.

Standing amongst the smouldering ruins, they raised slogans praising father. A few Biharis joined them. It was a strange sight to see stationmaster Pathan, Sharif Mullah, Mufti Salahuddin Qureshi and sub-registrar Sayeed Ashfaq Khan standing by my father and thanking him for mobilizing the villagers at a moment of grave crisis. I was so proud of my father, a man who was once an underground liberation warrior and now a pacifist. I regretted the times when some doubts had crept into my mind about his capability to protect us. A man who could protect so many was undoubtedly capable of protecting his family.

∾

Perhaps my conclusions were premature. Five days after the incident Rahman turned up at the kitchen door and silently waited for mother. 'Anything you want Rahman?'

'Ma, people are ungrateful. They treat goodness as weakness.'

'What's new Rahman? Betrayal is a common human trait. Who deceived you?'

'Not me Ma. The ungrateful Pakistanis now think our karta is a barrier between the Bengali Muslims and the Biharis. The villagers did not move out to save the Biharis till karta reached the spot. The Mufti held a meeting in the mosque with some leading local and Bihari Muslims. They think our karta should leave the area. With him around Pakistan would not be complete. He is one Hindu who is standing between Pakistan and Bengali Muslims.'

Mother stopped stirring the ladle in the boiling rice pot. Her fair face glowed in the hearth fire and her large eyes narrowed down to slits. I sensed a whiff of trouble. 'You mean Rahman that they want to kill your karta?'

'Nobody used that word. They want you people to go to Hindustan at the earliest. These are mad days. People have forgotten Allah, and the devil is ruling over human minds. Ma, tell karta to listen to the rumblings. We are there to protect you. But he moves freely and goes everywhere. I feel he should be more careful.'

'Thanks Rahman. We won't leave you people just like that. This is our motherland. Let's see what they can do.' Mother resumed cooking rather nonchalantly. I was foxed. She had been imploring father to escape to the safety of India. Why did she talk to Rahman like this? Was she telling a lie?

On this occasion, I did not have to eavesdrop. After dinner we sat around the Aladdin magic lamp, all four of us. This was a unique moment of togetherness. Benoy was busy reading a book. He normally did not take an interest in these grave matters.

'Baba, your firefighting has not earned you appreciation and recognition.'

'When did I hanker for appreciation?'

'They think you've a magical hold on the local Bengalis. They want you to go. They think you're a stumbling block between them and Pakistan.'

'We live in Pakistan. And who are 'they'?'

Mother explained what Rahman had said about the discussion in the mosque and the instigation of the fanatic fringe by the core Muslim Leaguers and Bihari leaders.

'Why did you tell Rahman that we wouldn't like to escape from Pakistan?' I charged mother.

'I lied. It was an act of reassurance. Rahman has been loyal to us and in all likelihood, the likes of Dhala and the Biharis would torment him. He requires our support. Haven't you read in the Mahabharata that even Yudhisthir had to resort to a lie at least once for a greater cause? Always tell a lie if that means saving faith and the lives of many.' I was stunned by her reply. It was an education that stayed with me like a shadow of truth.

'Go to bed. When you grow up you will realize that every action has several reactions. Most reactions are not under your control. That does not mean you'll never act in a crisis. You've to manage every crisis with newer ingenuity. When the time comes you've to act, and act decisively.' Father spoke like he was opening up his heart. It was my second major interaction with him.

❧

Suddenly a flood of events inundated our very existence.

Subhan kaka dropped in around midnight. A man called Nazrul accompanied him. Father was woken up and mother prepared tea.

'What's the matter Subhan?' father asked.

'This is Nazrul Islam, a friend of Sheikh Mujib. The young leader is visiting our area to hold a meeting in support of Fazlul Haq and Suhrawardy. We want you to be there.'

'I have never known him well. He is a young leader.'

'We require young people. Let us join his group. Our old movement has become irrelevant. We must be with the new progressive forces.'

'That sounds reasonable. But Subhan, you know that Maulana Sharif and Qureshi are inciting people against me. They think I am a barrier between the Pakistani and Bengali Muslims.'

'We know their machinations. It is better if you join with Fazlul Haq, Suhrawardy and Mujib. You will get a new political umbrella.' Nazrul spoke with a heavy voice.

'Fine. I will join you people. Just ensure that my family is not disturbed.'

'We are with you Deben. No one can separate us.'

The visitors left at around three in the morning. They were on a mobilizing mission. The chief minister of East Pakistan was from our area and he had mobilized his own forces to blunt the influences of Fazlul Haq and the Suhrawardy-Mujib team.

'Don't get involved. Ours is a Muslim majority area and Nurul Amin will do his best to drive away all Hindus opposing him,' Mother intervened after the guests left.

'Let's see.'

∾

The future held many painful shocks. It happened in early June 1949.

Mother asked me to visit Girish Bank at Bhairab Market and collect fifty rupees from Uncle Hirendra. She needed the money to procure clothes for Benoy, now preparing to go to a Calcutta college. Our flourishing river-port boasted of two banks, Comilla Bank and Girish Bank. Grandfather's brother Girish had established the latter. It flourished until the debris of the World War inundated it and the money market slump and Partition made it worse. Uncle Hirendra managed the bank more by virtue of his amiable nature and the goodwill of his late father. Business was dull. Besides him, Dhiru, the family retainer and two other clerks managed the daily transactions.

In those days to carry fifty rupees was as good as carrying a treasure chest. I took Saifi along. Saifi had a habit of dancing along the street and humming folk tunes. But my mind was not at peace. I felt sad that Benoy would be leaving us.

We were inside the bank when suddenly five hooded men with swords and a gun in their hands stormed in. Dhiru dropped his gun and stood aside like a frozen statue. The clerks were pushed to the ground and one of the intruders placed the gun at Uncle Hirendra's head and demanded the keys. A fair complexioned man with big expressive eyes, Hirendra looked at the raiders with surprise and fear. 'Don't kill me. What do you want?' he begged.

'Open the safe and hand over all the cash,' one raider ordered gruffly. Uncle obliged and the raiders emptied the safe and retreated after shouting Allah ho Akbar.

Saifi and I stood frozen behind an almirah and watched Dhiru. He picked up the gun, rushed out and fired two shots in the air. He cried out loudly for help. Even to my young inexperienced eyes the scenario appeared to be too dramatic and rehearsed. Was Dhiru involved with the robbers?

We helped uncle to his chair. He was speechless and trembled in fear. 'I'm sunk, totally sunk. All the cash has been looted. What will happen to me?' he wailed.

Some traders had summoned the police who arrived in force and further ransacked the bank premises. We stood aside with our hearts pounding. Dhiru related the incident like he was a movie scriptwriter. I had known him as a con artist, but I was impressed by his storytelling and acting. The police sealed the bank. The doors would be reopened only after a senior officer from Kishoreganj inspected the scene.

I ran to Nazar kaka's place, dragged father out and helped Uncle Hirendra return home in a cycle rickshaw. He was a ruined man. His father had single-handedly built up the business empire and had added more landed property to the family kitty only to be deceived by his own brother.

We were stunned by the day's event. The raiders had plundered Rs 200,000, the entire fortune of the bank. Investments in various shares in Calcutta were too uncertain. My good-natured uncle had become a pauper overnight. One could live without enough cash in hand but what about the depositors and lenders? They would demand their money back at the earliest.

Several investors and depositors started visiting our home and demanding their money back. Most of them had deposited money in the bank because of the goodwill of the family, its assets and reputation. Now everything except the goodwill had been devastated by the Partition of the country. Girish Bank was a private banking venture that had sprung up during the trading boom in the late Forties. Besides Bhairab, it had a branch at Dacca, which had closed down soon after Partition.

It was a grim struggle for Uncle Hirendra to fend off the depositors with uncertain promises. Some depositors flexed their arms and others hurled indescribable abuses. The promise of returning their money even by selling landed property did not pacify them. They were seen confabulating with Dhiru whom I considered to be a double-dealing villain. I had lost trust in him after the shameful incident involving my lecherous cousin Adhir and Rani didi.

Uncle Hirendra and his wife had taken shelter in our house leaving their old mother alone at her home. I broached the subject during dinner. 'I suspect Dhiru of the robbery.'

'Why? He was there in the bank all the time,' Uncle Hirendra replied.

'I was also there. He just dropped the gun and pretended to be unconscious. He stood up as soon as the robbers left and fired a few shots. It's Saifi and I who helped you get up. Dhiru came much later.'

'What does it prove?' Father asked.

'His involvement with the robbers. He allowed them in and he may take a share of the money.' We dined in absolute silence and reassembled around a cane table.

'What do we do with him?' Mother asked.

'Nothing. Just take the gun away from him and give it to Gulab Misr, the chowkidar. Don't give the impression that we suspect him. If he's a collaborator he might invite the robbers to our homes.' Father's analysis was accepted as reasonable.

'What do I do now?' Uncle asked.

'You escape to Calcutta. You can't pay back the money. No one is buying landed property now. Like scavenging vultures, they'll wait for us to leave and then loot our land. And your brother and sisters might not agree to sell the land.'

'What about you?'

'They know I'm a faqir. I don't possess any wealth and I'm a disinherited son. They may kill just for the fun of killing another Hindu but not for money. You go.'

'Let Benoy accompany you,' Mother added. 'Let him stay with you and get him admitted in a college. He's good at studies.'

'That's a good idea.' Our aunt spoke for the first time.

'When do we leave?'

'Tomorrow.' Father stood up. 'Let me send Dhiru out of this area on some errand so that he does not inform the creditors.'

～

The next day Uncle Hirendra could not leave for Calcutta.

The Chittagong–Calcutta Mail normally arrived at Bhairab early in the morning between 4.30 a.m. and 5 a.m. Father, Rahman and Gulab Misr accompanied them to the station. Dhiru was sent out to Brahmanbaria to deposit the annual land tax for our family land at Sarail. The plan was to keep him away from the village. Subhan Ali bought three tickets to Calcutta for uncle, aunt and Benoy as we didn't want them to be seen at the booking counter. They waited behind cargo stacks.

However, the Chittagong Mail arrived late, around 8 a.m. It presented a ghastly scene. The station staff and a few general railway police personnel rushed and surrounded two passenger bogies that were practically empty except for over twenty slain human bodies and a few naked female bodies. No one noticed that Jasim and I had also followed. We rushed through the milling onlookers and witnessed the carnage. Over ten female bodies, some clinging to their babies, were lying naked amidst pools of blood. Two severed heads rolled out on to the platform as a GRP constable forced open the compartment door.

Before a police party arrived from Bhairab, Subhan Ali forced father and the escaping passengers to return home. He accompanied them saying that some friends would have to be mobilized to protect our family and the other Hindus. We lingered on unnoticed by our elders. The curious crowd would hardly have been able to determine if I was a Hindu and Saifi a Muslim.

A strong police party secured the station and an extra engine was pressed into service to disengage the affected compartments and take them to a secluded place. Zahur Pathan and Sahzad Khan, the SHO, conferred briefly and allowed the rest of the train to steam towards Dacca. Soon after, a shuttle arrived from Kishoreganj with a strong police party and a senior police officer. They opined that the killing might have taken place between Laksam and Comilla. These Hindu families were escaping to India and a few of them carried cash and jewellery. The Laksam, Comilla and Begamganj line extended up to Noakhali, the scene of the worst communal carnage.

Jasim and I left the ghastly scene. We were horrified and filled with extreme repulsion for our fellow human beings. It appeared that mad demons had replaced the simple village folk who had lived happily side by side.

'What are you thinking Krishna?' Jasim asked.

'How can they kill so many people?' I was stunned.

'Only men can kill men. Tigers don't kill so mercilessly. Even hurricanes are not so merciless. Something has gone wrong with men. Must be the demon called Pakistan.'

We returned home silently. I felt angry, ashamed and helpless.

Rahman's face was a mask of anxiety and father did not present a picture of confidence. I did not feel reassured when Subhan Ali brought in four Muslim youths to guard us. Even a nightly visit by Chand mian, son of Ramzan the pirate, to reassure father that our security was their concern could not erase the ghastly scene I had witnessed.

Uncle Hirendra could not be kept hidden from the creditors. They disturbed us at odd times. Mother had devised a strange way to hide them. She pulled out one of the huge circular wooden storage vats, used for storing rice and paddy, to make a bed for them. Most nights, they slept there. Their days were spent hiding inside our home.

Finally, they succeeded in boarding a train for Calcutta when the authorities placed additional police guards in each compartment. Once again, we went to the station in the wee hours. Subhan Ali again bought tickets for them and pushed the three scared members of our family into a compartment. He spoke briefly to a policeman and slipped some currency notes in his palm. I did not realize that such bribes could buy safety even in the midst of war. Money was a stronger force than war and peace.

I waved and ran along the platform until Benoy's face disappeared beyond the outer signal post. Jasim ran with me. I sat down on the track. For the first time I realized that Benoy was dear to me and a part of me had left the village, never to come back. We had hardly interacted but his personal lifestyle, honesty, and enormous power to absorb shock and pain had instilled some lessons in me subconsiously. I wept for my brother for the first time. I felt angry with the train, the dear old station and everything. This station and the trains were devouring the people that I knew and disgorging them in an unknown land called India.

Jasim took out a few pieces of dry green mango slices mixed with salt and red chilli powder and pushed them into my mouth that automatically stimulated the secretion of saliva and helped the flow of tears from my eyes.

The sun had come up above the trees and the gloom around had started melting. I returned to a near empty home. There was just father, mother and my grand-aunt, Hirendra's mother. Oh yes! How could I forget cousin Dukhia? He was there with his wife and three brothers-in-law. Dukhia never tired of making his presence felt by doing the oddest things.

The unscrupulous son of my late senior uncle continued to flourish even in a seemingly hostile Pakistan. He cared very little for family tradition. His brothers-in-law suddenly erected a bamboo and tin shed next to the decorated front garden and started a clothes-laundering business. Dhiru joined the gang. Some non-resident members of our extended family objected to this defilement of our ancestral property. Dukhia as usual replied that he too was a shareholder of the ancestral property and he had the right to conduct business ventures from his own premises. The last of the resident members of the family, our parents, just cold-shouldered the smuggler-turned British agent turned-washerman.

The temporary lull was disturbed by three unforeseen developments.

Subhan Ali and others complained to father that Dukhia and his cohorts had started a facilitation company. His people in collaboration with some Muslim toughies helped fleeing Hindus cross over to the safety of India to Tripura and Assam, at a premium of Rs 1,000 per head. Within months, Dukhia acquired a BSA motorcycle that plied with annoying sounds between our home and Bhairab Market. A daily queue of villagers from near and far off villages who gave him money for securing a 'Dukhia passport' to India added to his affluence.

The second problem arose out of a much-awaited and a pleasant incident.

We were told that Rahman would be going to Brahmanbaria the next day to bring Lutfa home. The independent government of Pakistan suddenly woke up to the reality of a minor girl in prison for helping the 'swadeshis' against the British. It had finally responded after my father, Subhan Ali, Karamat Ali and others repeatedly sent representations to the government in Dacca. We did not know the legal intricacies but Lutfa was released on 14 August 1949, on the second anniversary of free Pakistan.

Her homecoming was not greeted by fanfare. A few of us received her at the station and father carried a floral garland to honour the sixteen-year-old hero, who like many others went unsung in the annals of India's Independence struggle.

Lutfa had really grown up. She looked taller and more feminine. Rahman's wife, our Aunt Anguri, embraced her daughter and they wept in each other's arm. Mother took her inside our main room, and offered her sherbet and payas. She caressed the rough locks of the young girl and combed her hair gently.

'How have you been Lutfa?' I asked.

'Call her Lutfa didi. She is older to you.' Mother chided me.

'I was fine in jail. I cooked for the jailor and massaged his wife. How have you been?'

'Don't know. Things are changing and falling apart.'

'Don't worry. We'll fight again. One day we will again be united.'

I do not know from where she got her confidence. Within a few days she settled in. But the changes took her by surprise. The people she knew were not there. The new people, especially Dukhia's gang disturbed her, as did Bhanu, one of the three brothers-in-law of Dukhia. A hefty looking human bull he fraternized more with the women visitors who queued up daily seeking a 'Dukhia passport' to India.

Dukhia, miserable fellow that he was, had learnt the tricks of making others miserable and earning quick money by exploiting the situation. As a contractor to the British garrison, he had minted a fortune and now his treasury was piling up with 'money to freedom' that he forced out from those seeking favours. A brother of Dhala mian, to whom everything Hindu was to be avoided, also joined the strange venture. Mintu, Dhala's brother and Bhanu launched another joint venture that we came to know about rather accidentally.

One lazy evening Jasim, Majid, Mani and I were busy playing marbles. I was concentrating on a red marble with my body and mind completely aligned to the line of throw that was about five yards away. A sudden cry disturbed my rhythm and concentration. It came from the direction of a croton bush at the back of the community hall.

'Someone is crying. I think it's a female voice.' I alerted the others.

'Must be some dry wood creaking,' Mani said.

'No,' Jasim said, 'I hear didi's voice. She's in trouble.'

We rushed there. Indeed Lutfa, the lion-hearted fighter lay pinned down on the barren earth with the hefty Bhanu on top of her. The scene was not new to me. I had seen Mano didi pinned down by Dhala's goons. Dhala's brother Mintu had immobilized Lutfa by forcibly pinning her hands on the ground. I took out my rubber catapult and fired a few marbles at Bhanu. He jumped in pain and chased us. Lutfa kicked Mintu in the groin. The two bulls ran towards the laundry hut and we chased them, shouting and firing marbles at them.

Dukhia emerged out of the hut with a long bamboo rod. However, our cries had attracted the attention of Rahman, Ramdin and the others. Father came running. I saw a weapon in his hand.

We did not have to describe the scene to our elders. Lutfa's body was scratched at several places and her clothes were torn. Rahman's wife ran in with a long fish-carving contraption known as a *bati* in Bengali. She charged at Bhanu, Mintu mian and Dukhia and set fire to the bamboo and tin shed, swirling the bati above her head. Dukhia and his gang of 'freedom passport' cohorts bolted. The hut was reduced to ashes in minutes.

That was not the end of the episode. The next day a meeting of the clan, elders and a few important Muslim leaders ruled that Dukhia should finally leave the village with his family. I felt sorry for Dukhia's wife, a lady with an enlightened mind and many accomplishments. That was not our last brush with Dukhia, Dhiru and their cohorts.

We realized that Lutfa had fought to the last puff of her breath. Her withdrawn disposition, measured words and newly donned maturity had drawn an unseen barrier between her and us. I had seen the same disposition in Mano and Rani didi.

Our troubled days were lit up temporarily with the solemnization of the nikah of Lutfa with Babloo Sheikh of Raipur village. One fine morning she took the train towards Dacca and disappeared from my life.

But we were to meet again. I rediscovered Lutfa in 1971 somewhere in the Sylhet sector along with her two sons—again fighting for freedom, this time freedom from Pakistan. She and her sons survived the war and enjoyed the freedom that was denied to her during the war for Independence.

The Vicious Storm Spirals

The year 1949 ended on a few happy and sad notes. The happy note was Lutfa's marriage and a few celebrations and community feasts. We Hindus had no reservations sitting with Muslim guests and sharing meals with them. Lutfa's husband Babloo Sheikh alias Sheikh Bardrudduja was a soldier in the Pakistani army posted somewhere near Jessore. Lutfa stayed in Babloo's village Raipur and often visited Kamalpur. The old days of our close friendship were gone. She often wore a burka. This was new to us. In our part of Bengal, Muslim women worked in the fields, tended cattle and never wore a burka. Like most Hindu women, they drew in a *ghomta* (the part of the sari that was used to cover the head) in front of strangers and elderly persons. They traded merchandise in the markets and often climbed the stage to sing devotional songs. The purdah system was not prevalent in rural Bengal.

Lutfa explained her new way of dressing. Her husband's family had been to Lahore and they followed the Shariat rules scrupulously.

'Do you like it?' I asked.

'Who cares? At home, I am a Bengali woman. This dress is for satisfying my in-laws. I don't mind, my husband loves me.' Burka or no burka Lutfa had not changed. Her charm, her warmth had not diminished.

Late that evening Lutfa brought in the first bad news. Our family ducks numbering about fifteen normally came ashore before sundown and returned to their coops. Sonai was in the habit of waiting near the kitchen door and cackling to remind mother of the rice ball she received as extra ration. It had become a routine and we normally did not do a head count.

'Kaki, Sonai hasn't come for the rice ball,' Lutfa announced in an anguished voice.

'Look inside the pen. She might have settled in to hatch eggs.'

'She's not there. Sonai hasn't returned from the pond.'

It was time to panic. Marsh falcons were common in our area and these hunters swooped down on the chicks. But Sonai was a fully-grown mother weighing over three kilogrammes. Her majestic gait and wing flapping often scared the midget-sized marsh falcons.

We searched the pond and the surrounding areas over and over again. Sonai was not the sort of bird to elope with a male from a neighbourhood pond. Anyway, we searched the ponds of our relatives and the one owned by Chandradhar Sutar, the only carpenter of our village. Sonai was not there.

'Someone must have stolen her,' commented Lutfa.

'Who would dare? They know it's the favourite duck of choto karta,' Rahman tried a wild guess. 'It must be Fazal, the petty thief.'

Fazal was a known bad character. A petty criminal from Jagannathpur, he had been convicted several times for petty thefts. However, he had never dared violate the limits of our homestead.

Rahman crossed the canal and made straight for Jagannathpur. Mostly inhabited by Muslims, a few Hindu families still lingered on to protect their landed properties.

Rahman was a known face. He commanded as much respect as any of our family members drew during the halcyon days of feudal glory. That day Rahman was not so lucky. He ran back from Jagannathpur with bleeding wounds on his hand and back. Chased by Fazal and his gang he crossed the canal and reached our home an anguished and bitter person.

'What's happened Rahman?' Mother rushed to his aid.

'That Fazal is a thief. He killed Sonai and was feasting with his friends over glasses of toddy. He chased me saying that the zamindar's days were over and they had every right over everything of the Hindu overlords. They were drunk, Ma. Poor Sonai is in their stomach. I'll kill that thief.' Rahman sat under the porch and wept like a child.

I was stunned. Five-year-old Sonai was an old duck. Her twenty odd progeny were a part of our life. Never before had a family duck been killed for table meat. We enjoyed some of the eggs and the rest were cycled for hatching. Mother knew the best way to rotate the eggs. I felt a part of my mother had been killed and consumed by the drunken thieves of Jagannathpur.

'I'll kill him,' I announced and took out my Sheffield knife.

Lutfa ran and stopped me. 'Are you mad? They are thieves and killers. This might take on a Hindu–Muslim colour. Let's wait for kaka to return. He'll take up the matter with Sabur mian, the Jagannathpur village chief.'

Sabur mian visited our home with three villagers. They were polite, shared our distress for the fine bird and finally said that very little could be done to Fazal. He had enrolled as a member of the Pakistan Muslim League and headed a unit of Ansar Bahini, an armed civilian vigilante force. He was tipped to contest the union board election, backed by Jalil Sarkar of Kalipur and Chhoban Khondakar, the top Muslim League leader of our area. Fazal was no more a petty thief. He had become a kind of political leader.

'Karta, I'll send a few more ducks for your son.'

'The thieves should be punished Sabur.'

'I agree karta. But the criminals are with the League. Please forget the incident. A bird should not whip up a Hindu-Muslim riot. We're afraid of the Leaguers and the Biharis. Accept our apology.' Sabur mian left with pain writ large on his face.

That night I went hungry though Lutfa and Jasim tried their best to comfort me and wipe my tears. Would they steal Pintu, my bearded goat? I knew they did not eat dog meat. But would they kill Tomtom just to hurt us and warn us to quit the village. Had the time come to quit our village?

Uncle Hassan Ali Mintu's visit brought in tons of information. 'I smell blood in the air Deben. India and Pakistan are fighting over jute and coal. They say Pakistani barges loaded with jute are waiting near Noakhali and Chandpur. India is pressing for a speedier supply. Karachi wants to go slow. India has stopped coal supplies. Our railway trains might grind to a halt anytime.'

'This is serious. We should appeal to India to release coal.'

'I smell dirty politics. The Muslim League is under pressure from Fazlul Haq sahib. Karachi is yet to finalize the agreement with India on coal and jute supplies. Nurul Amin is under pressure from the lobbies against him and wants to flex his muscle against the Hindus to divert the attention of the people. His police have started killing Bengali communist leaders in the Khulna area. Most of them are Hindus. I fear a general attack against Hindus. Haq sahib has called for a meeting at Munshiganj near Dacca in February. We'll find a way out. Just don't panic. Our boys are there to help you.'

'That's fine Hassan. But I am worried for my family. Loss of property can be suffered but honour of the family is more precious. I think I'm losing faith.'

'Don't lose faith. We Bengalis will stay together. I'm worried about the Muslim killings in Calcutta and Bihar in protest against the Khulna and Barisal killings by the Ansar Bahini. Killing has a ricocheting effect, you know Deben, from your own revolutionary days.'

Mintu kaka explained that the communist leaders of Khulna, Jessore and Barisal areas were inciting the rural masses against the League government of Nurul Amin. They were receiving tacit support from Fazlul Haq and even Maulana Bhasani. Clashes between the police and the communists were being given a communal colour by the League. They wanted to suppress rural unrest, near famine conditions and massive economic failures. League politics was again taking on a communal colour.

Father pondered over the situation and finally said, 'Let's look forward to the February meeting at Munshiganj. Hope the League won't go on a communal rampage before that.'

The next catastrophic event that rocked us was the news of revolt by the crew of two steamer boats belonging to our extended family. The captains and crew had unfurled the Pakistani flag and declared that as true Pakistanis they were the real owners.

After the clandestine departure of Uncle Hirendra, his bank creditors were sniffing around for some of his assets, which they hoped they could grab as compensation. The landed property was not clearly demarcated and thanks to my scheming grandpa, his brother's sons and daughters were deprived of most of the properties in nearby villages. The most visible assets they had included an ice factory, two steamer boats and some business ventures at Mymensingh.

Father suspected Hirendra's creditors for the misdeed. He proceeded to Mymensingh to lodge a complaint with the district authorities and to request Dhirendra, the eldest son of Girish Chandra to visit the village home and take charge of their family properties and their old mother. A beauty in her youth, my grand-aunt had developed some spinal problems and could not stand erect. She was dependent on my father—there was no one else.

The district authorities were not in a hurry to meet the progeny of a bygone landlord. They were busy with larger issues like communal riots, the shortage of coal, and ethnic cleansing in certain areas of the district. Finally, the additional district collector called my father in and expressed surprise that a few of us were still there. It was time for us to go. His message was clear.

The other part of the plan was successful. Dhirendra visited the village reluctantly and in a way was forced to help the old lady pack up. She did not like to leave the home her husband had built and where she had arrived at the young age of fifteen.

Putting my great-aunt on a train to Mymensingh turned out to be a war against a determined person willing to die at her post. Dhirendra cared little for sentiments but my father did.

The old lady repeatedly shouted at my father. 'Deben, kill me and burn my body here. Don't send me out of this home.'

We all wept. The old aunt was fond of me as I was the only young one who gathered fruits and flowers for her from the family garden. Propped up by mother I fed her a few spoons of payas, the only food she had accepted in the last two days. She looked at me and I could see the emptiness in her azure blue eyes. I have never seen such an empty and disillusioned look.

The pauperized wife of a wealthy person did not have even a few coins to give to the house staff. Father pushed a few coins into her hand and whispered in her ears. She summoned the house staff and blessed them with borrowed symbols of prosperity.

She was forced into a wheel chair and carried to the Bhairab railway station. She could not die on the soil where she lived for sixty years. She died in 1954, at the age of eighty-nine, a pitiable death on the floors of a coal-vending shed.

In those days of turmoil only lion-hearted and chronically caring people cared for their near and dear ones. Dhirendra was the antithesis of my father. He lived only for himself and cared very little even about his own progeny of ten.

Destiny had forced me to be by the side of the dying lady inside the coal-vending shed at Calcutta's suburban town Bali, next to the town of Uttarpara in the district of Hooghly, where our family was dumped by the Great Manmade Partition of India. The beauty queen, Girish Chandra's widow, was cremated on the banks of the Ganga. Her death did not inspire her descendants to write an epitaph.

We had no time to cry or think. Another twist of fate suddenly dumped some unexpected guests on us.

Father's sister and her family of ten suddenly arrived from Baghapura, a village down stream on the Meghna. My cousins were permanent guests at our village home during the heydays. A few of them had flown out to greener pastures but the rest had to face the marauding Ansar Bahini attacks. The entire Hindu village was torched, several young and not so young women were abducted, and everything that could be taken was carried away. My aunt was fortunate to find shelter in a Muslim tenant's home and a boat to escape to her paternal home.

A cluster of empty buildings with a few souls still hoping for the best to happen greeted her. We still had plenty of food, water, vegetables and fish to offer. But no one was in a position to offer security.

They intended to take a train to Brahmanbaria, a flourishing town still inhabited by affluent Hindus. Uncle Birendra and a few other members of the extended family had taken shelter in the burgeoning town hoping that Partition would spare this satellite of peace. However, taking a train to safety was not easy.

Stationmaster Zahur Pathan mostly declined to issue tickets to Hindu passengers on the plea that India had intentionally closed the pipeline of coal supply. Only Muslim passengers were given preference. Ordinary Hindus had to request their Muslim neighbours or well wishers to purchase tickets for them. On special occasions, when directed by Ansar commanders and Muslim League stalwarts, Hindus were issued tickets. Such occasions often ended in gory tragedies. Probably directions were given from somewhere to the Ansar and Bihari commando leaders to carry out a pogrom on wheels. Those were the days when Hindu passengers were stabbed, looted and thrown out of trains and their women were abducted.

These gangs were deputed on different routes according to a centralized scheme of action. These were not random train robberies. The meticulously planned actions were directed at killing Hindus on internal journeys or those escaping to the safety of India.

In December 1949, the newspapers carried reports of mass Muslim killings in Calcutta. This was an exaggerated report. However, within the next seven days, two trains were targeted and over fifty Hindus were killed.

On 15 December, a train from Dacca to Comilla was stopped at Khalilabad, between Bhairab and Narsinghdi, and all the Hindu passengers were ordered out. They were lined up by the side of a paddy field. The womenfolk were separated and the men and children were killed with machetes and swords. The victors carried away the women as if it was an integral part of the gains of war. It was a war indeed, a war against unarmed people fleeing their homeland for a new undefined home somewhere in a new India.

My father approached his political colleagues to buy tickets for my aunt and her family. Brahmanbaria was only forty odd miles away though the metre gauge train took nearly an hour to cover the distance. Some of the trains had switched over to wooden logs instead of coal which was in short supply from India. The jute and coal politics had deteriorated the political and diplomatic ambience. The Communist Party of East Pakistan, in which several Subhasists and Congress activists had taken shelter had generated greater suspicion amongst the Muslim League leaders. Uncle Subhan often said that these petty political miscalculations had prevented India and Pakistan from smoothening their relations.

He and Karamat visited Bhairab station and were told that passenger trains to Comilla and Chittagong had been suspended due to coal shortage. There was no motorway and no river-craft connectivity. The one and only Anderson Bridge over the Meghna at Bhairab provided the vital rail link. My aunt and her family were stuck for five days. However, after spending a princely amount of Rs 5000, some accommodation was secured for them in a goods train.

Karamat, by profession a jatra artist, used his theatrical charm to influence stationmaster Pathan. I watched the drama with amusement and apprehension.

'Pathan sahib, you're the descendant of a great Afghan warrior. Help me to win this small family battle,' he pleaded with a theatrical flourish. 'My sister's daughter is getting married at Brahmanbaria. She and her relatives must reach there tomorrow. Please help me.'

'How can I, Karamat sahib? This bloody Hindustan has stopped supplying coal to us. My home state of Bihar is full of coal. We were foolish to give Bihar over to Hindustan.'

'You're right sir. But some goods trains are plying on this route. Can you put them in one of those wagons?'

'It's difficult sir. You know I am a servant of the railways.'

'I know sir. It's also correct that your ancestors were so benevolent. Please help me.'

'Help comes at a cost.'

'I'm a poor jatra artist sir. I can give you Rs 3000.'

'Five?'

'Okay sir.'

'Deal. Bring them tonight near the loco shed and put them in one of the cattle trucks marked for Brahmanbaria. But they have to travel with cattle.'

'Cattle are precious to us. These bloody Indians have stopped supplying cattle to us. How do we meet the need of our meat?' Karamat, himself a vegetarian, told a lie to humour the stationmaster.

'Exactly. Don't worry, one day we will take back the whole country as our ancestors did.'

'Inshallah.'

'Bring them around 8 p.m. A railway employee Ratan Mochi will be there to help. Tell your sister to get out of the wagon when the train stops at Brahmanbaria for refilling water and coal supplies. If they are caught, I don't know them. Is that clear?'

Zahur Pathan pocketed the money and called Ratan Mochi, one of the few Hindu employees who was still with the Bengal Nagpur Railway, renamed the East Pakistan Railway.

I accompanied my aunt and her family to the loco shed located at a considerable distance from the station building. Dressed like ordinary Muslims they were helped into the cattle truck and sat on haystacks. Ratan closed the door and assured Karamat that the wagon would be shunted and tagged with the goods train arriving around 9 p.m. He happily pocketed Rs 100 as service charges and asked one of the inmates to bolt the door from the inside.

I was forced to return home. Karamat stayed on to ensure the shunting and tagging of the cattle load with the main goods train carrying rice, wheat and other merchandise to Chittagong. A few wagons marked for Brahmanbaria were to be shunted out on arrival at the target station. Karamat wished them godspeed and reported back to father that, Allah willing, they would reach Brahmanbaria by midnight.

Father had not shown up at the railway station so as to protect his sister's identity but he was immensely pained. I overheard my parents at night.

'Everybody is leaving for India. What is your plan? How long do you want to experiment with our lives?' Mother asked.

'Sorry Su. I know I've been a foolish idealist. I think I was made to be a wandering troubadour and not a family man.'

'I haven't questioned your personality. It's our safety that I'm talking of. What's left for us here?'

'Su, this is our land, our home for generations. We don't live in a sarai. Allow me one final effort to meet Haq sahib and decide if we have any future in Pakistan. We never prepared for this eventuality, never cared to transfer assets to Calcutta.'

'I appreciate your sentiments. But there are reports of riots from everywhere. How long do you think peace will prevail here? They are after your family land and other properties. Salvage whatever you can.'

'Fine. Ask Rahman to arrange for the disposal of the Raipura land and some land and other properties here. Do it on the quiet. People may not pay the right price,' said Father. 'I should accompany a delegation to Dacca or Munshiganj to meet Fazlul Haq and Bhasani. Our Sylhet rival Mujib has also agreed to take up the matter with Suhrawardy. I hope we can arrest the slide.'

'You won't change. Now go to sleep.'

'One point Su. Nazar and Asgar Khondakar, the student leader are coming tomorrow. They want to hold a peace meeting with all the village elders of the area. Ramzan has sent word for to me to stay here and mobilize people for the peace committee meeting. He wants me to preside over it.'

'Your brother Birendra is the Union Board president. Let him preside. You had better concentrate on the Dacca visit. I'll prepare for the final train to India,' said Mother.

Perhaps the time for taking a jump into the uncertain country called India was approaching. What would happen to my school, friends and my Tomtom, Pintu and Chandana? Where would we stay? Would there be a river like Meghna and a lake like Satmukhi Beel? I woke up and went out of the bedroom. Since the breakout of communal tension, Rahman kaka and Jasim used to sleep in an adjoining hut. He kept a long ramdao by his bed. I slept by Rahman's side and called him softly. 'What're you doing here chhoto karta?'

'I'm afraid.'

'Why? Who threatened you?'

'No one. Where would I stay in the new India, kaka? Can I stay with you when my parents leave?'

Rahman took me under his light kantha and embraced me. 'You're welcome. But no one is going to hurt you and your parents. Everyone in the area likes them. They like your ma's benevolence and your baba's free medical treatment, his music and selfless identification with the downtrodden. Allah will never punish you.' Rahman held me tightly and I felt reassured. 'Sleep well. I'm here to die for you.'

The New Year brought in some good news. I was promoted to class six with distinction. While Meboob Alam stood first, I stood second. As usual, my arithmetic score was abominably poor. I compensated by scoring very well in the other subjects. Headmaster Abdur Razzaq announced a monthly scholarship of ten rupees for Mehboob and five for me. It was time for celebration.

I walked down to Nazar kaka's shop and broke the news, bought some sweets and rushed home to mother. Father had a surprise for me. He had never purchased any presents for me. That day he took me to a store and bought me a new shirt and knickers. To top my surprise he also bought canvas shoes to wear while playing soccer and other games.

In our joint family fathers never bought presents for their own children. Presents had to be bought for all the children of same age group. During the annual village fair, each child was given an equal amount ranging from four to eight annas. These were the unwritten rules of a rural joint family.

For the first time I returned home a doubly blessed person, second topper in the class and with a boxful of presents from my father purchased exclusively for me. My happiness knew no bounds when mother also presented me with a rare dish of duck meat for lunch. Hindu homes were not supposed to eat fowl, presumed a Muslim dish.

From the time when Mano was attacked by the goons of Dhala mian I often felt that I could hear the lightest footsteps of the saddest moments approaching us.

Dinanath, followed by Purno Sangma, one of the family aides ran towards mother and suddenly tripped in front of the door. Blood was gushing out of his back. Purno followed and tried to stop the flow of blood by pressing a piece of white cloth on the wound.

I cried out. The pleasures of the day yielded to the pain lying in front of me. Mother followed by Rahman, Ramdin and others rushed in.

'Two goons of Dudu mian attacked Dinu babu and looted the day's income from the ice factory. Babu refused to surrender and they stabbed him in the back.' Purno spoke in a half Bengali and half Garo dialect.

'Rahman, send someone to the market to call your karta.'

Mother kneeled before the writhing body of Dinanath and asked Ramdin to collect as many calendula leaves as possible. She crushed the leaves, poured some juice on the wound, pressed the wet paste on the gaping hole and bandaged it with a clean piece of cloth. She directed a housemaid to prepare a concoction of milk, turmeric and ginger which was normally used as a pain killer. The juice and paste of calendula could stop the bleeding instantaneously.

Dinanath was made to sit against a cotton pillow and drink the concoction. He passed out under the impact of fear and trauma and perhaps loss of blood. As a family employee, he was a known face in the nearby villages. He collected land revenue, half of the produce of the land and often worked as clerk to our grandpa in lending money. He was not a universally loved man just as the landlords were not. He interacted more with the villagers and borrowers than his employers did.

An object of hate, Dinanath continued to glow in the reflected glory of his masters. The frustration of losing command of the serfs and villagers who were in debt, had transformed him into an abusive person. He still felt that he could get away by abusing and threatening people. In fact, we young kids used to call him *langda* Dinu, because of his gait and slight limp. Today the langda, sans his borrowed crown, was almost unconscious. Our usual game of mimicking the limping tyrant was replaced by a sense of fear and pity. All said and done, Dinu was a loyal servant and had continued to look after the fast disappearing interests of the family.

Father arrived with Nazar kaka, Shorab Ali, a Congress leader, and Jamil Ibrahim, a junior police officer. Father injected a painkiller and antiseptic and administered two sulphonamide tablets. 'What happened Dinu?'

'Two goons of Dudu tried to snatch the cash box. I resisted and they stabbed me.' Dinu managed to give a graphic account of the incident.

'Can you identify them?' asked Jamil Ibrahim.

'Yes sir. They are Sohrab Mondol and Amzad Bihari.'

Sohrab Mondol's father Jatin Mondol had converted after he fled Bhairabpur chased by the tax collectors of our grandpa. His homestead was seized and his cattle sold to realize the accumulated taxes and the five maunds of paddy he was supposed to pay as sharecropper's dues. Sohrab, like Dhala, nursed a personal grudge against our family. But this Amzad Bihari was an unknown character. Someone announced that Amzad was a young Bihari Muslim who had joined the Ansar Bahini under the command of Dudu.

The police officer left after recording Dinu's statement and being served Brook Bond tea and coconut barfi. An impromptu meeting between father and his friends followed Jamil's departure. Dudu had become unassailable since he was appointed a commander of the Ansar Bahini. The ill reputed force acted as the armed wing of the Muslim League and enforced the programme chalked out at Dacca and Mymensingh. Even the police and civil officers were afraid of them. Some Bihari newcomers had also enrolled in the Ansar Bahini and were issued firearms. The Muslim League did not have a strong presence in our area and the leaders in Dacca hated the idea of conceding an important place to the revived Praja Parishad Party of Fazlul Haq and Awami Muslim League floated by Maulana and Suhrawardy. My father and his colleagues were more inclined to support Haq and Suhrawardy. They never considered the Muslim League as a political product of the soil.

A delegation headed by Subhan Ali visited Munshiganj in late January 1950. The leaders of the Praja Parishad and Awami Muslim League were scheduled to meet there and formulate lines of action against Nurul Amin, the trusted man of Karachi.

Despite the ugly incident of the day, I noticed a glimmer of hope and some determination on my father's face. He was a chronic optimist. Even at that point of near defeat he refused to be defeated. His determination to stay back and fight amazed me.

eleven

The Cyclone Batters Mercilessly

January 1950 was not the best of times for the people of Bengal—in the east or the west. Bengalis had accepted the fait accompli of Partition and were aware that this Partition was not like the one of 1905. It could not be reversed because religion had taken centre place in our subcontinental politics and India was permanently divided. The Empire had experimented with the 1905 Partition at the cost of a nationwide agitation, severe communal clashes in Bengal and finally sowing the seeds of a separate Muslim state. Historians have recorded these events. But at the grassroots level the Hindus and Muslims had maintained the solidarity of cultural nationalism till political nationalism had mutilated the unique unity of the Bengali speaking people. Even we as young children had figured this out.

Moinul Haq, our class teacher was a bitter critic of Partition, as was Asgar, the student leader. Both of them were of the view that Muslims did not require a separate homeland. They required social, political and economic justice. However, their voices were drowned in the cacophony of bloodthirsty cries of the likes of Dhala and Dudu at the grassroots level, and Liaquat Ali and Nurul Amin at the higher political levels. They behaved like neo-invaders of Bengal by a strange Muslim power that was alien to the cultural nationalism of Bengalis.

A peace committee meeting summoned by Moinul Haq and Asgar near Bhairabpur was disturbed by certain elements owing allegiance to the pirate Nibharsa, and the volunteers of the Ansar Bahini headed by Dudu. They forcibly occupied the podium and delivered hate-speeches. Efforts by Asgar and Moinul Haq to spread the message of peace and amity were drowned out by shouts of Allah ho Akbar. Dhala and Maulana Qureshi described the creation of East Pakistan as the second successful march of Islam to the soil of Bengal. One of them described Nurul Amin as the Qaid of the Bengali Muslims and an incarnation of Bakhtiar Khilji, who had originally conquered Bengal from the Sena kings in the early thirteenth century.

We had very little hope of peace despite the efforts of saner elements. After the looting of the ice factory and the fatal stabbing of Dinanath we were not surprised when the clandestinely smuggled in Calcutta newspapers, *Amrita Bazar Patrika* and *Jugantar*, reported disturbing news. It started with news about joint Muslim and Ansar Bahini attacks on Hindu houses at Bagerhat in Khulna. This was followed by reports in *Ittehad*, a paper published from Dacca, of hundreds of Muslims being killed in Calcutta and certain places in Bihar and UP. Calcutta newspapers however reported the killing of twelve Muslims in communal incidents. Contradictory reports confused us and inflamed the communal leaders.

Disturbing news poured in from parts of Bakharganj, upper Mymensingh bordering Assam, Chittagong and Sylhet. My newfound maturity prompted me to maintain a file of paper clippings of these incidents. I did not share it with my friends.

It was around this time that father composed two songs that were sung by Nazar and others. The songs were symptomatic of the mood of the people—both Hindu and Muslim Bengalis. Rendered in our Mymensinghia Bengali dialect set to bhatiali tunes these songs had become popular and instilled some sense of unity in the people. A few lines are still vivid in my memory:

My aunt's home is at Kishoreganj,
My maternal uncle lives at Chatalpar,

My father's home is at Brahmanbaria,
I don't have an abode for myself.

Don't kill men, brother don't kill men,
Blood is red in the veins of
Both Hindus and Muslims
Allah and Krishna live in the
Same heaven,
They bless and curse evenly
For our good and bad deeds.
Love men.
Love is Allah and Krishna.

I feared that this time too songs and the re-enactment of traditional camaraderie would not be sufficient to avert the final disaster.

My father's second widowed sister who lived at Kuliarchar, about twelve kilometres from our home towards Kishoreganj, ran into trouble around 13 January. Her only son, a medical practitioner of sorts lived at our place with his rather enterprising and hardworking wife. We called him Sanu kaka. My aunt's daredevil attitude had earned her the respect of the villagers. This grand lady had changed the life of my uncle, so ill prepared for the battle of life.

However, my aunt's second son who was a cloth merchant was attacked by a Muslim mob and his young son was killed in the skirmish. Her third son, a wilier creature and manipulator, managed to flee to Calcutta leaving the old lady at the mercy of her neighbours and a few relatives. Her frenetic message prompted father to visit Kuliarchar and bring her to our place. Two days after her departure the entire Hindu part of Kuliarchar village was set on fire followed by mass looting, killing and dishonouring of women. Some Hindus managed to escape and reached our home. They were accommodated in a vacant building and some relief materials were collected to enable them to take an onward journey to Agartala. Obviously, the onerous task could only be completed with help from father's Muslim colleagues who still hoped to neutralize the fanatic Muslim League and the Ansar Bahini.

Disturbing news also trickled out of Calcutta. Benoy had to forget about college as our eldest brother pointed out that it was time for him to work to survive. He refused to support him financially. Each one was on his own. Relatives seeking shelter were construed as unwanted beggars. Benoy wrote in his letters that he had taken up a job as a low paid government relief-worker helping the flow of refugees from East Pakistan. The irony of one rootless refugee offering succour to other uprooted people had struck us. Mother was particularly fond of her second son. He was a delicate dreamer, a studious and steadier person. Mother was optimistic of his grand success in life. Her elder son had carved out a career for himself in the department of public works. He was a self-centred person, impatient and impulsive, in many ways the antithesis of his parents.

The premature termination of Benoy's studies had disturbed us. But days were difficult and the waves of Partition had forced people to plant themselves wherever they could and to take whatever position was available. This philosophical advice from Rahman kaka could not console me. He had just returned from Raipura with some good news. Rahman had managed to dispose off some land at Raipura, a few dozen valuable trees and some business assets. He faithfully handed over a royal sum of Rs 50,000 to mother.

He took me to the family pond. 'Take this rod. Let's try to catch a few fish for dinner.' He prepared bait and handed me a rod.

'I feel unhappy kaka. Bloodshed everywhere, people killing people. Benoy has been forced to take up a job.'

'Look beta,' Rahman addressed me for the first time as his son and not as choto karta, 'this is a stormy time. One has to take shelter even under the small arum leaves of the giant mankachu. The storm subsides and the sun shines again. That's Allah's rule.'

'I'm afraid I've to leave this village.'

'You have to in any case when you pass out from school. Look at your father. A man with so many qualities has suffered because he never tried to sell what he had to sell. He treated people free of cost; he composed music and sang for free.'

'He is a noble person, kaka,' I said.

'Yes he is. He is a living saint. But son, this life is a battle. To live you have to fight. Look at me. I was the son of a serf. I wouldn't like Jasim to be one.' Rahman kaka spoke with a sense of pride and dreams.

His pep talk soothened my nerves. I felt sorry for Benoy. We were not close, but we loved each other silently.

～

Sometime in the course of night, I woke up to the shrill cries of Rahman. He was shouting as loudly as he could. 'Karta wake up. There are thieves in the compound.'

Mother lit the lantern and father fished out his torch and a gupti. 'What's the problem Rahman? Where are Purno and Ramdin?'

Rahman rushed towards the family pond which skirted a barbed wire fence leading to the canal. Ramdin, Purno and few others followed him. Two thieves succeeded in negotiating the fence but the third one was entangled in the barbed wire and was caught in the stranglehold of the arms of Purno Sangma.

Verbal and physical abuses made the poor thief almost unconscious. Finally, mother rescued him by saying that no one should take the law into their own hands and the thief should be handed over to police. After drinking a glass of water, the thief, a low caste Hindu, admitted that his partners Habib and Harun of village Saidpur were the kingpins. They had planned a daring break-in on being tipped off that the nearly empty 'bara bari' had many hidden treasures buried under the floors of the northern and western court buildings. Since some visiting relatives occupied both the courts, they targeted the goat pen where we reared about ten female goats. Pintu was the only bearded male. Habib and Harun succeeded in lifting Pintu into a gunnysack but his braying sounds had woken up Rahman.

We rushed to the goat pen. Pintu's female partners and the kids were there but Pintu was missing. We fanned out with lamps and torches and called Pintu loudly. Pintu was a plump goat. Well fed and cared for, he was as dear a friend as Tomtom was. My heart sank. The merciless thieves were sure to sell Pintu at a hefty price or slaughter him for fatty tangri roast and spicy salan curry.

A police officer arrived well after eight and perched himself under the shade of the eastern court building. Over a cup of ginger tea, he interrogated the unfortunate thief. He finally declared that Habib and Harun were habitual offenders and had come out of jail only ten days ago. Father suggested a raid to recover Pintu.

'Deben karta,' the police officer pointed out politely, 'it's our duty and we would do that. Please don't go to Saidpur. Mufti Salahuddin has set up a mosque and a madrasa in that village. Some Biharis have also taken refuge. They won't welcome a Hindu visiting and I don't want a communal riot over the carcass of a goat. Better send your family retainer Rashid to enquire and report.'

'They'll kill the goat,' Father protested.

'Stolen cash is spent fast, abducted women are dishonoured and stolen goats go to the cooking pot. Obviously they would sell at a hefty price, maybe to the meat hungry Biharis. We Bengalis prefer fish.' The polite police officer asked a constable to tie a rope around the waist of the apprehended thief and promised to send a team to arrest Habib and Harun. If alive, he reassured us Pintu would be traced and returned.

That was 5 February 1950, a very depressing day. I knew in my heart that Pintu was lost forever. The fear of being found out might prevent them from killing it for a family or village feast. They might shave its goatee and sell it at a neighbouring market.

I did not feel like eating, I walked down to the stairs of the pond with Tomtom following me. I did not notice Jasim following quietly. I stood near the edge of the water and threw in flat clay pieces that created small ripples and disappeared. Pintu and I had been friends forever. Rahman often made me mount the old faithful and took me around the lawns.

I started weeping. Tomtom gauged my mood, looked at my face, and licked my big toe. That was his intimate way of expressing solidarity with an old faithful friend, three years senior to him.

Jasim dug into his pocket and took out a packet wrapped in green banana leaf, delicious rice dumplings mixed with gur.

'Allah has his way of punishing such thieves. Now eat. You must go to school.' Jasim forced the dumplings into my mouth.

'I don't feel like going. Father is going to Dacca the day after tomorrow. I'd like to be with him,' I replied in a pensive voice. All the people I loved had started going away gradually. Manorama, Rani and Lutfa didi had left. I had lost Sonai and Pintu. Most extended family members had gone over to Agartala or Calcutta. The manicured gardens were turning into wild forests. There was no one to trim and maintain the gardens and orchards. I felt like I was suffocating.

∼

7 February 1950.

Father Debendra accompanied by Subhan kaka, Karamat kaka and others left for Munshiganj to attend a meeting with Fazlul Haq and if possible with Suhrawardy and Mujib. Our student leader Asgar accompanied them. We saw them off at our dear old Bhairab station. As I started walking home in a pensive mood Rahman kaka bought me a piece of cake from Jagannath Jola's shop.

'Don't worry. He'll be back in a few days. Things will be alright.' Rahman tried to cheer me up.

My eyes were drawn by the bold headlines of *Jugantar*, the newspaper from Calcutta: 'FRESH COMMUNAL KILLINGS IN EAST PAKISTAN.' 'Communal clashes in Hooghly, Burdwan and Murshidabad—several Muslims killed' in a box item followed it. I picked up the paper and paid two annas to the shopkeeper.

Rahman gauged my changed mood. 'What's in the paper?'

'More bad news kaka. Muslims and Hindus are again killing each other. I won't show it to mother. She'll feel scared.'

'Better show her. She should know. Don't worry. We'll protect you. No one can harm you while I'm alive.' Rahman drew me near and we walked home in silence.

The next day, Jasim had gone to the railway station to collect empty cigarette packets. We used to cut the cigarette packets into small rings and make long garlands and artistic figures of animals from those paper chains. We often gathered the empty packets from the hawkers and from the railway tracks.

He came scurrying like a scared rabbit. 'Abba, Abba,' he shouted at the top of voice. 'The Noakhali express train has just arrived. It has over fifty dead bodies most cut into pieces. Allah kasam. The police are guarding the platform. All the vendors have run away. Most Bihari coolies have disappeared. Go and see for yourself.' He sat down under the shade of our porch. Mother offered him water and gave me a frightened look.

'Let me go and see,' I implored my mother.

'No, you won't. Stay home.' She asked Rahman to walk up to the station and see the situation for himself.

Rahman returned after an agonizing hour and informed us that Jasim was correct. The dead bodies of Hindus were dumped in an adjoining ground and the bogies were detached to be cleaned and washed. A special police party had arrived in a special train and two policemen were detailed for each compartment. He also informed us that groups of Bihari Muslims and Kuttis—South Indian non-Bengali Muslims settled in the Dacca area for generations and mostly engaged in plying tongas and other small businesses—who spoke a queer mixture of Bengali and Urdu—had been attacking trains and robbing Hindu passengers.

More bad news the following day as well.

Kirit Dhar, a junior commissioned officer in the Indian army had visited his father Gagan Dhar, a retired legal practitioner. He had boarded a train for Calcutta promising to return and take his parents to the safety of India. Someone from Dacca informed Gagan Dhar that Kirit had been attacked by a mob of Kuttis at the Dacca railway station and had been killed. His dead body was brought to our village by two policemen.

In the absence of my father, mother deputed me to attend the cremation and offer condolences to Uncle Gagan Dhar, a distant cousin of my paternal grandfather. The funeral party was accompanied by our near relatives who still lived in the village hoping for better times.

On reaching the funeral ground, we found a crescent flag perched next to the small temple. The Brahmin who lived there and performed the rituals was also missing. Frenetic enquiries revealed that the cremation ground was occupied at the instance of Maulana Qureshi on the plea that Hindus had no right to be cremated on the soil of Pakistan.

No one dared remove the flag. Finally, a few saner Muslim leaders of the western side of the village removed the flag and produced the Brahmin who had taken shelter in the railway colony. Kirit Dhar was cremated in the presence of Muslim leaders. That was my last visit to the cremation ground that had been donated by our family.

My friends in Bangladesh inform me that the ground near the banks of the Brahmaputra still continues to be the Hindu cremation ground.

At home, Gulab Misr and Ramdin approached Mother around 3 p.m. with folded hands. 'Mataji, we want to go home. Most Bihari coolies and businessmen have left Bhairab. It is no longer safe for us.'

'How long have you been here Ramdin?'

'Twenty years. Now I want to go home to my family.'

Mother went in, brought out a couple of currency notes and divided them between Ramdin and Gulab. 'Thanks for your services. Take care. Have a safe journey.'

Both the Bihari house-guards fell flat at mother's feet and stood up wiping their eyes and cheeks. 'Here is our address Ma. We live in Bhagalpur, if you ever need us get in touch.'

The two old faithful guards had been so much a part of our home. We grew up playing on their shoulders and laps. They guarded us against many odds. We considered them more formidable than the giant bottle palms which lined our front gardens. Their departure created a vast emptiness. The only one left was Purno Sangma, the faithful Garo tribal. He patted my head and spoke softly. 'Choto karta, I am afraid too. I want to go back to my village. Tell Ma to relieve me. Let me wait for your baba to return. I cannot leave your mother and you alone. Have you noticed that the three Muslim guards deployed by Subhan sahib have not turned up for two days? Something is wrong karta. Something bad is going to happen.' He lamented in a miffed voice. 'They must have been scared away by Dhala and Dudu. I am alone. How can I protect you? I don't even know how to fire a gun.'

'I don't think one gun can fight so many attackers. And why should they attack us?'

'We are Hindus. In a war you need not be a soldier to be killed. Even innocent people get killed,' was Purno's wise comment. I was rattled. I did not show it apprehending mother would get more scared. It was my duty to protect her. I clasped the butt of the Sheffield tightly with a determination to use it against any attacker.

～

10 February 1950.

Shock after shock greeted us that morning. Jasim ran in crying at the top of his voice. 'Master, the worst event has taken place.'

He panted, cried and retched from his empty stomach. He had gone for his morning evacuation to the side of the dried canal bed. As he settled down, he heard a groaning sound. On inspection, he found the body of Purno Sangma lying in a pool of blood, his throat slit and blood gushing out. He ran for help.

Rahman called out for help and was joined by one of the guards posted by Subhan kaka. I followed them. They carried Purno's body up into our courtyard. Mother tried to bandage his throat with a long piece of cloth. Her efforts did not prevent the gushing flow of blood. Purno's hand involuntarily touched mother's hand and he whispered a few words.

'Dhala's man Kadir Sheikh . . . my wife and daughter . . . home . . . ' Purno stopped talking. His eyes were riveted to an unknown spot in the sky and his mouth hung open as he vainly struggled to breathe. He was dead.

Mother covered his body and requested Rahman, the last of our faithful retainers, to seek help from the village carpenter, the barber and a few fishermen to carry out Purno's last rites. She sent the other guard posted by Subhan kaka to Bhairab market with a letter to Uncle Birendra. His establishment, Dhar Trading Company was located in the main market. Besides being a prominent businessperson he had the distinction of being elected as the Union Board Chairman. For a Hindu in Pakistan it meant a lot to be chairman of a local self government body. It meant that our family still carried some respect and recognition; our people had not yet succumbed to blood-curdling communal cries. They maintained a fragile shield of harmony despite attempts by Biharis and Ansar Bahinis floated by the Muslim League.

I did not join the procession to the cremation ground. The very ambience of that place sickened me, especially after my last visit to cremate Haripada and Kirit Dhar.

The police made a routine visit, inspected the murder spot and recorded Jasim's statement. After they left, Jasim and I sat down and talked about Purno's murder by Kadir Sheikh. I was not in a mood to talk. I missed the presence of father and hoped he would be back soon and finally decide to take us to the safety of India.

'Are you thinking of leaving us?' Jasim asked as if he was able to read my mind.

'I am worried about my father and mother.'

'Why worry? No one would dare attack your house. You are the landlord.'

'Things and people have changed Jasim. I love this village; I don't want to go. But what happens if they kill my mother and father?' I knew I was not talking coherently. I was just venting out my fear and imagining that I could hear the footsteps of another murderous mob headed by Dhala mian attacking our house like he did in 1947.

With darkness descending, a pall of gloom overwhelmed me. I would wake up from involuntary slumber and place my ears against the darkness of the night to pick up distant footsteps. Jackals howling often appeared to be war cries of an advancing mob. The movements of giant lizards and tortoise on dry grass produced the sound effect of stealthily crawling killers with arms.

I closed my eyes and tried to imagine what India would be like. I had been to Agartala. It was not a part of India when I last visited. Would India be full of rivers, lakes, forests, orchards and big homesteads? Where would we live? How would we live without income from land and other establishments? Would our father take up a job? These big questions of life haunted me. I slid down from my bed and crawled to mother's side. She was awake too. 'Sleep. Let your baba come. We'll decide in a day or two.'

'What would happen to Tomtom and Chandana? Can we take them?'

'I'll try. If we cannot I would free Chandana and gift Tomtom to Jasim. He also likes Tomtom.'

'Rahman will take care of our home. We will be back soon after the disturbances are over. This is our home and country. We can't be in India permanently.'

'Why does Baba not care for our safety? People are getting killed everyday.'

'Don't be angry with him. He loves us like the air and waters around love us. You don't hear them talking, but they talk. Calm your mind and listen intently. You'll here them singing to you. He's a mendicant by nature. He has everything but he possesses nothing. He lives for his ideas.' Mother spoke for the first time to me about the man with whom she had spent nearly thirty-five years. I do not know if she ever had a chance to express her appreciation to the man who mostly lived for others.

'Has he no dreams for us?'

'He wants you to be a big poet and artist. He hopes that your elder brother will be a Collector. But son, most dreams burst like coloured balloons. Only a few dreams materialize and only when you work hard for it. Don't stop dreaming even if most of your father's dreams have not materialized. He is limited by the times and situation that we live in.' Mother tucked me under a light kantha and hummed a song she always sang in my childhood.

We could not sleep. Rahman and another helping hand slept outside our bedroom with swords and spears by their sides.

We heard his agitated shouts and banging on the door. 'Ma, open the door. Give me the gun,' he shouted repeatedly.

Mother opened the door after lighting the lamp. Rahman had a hurricane lantern in his left hand and a sword in the right.

'What has happened Rahman? Have thieves struck again?'

'Come out and look Ma. Look at the skies of Bhairabpur. It's all red. There is fire and can you hear the cries?'

Mother stepped out and looked up at Bhairabpur about three kilometres across the yellow mustard fields. The skies were red and we could see silhouettes of burning homes and hear shrieks and cries. She stepped back into our room and brought out two guns, one double barrel gun used by Ramdin and another that looked like a military gun with a magazine. 'Use the double barrel. There are thirty rounds. I have fifty rounds. Don't allow the gang of Dhala and others to force entry.'

She crouched behind a cement block that was used as a grain-thrashing platform. Rahman and his associate took positions behind huge bottle palm trees. A few other relatives also lined up with whatever weapons they could lay their hands on. I stood by my mother with the fully stretched Sheffield knife, determined to hit anyone daring to attack her.

No invader stormed in. After about thirty minutes, some twenty tired and injured persons ran across the mustard and lentil fields and tried to enter our front gate. Rahman stopped them with a pointed gun. 'What do you want? You can't enter this house. It has been the house of your providers.'

'We're Hindus. A Bihari gang aided by the Ansars from other areas has attacked our homes. Hindu homes have been put on fire. Some have been killed. Hrishikesh Das, the prominent businessman has been attacked. We don't know if they have spared his life.' An elderly villager pleaded with Rahman.

'Open the gate Rahman. Let them in.' Mother came out from behind the cement block, the rifle in her hand, 'What's happened Baikuntha?' she asked one of the wailing villagers.

'It's the Biharis, thakurain. Some Ansars were with them. Over twenty houses were torched. I saw three bodies lying on the ground.' A person with blood oozing from his abdomen lamented loudly.

'Take some clean cloth from me and some antiseptic lotion. Rahman, open the eastern court building. Stay there until daylight. We'll see what can be done in the morning.'

That night we did not get back to bed. We tended the injured and provided them with tea and sweetened puffed rice balls. They huddled on the floor like injured and cornered animals. In the melting darkness of that 11 February morning I could visualize those butchers, eager to slit throats, chasing about twenty villagers from Bhairabpur.

∽

11 February 1950.

No police party came to the rescue of the villagers. Mother sent Rahman to Bhairabpur to contact Abdur Rauf, a leading businessman and member of the Union Board. Rauf arrived after about an hour and submitted that he was not in any position to protect the villagers from the marauding gangs of Kuttis, Biharis and Ansars. They were directed from Dacca by some forces that he did not know.

'What should they do Rauf sahib? You're an old friend of our family.' Mother spoke from behind her veil.

'Thakurain,' Rauf spoke haltingly. 'They can go over to Agartala. Mejo karta should stay in Agartala for some time. Like in 1946 hopefully this madness should also subside.'

'He's in Dacca for a political meeting.'

'Send a man to him and ask him to come back. Should I send word to Ramzan the river pirate to send some men to guard your home?'

'As you think best Rauf sahib. I could never have imagined that this would happen to our Bengali people.'

'We've lost control to the Biharis and Punjabis. They are the masters. It is better that you leave for sometime.'

'Please ask Ramzan to send someone to Munshiganj to inform your karta. He should return at the earliest.'

Abdur Rauf bowed profusely and left for his village with a couple of bodyguards accompanying him.

Mother called me aside after breakfast. 'Take this letter to Uncle Birendra. Ask him to see me. Take Jasim with you and bring some fish and mustard oil from the market.' She gave me a rupee and eight annas and saw us off with an anxious look.

Jasim and I reached Bhairab railway station in no time. We decided to take a short cut through the graveyard. The station hummed with activity. Over two hundred people waited at the platform with some police guards loitering with disdain and hate writ large on their faces.

'I've never seen so many people in the station so early in the day,' I commented curiously.

'They are Hindus escaping to India. Where is India, Krishna?' he asked.

'Agartala must be in India. I know Calcutta is also in India. It must be a big place.' I commented with an air of authority. A sixth class student should know more than Jasim who never attended school.

Uncle Birendra asked when father would be returning.

'He's in Dacca, attending a meeting.'

'I know. But he had better attend to things here. Tell your ma that I'll come home tomorrow. Ask her to cook a meal for me.'

On the return trip from the market, we decided to take the road that passed in front of my school. Cycle rickshaws and peddlers crowded the pebbled road. The bakery was our main attraction. Two muffins could be had for two annas. I had saved four annas after all that shopping and decided to purchase four muffins, one each for mother, Rahman, Jasim and me.

We were stopped by a loud shout. 'Hey Krishna, Mehboob here.' I turned back and saw the boy from my class walking briskly towards us. We stopped.

'You haven't come to school for two days.'

'You know what's happening around. Our servant Purno was killed and several houses at Bhairabpur were attacked.'

'We know. Actually, my father wanted to speak to your father. Where is he?'

'He has gone to Dacca for a meeting.'

We walked back with Mehboob. His mother greeted us with sherbet. His father Shaukat Alam, a tall handsome man appeared from an inner room.

'Look son. You're Mehboob's friend. I hear bad news. They want to attack your house.'

'Who are they uncle?'

'Difficult to say. Must be the Leaguers and Ansars. They think your family is standing in the way of the integration of this area with Pakistan. Tell your father to see me. And tell your ma to go to a safer place for sometime.' Shaukat Alam patted my head gently. Mehboob's mother mumbled a prayer and wished us godspeed.

I was puzzled by the intervention of a sane and respectable person like Shaukat Alam. He was a prominent figure and Mehboob often said that he was a poet of some kind. I mulled over his suggestion and decided to warn mother. She listened carefully while talking to a man I did not know. 'Jaman bhai, please go to Munshiganj and tell your karta to return home urgently. Things are not going well here.'

Jaman touched my mother's feet and said that he would take the evening steamer and bring father back with him.

'Who's this man, Ma?' I asked.

'He's Jaman, a man of Ramzan the dacoit.'

We spent that evening planning the defence of our house with two guns and a few spears and swords. In all, the strength of our army consisted of four able bodied males, mother, the housemaid Ranga, Jasim and I. Our weapons included the precious Sheffield knife, plenty of marbles and two catapults. We thought these were good enough to hit at least a couple of enemies.

Nothing happened. We did not talk much but anticipated the loud stomping sounds of the marauding mob.

twelve

Train to Disaster

15 February 1950.

Uncle Birendra reached home around ten thirty in the morning. As usual, he was dressed in a fine dhoti, an off-white silken punjabi, a light woollen shawl and brown moccasins. My stylish uncle was fond of his gold-rimmed eyeglasses and gold Parker pen. He looked elegant. A man of means and position he never neglected his attire and never shied away from exhibiting wealth. He was the president of the Union Board dominated by non-Muslim League Muslim members. Traditionally our family by virtue of being the largest land owning aristocrats bagged the post.

He was the antithesis of my father who dressed indifferently, did not shave for days together and kept the company of people considered lesser specimens of human society. He listened to all and sundry and spent all that he could afford to help them. Uncle Birendra was born to be a successor to his worthy father, wielding influence on the tenants, controlling their destinies and gradually climbing the ladder to political power and patronage. The only person he was scared of was his wife, our youngest aunt, a modern lady from an urban family.

Rahman greeted Uncle Birendra with a chair and a glass of water.

'Boudi,' he addressed mother rather impatiently, 'come to Brahmanbaria with me. There may be disturbances in our village.'

'Your brother is in Munshiganj. How can I go leaving him behind?'

'He'll be okay. His political friends will take care of him. Here you're alone. I'll send a message to him to come over to Brahmanbaria. Things will cool down in a few weeks.'

'Are you shutting down your business establishment?'

'No. My nephew will look after the business. Come with me. Don't carry all your valuables. In any case we'll be back in fifteen days.'

This was a tricky moment. This was a moment of destiny. To go or not go was a vital decision. Mother took most of the family decisions. But today she hesitated. This decision involved leaving her husband behind and leaving the home on her own. How could she leave home without consulting him?

Mother looked at me for an answer. 'What do you say?'

I was confronted with a grave question of life and death. I was scared, but leaving father behind did not sound right.

'I don't think that we should leave till baba comes back.'

'Don't be foolish. Who would protect you if the house is attacked tonight? He is safe in Munshiganj. Do you think Rahman alone can save you?' Uncle Birendra could hardly hide his impatience and annoyance.

'What would happen to the temple? Who'll light the daily lamps and offer worship?' Mother confronted uncle with a tricky question.

Uncle Birendra spoke in a decisive voice. 'The marble statues can't protect themselves, how would they protect you? You should think of your young son. Do you think God would come down to save him? Let Rahman take care of the home. The home temple should be closed for a while.'

Uncle's argument about my safety clinched the issue. Mother looked at me and asked her brother-in-law to have a quick bite before we boarded the train to Brahmanbaria.

I packed my books in a small carry bag, tucked the Sheffield in my half-trouser pocket, and hid some coins in the hollow of a bamboo pole in our kitchen. That was the safest way of saving small coins. Mother packed a small suitcase with essentials and asked me to help her bury a rubber-sheet covered box that contained cash and jewellery. We dug deep and placed the box and evened out the earth. Finally, a big water filled jar was placed on the spot to mislead prospective thieves.

We went to the temple, lit a camphor lamp and prayed for a few moments before locking the door. Rahman took charge of the keys of all the buildings and the temple.

The trickiest part of leaving was pacifing Chandana and Tomtom. Animals are known to be finely tuned to seismographic shifts.

Chandana rebelled. '*Kuthai jaitacha* (Where are you going)?' She pranced inside the cage and asked repeatedly.

'Going for a few days. Rahman will take care you. I'll bring lots of good food for you,' I replied as if I was pacifying a kid.

'*Jais na, baro bipad. Eka thaikbona* (Don't go, grave danger, I won't stay alone).' Chandana kicked her water and food plates in violent protest.

Tomtom caught hold of the belt of my carry bag and dragged it under the bed. He buried his face in the bed and simply refused to look at me. Rahman's efforts to retrieve the bag with a bamboo stick were received with barks and growls. I had to crawl under the bed to pacify Tomtom promising to take him along. I felt sorry that I lied but there was no other way. Tomtom was never on a leash but that day I put a leash and chain on him and requested Jasim to hold him.

I was never pally with our cat Victoria who lived behind our kitchen. Tomtom never allowed her to enter the house. The cat suddenly started showing her affection by brushing her body against my feet. That day I patted her for the first time and promised to come back.

Many years later while reading Kalidasa's *Abhignana Shakuntalam* and other treatises on animal behaviour I understood what they really feel for us though we may not understand their way of expressing their affection and love.

It was time to embrace Jasim and Saifi. Saifi had brought me some coconut candy made by his mother. I kept a few in my kit bag and we shared some.

Uncle Birendra was in a tearing hurry. 'Let's go. The train leaves at exactly 1.30.'

Mother bowed down to the images of the gods and goddesses which she kept in a corner of the bedroom, locked the house and handed over the keys to Rahman. 'Take care of Tomtom, Chandana and the ducks. You are in charge. Guard everything carefully.'

Rahman touched mother's feet, wept and said in a broken voice, 'Don't worry Ma. I will protect everything until my last breath. May Allah protect you. Come back soon.'

We walked to the railway station with Rahman, Jasim and Saifi following us. It was not a common sight for a woman of our family to walk down to the railway station without a couple of escorts. Most shopkeepers and some visitors to the sub-registrar's office lined up and raised their hands to greet mother and uncle. This was an age-old practice. It pleased me.

But the station platforms did not please me. The day before the platforms had been swarming with people, in groups here and there. That day all the three platforms were nearly empty. Even some of the regular hawkers were conspicuously absent. Only a junior station staff member greeted uncle and informed him that the Dacca–Sylhet Express would arrive at platform number two. He courteously offered to purchase tickets for us. Uncle always travelled first class. The train would stop for five minutes.

The empty railway station disturbed me. 'There is a problem Ma. The station is almost empty.' I shared my anxiety with her. She knew very little about the station. 'What could be the problem?'

'You're a precocious child,' uncle reacted. 'The train to Sylhet normally goes empty from Bhairab. There will be more of a crowd at Brahmanbaria.'

We were never encouraged to argue with our elders.

Kala mian, a member of the Union Board appeared suddenly with three other people. 'Adaab Biren babu,' he greeted uncle. 'You'll be away for a few days. Please sign these papers. These relate to the water supply to our villages and the digging of an irrigation canal at Kalipur.'

This was normal business talk. Uncle signed the papers and said something in a hushed voice. They were intensely watched by about ten people standing on the railway overbridge. I didn't recognize them. They looked like outsiders, non-Bengalis. We Bengalis, both Hindus and Muslims mostly looked alike with somewhat mongoloid features. There were some exceptions, mostly the descendants of north Indians settled in Bengal. The group on the overbridge looked fairer with features that looked Turkish or Afghan. Were they Biharis? As the train ground to a halt most of them rushed down and entered different compartments. Their demeanour agitated me. I murmured to mother. However, she did not consider it necessary to share my impressions with uncle.

The train arrived on time. As we boarded the first class compartment I noticed a huge tick mark in white chalk on the side panel. This sign worried me. As one who often visited the station, I was acquainted with the passenger bogies. Only cargo bogies were often tick-marked below the name of the destination station. Ours was not a goods train. I dared not share the thought with my uncle.

Jasim, Saifi, Rahman and Tomtom lined up to bid us farewell. Tomtom almost jumped on me to lick my face. Rahman took charge of the leash and we boarded the compartment. As the train started moving, Jasim and Saifi ran alongside waving.

Suddenly I noticed Mehboob Alam running beside the compartment and trying to tell me something. I thought I heard . . . don't go by this train . . . It could have been my imagination. The clanging and clamouring of the engine drowned out his voice. I managed to wave before a man in a black cloak pushed me aside and locked the doors. Two other men pulled down some of the window shutters on the platform side.

Uncle Birendra, in conformity with his official position and assumed dignity concentrated on reading a newspaper. Mother and I occupied seats in a row opposite him. I felt uncomfortable when my eyes met some of the eyes of the strangers who had boarded the compartment moments before our entry. I shifted my eyes and as the train moved, and peered out of the open window to enjoy the sight of the market area on the right and the fields on the left. Travelling by train and pushing one's head out to enjoy the countryside and feel the gushing wind were integral ingredients of the adventure. The gushing air always gave me a sense of freedom.

Suddenly a liquid blob hit my face. Spit, I thought, normally relieved by passengers from the compartments ahead. I felt irritated and tried to remove the dirt with my left palm. It was fresh red blood. I wiped the blood with my palms and looked out to check the source. The train had, in the meantime, slowed down near the outer signal.

There he was. A fat Marwari looking man with only an undergarment on his huge hulk was shouting at the top of his voice by raising one hand. His other hand was trying to stop the gushing blood from his punctured stomach. Obviously, he had been stabbed and pushed out of the compartment ahead of ours. Four more bodies with stab wounds, fountains of gushing blood and pitiable cries followed the first body. I knew what was happening. I had seen such Marwaris in similar conditions brought to our home for shelter and treatment. The Biharis, Kuttis and the Ansars had attacked our train. I now realized what Mehboob Alam had been trying to tell me while running along the speeding train. He was warning us not to travel in the ill-fated train.

The realization helped me prepare for the worst. I moved closer to my mother and whispered that some people were killing Hindus and throwing them out from the train. She looked at my blood smeared face with an ashen face. She clutched my hand, perhaps to derive strength and to reassure me that nothing would happen to us. A mother's instinct to protect her child propelled her to embrace me with her right hand and caress my hand.

Her instincts and wishes were not enough to save us from the killers. I looked up and noticed fear writ on her face and her fragile body writhing in some sort of inner convulsion. She was afraid, I realized. I instantly remembered what my father had told me about protecting mother. I gripped the Sheffield knife tightly.

The train had just entered the Anderson Bridge and slowed down further when three men who looked like Biharis stood up and walked towards uncle Birendra. One of them removed his gold-rimmed spectacles, the other his gold Parker pen and the third one his woollen shawl. Uncle looked at them with a stunned expression and started touching their feet. 'Don't kill me. Take all the money you want.'

One of the Biharis slapped him and hurled abuses in a language that I did not understand. What should I do? I was perplexed for a moment. The next moment I decided what I would do. I took out the Sheffield knife, flicked open the blade and tried to charge at the Biharis.

But mother stopped me. 'You can't fight them. They are big and too many. Come, let us jump off the train.'

I looked out. We could not jump on the bridge girders. I looked out and saw several human bodies rolling down to the river below, all drenched with blood and severe wounds. I counted twenty bodies.

The fearsome sight parched my throat. I tried to swallow my saliva. My fearful eyes caught the slow motion of a young woman clutching her baby and falling head down to the river below. I felt dizzy, but did not lose my head. I dragged mother to the compartment door. It was locked. I forced open a window and preened out, my hopes up as I saw the platform of Ashuganj station just rolling under the foot rails of the compartment. My other eye was directed at my uncle. The goons were in the act of throwing his body out of the compartment. They lifted his heavy body and threw him out of the window. I was afraid that he had been stabbed.

As I approached the window to push mother out on the platform, I encountered a young Bengali Hindu deserting his small daughter and jumping out to the safety of the platform. She stood near the window and cried out for her father. I picked her up and threw her on to the platform more as an act of clearing our way to safety than as an act of mercy. There was no time to check her condition.

As one of the Biharis tried to shove past the bewildered Muslim passengers towards us, I lifted mother with all the strength I had and pushed her down to the platform. Next was my turn. The Bihari almost caught up with me with an open dagger in his hand. I pointed my Sheffield at him and the Bihari paused for a few moments. I took the opportunity and jumped out of the compartment. The train clambered ahead for a while and stopped.

We, mother and son stood on the platform as if we had landed on another planet. Some people looked at us curiously, especially at my open knife. I saw the young Bengali Hindu picking up his daughter and running down the steep slope of the platform that ended up at the base of the embankment nearly a hundred feet below.

'Where do we go?' Mother looked at me helplessly.

'Don't worry. Let's rush to your maternal uncle Shome's home.'

'Do you know the way?'

'I remember the road leading to his house. Hold my hand firmly, walk fast and don't panic. I still have the knife with me.'

Mother looked at me in disbelief while chanting the name of Chandi, her family deity. I did not have time for gods and goddesses. Every passenger, every human figure appeared to be a likely killer. I avoided their eyes and helped mother climb down faster.

I reassured her, a veteran of many social movements and a progressive woman, now totally shaken by the unexpected turn of events. We ran and partly rolled down before landing at the base of the embankment. It was covered with soft greens. We took shelter behind a bush. I checked to see if mother had any open wounds that she might have suffered while rolling down the slopes. Except for a few bruises she appeared to be in one piece.

'How do we go to uncle's home?' she whispered.

'Wait Ma. People are still coming down from the station platform. I see some coming our way. Hold your breath and lie still.'

We remained still for about ten minutes. The stillness was punctuated by a groaning voice. I looked around. A woman, almost naked, lay about ten feet from us bleeding from her stomach. Mother's instinct made her crawl to the woman and rearrange the clothes on her body. She looked at us as if we were angels from heaven.

She was not alone. A baby, unmindful of its mother's injuries, suckled at her breast. The wounded woman comforted her baby with one hand and raised the other asking us for help. Mother bandaged her wound and covered her exposed body.

In a surprise move the young woman shifted her position and implored mother to take charge of the six-month-old baby girl. Mother looked at me, a mute message in her eyes; she wanted to help the baby. I nodded my head. The dying woman looked at me and I felt that she was showering heavenly blessings on me.

A few feet from us lay three more bodies, one of a young kid and two middle-aged men. The elderly looking one was still. His eyes and body posture indicated that he might have died as soon as his throat was slit. The young kid was still too. I felt his jugular. Yes, he was dead too. The younger person was still breathing and croaking in pain. What could we do? We were also in the slaughterhouse trying to escape the butcher's hatchet.

'Let's go,' mother prodded me.

The injured woman croaked. She extended her hand imploring mother to take the baby. It was a moment of dilemma but mother clinched the issue. She picked up the baby as the dying mother closed her eyes.

It was not the time to grieve for slaughtered fellow human beings. I was more concerned about reaching the safety of great-uncle's home. We tried to move out of the thick greens. Our move was thwarted by the sound of footsteps coming our way. I moved a few leaves of the thick foliage and saw a group of three walking down. They were talking animatedly and I strained my ears to hear snatches.

'The Biharis are brave aren't they?

'What bravery is there in killing unarmed people? Did you see the Dhakai Kuttis and Ansars? They kill neatly . . . '

'What's neat, brother? These Biharis are killing Hindus unnecessarily. We were so happy together.'

'They killed Muslims in India.'

'Everybody kills everybody. What do we gain. Most of the lands will be taken away by the Biharis, most jobs would go to them. We will remain where we were.'

The group disappeared into the opening of a street that led to a labourer's colony.

I moved out with mother. Before doing so, I removed the vermillion mark from the parting of her hair and broke her conch shell bangles that identified her as a married Hindu woman, though some Muslim women too wore the same symbol. I took the socially deplorable step to be on the safe side. Two ordinary looking people like mother and I and a suckling child would not be suspected as Hindus fleeing the slaughter house that the train had been so horrifically converted into.

Great-uncle Shome's house was about two kilometres from the Ashuganj railway station. The route to his house was embedded in my mind. As we took the turn from the main road to the residential areas of the senior staff of the jute mill, I saw from the corners of my eyes two hefty youths approaching us. I dragged mother behind another wayside bush of datura and wild hashish plants. Both datura and ganja were considered holy by Hindus, and on occasion Muslims hardly shied away from sherbet concocted out of green ganja flowers and leaves, and licking a paste of datura seeds that gave a mild high.

'Where have those two figures disappeared?' one of the youths asked.

'Did you see them? Are they Hindus?'

'Who cares if they are Hindus or Muslims? Everyone is looting everyone. We could probably get a couple of gold ornaments from the old lady. Must be a Hindu. Muslim women don't normally wear gold jewellery.'

'Look around the bush. Must be hiding.'

The youths approached the bush we were hiding behind. My eyes met the eyes of one of the youths.

'Here they are!' he shouted in glee.

I did not take any chances. For the first time in my life, at the young age of ten, I used the Sheffield and slashed a deep cut in the goon's left calf muscle. He collapsed in pain. There was no room to hide. I emerged out of the bush with mother behind me and swung the big blade menacingly. I dragged mother, the baby clinging to her chest as if she was a piece of log. But that was not the time to carry her gently. The other goon hearing the agonizing cries of his friend rushed towards him instead of chasing us.

We got a head start of about ten minutes, time enough to drag mother to the doors of Shirish Shome's house, banging with all the might I could muster. Uncle opened the door. His two sons Pavitra and Soumitra flanked him with two sharp swords. I dragged mother in and closed the door. She collapsed in my arms which were not strong enough to hold her. Uncle took her inside and made her comfortable on a bed. Someone picked up the crying child.

My hands were still smeared with the blood of the goon. The sight shocked me. I had seen Haripada and Purno's blood and other blood-smeared bodies. The first human blood that coloured my face was still there. My blood-smeared palms unnerved me. A sense of guilt started seeping into my mind. Had I committed a crime? Was hurting others in self-defence a crime?

Pavitra, about six years older to me, offered soap and water to wash up. All the soap could not wash away the peculiar stench of human blood. It stayed with me for years. My first act of drawing human blood gradually changed my psychological make up. I started feeling that a knife could solve many problems.

Mother had in the meantime recovered and looked askance around her. The presence of her own kin comforted her. 'Where is the baby girl?' she asked.

'She is fine. Who is she?' great-uncle asked.

I narrated the gory human drama.

'Uncle, could you inform Ramzan that we are here?' Mother implored the senior Shome.

'The pirate?'

'Yes. Please tell him to rush and pick up my brother-in-law lying at the bottom of the slope on the off side of the station. He must have been stabbed. Please contact Dulu mian of Bhairabpur. He knows what to do. Send this letter to Ramzan.'

Bhairabpur was opposite Ashuganj and a motor boat could cross to the other side in thirty odd minutes if the tide was favourable. Uncle agreed to deploy his company's steamboat and depute a Muslim employee to contact Dulu. I had never met Dulu who was the public face of the Ramzan gang, rated as the topmost outfit that had in the past collaborated with the 'swadeshi' madcaps. He was wanted by the British both for acts of piracy and for assisting the rebels who fought against foreign occupation.

Dulu arrived in an hour.

'Please tell Ramzan bhai to send a group to search for my brother-in-law Birendra. They probably stabbed and threw him out of the train,' mother requested Dulu mian, who refused to sit in her presence.

'Pardon us thakurain. No local Muslim is involved in the crime. These are Bihari and Kutti gangs sent directly from Dacca. Please go back to the village. It's a shame on us that you have been treated like this.'

'No brother Dulu. I had requested Ramzan bhai to send someone to Munshiganj to inform your mejo karta. I am totally shaken. Please ensure that they don't ransack our house and brother Birendra receives proper treatment. We hope he is still alive.'

'Don't worry thakurain. Ramzan has already sent out a search team for Biren karta. I will request him to put some guards at your home. The Nibharsa gang, a rival pirate gang is supporting the Ansars. Don't allow his men to come near you. Let me go and inform everyone that you are safe.'

Dulu accompanied by four armed men walked down to the riverside. The unconscious body of Uncle Birendra was recovered by Ramzan's men. He was taken to the Bhairab hospital. He had not been stabbed but he only regained consciousness after two days but lost his mental orientation and for a considerable period failed to recognize anybody.

～

While mother was busy with the baby, I asked, 'Ma, what do we do with this child. We don't know anyone in her family.'

'We will send out word through Ramzan and Subhan bhai.'

'How do we trace her father and other relatives?'

'If no one claims her I will be her mother. I will accept her as Mother Chandi's gift. I gave a silent promise to the dying lady. Treat her as your sister.' That clinched the issue.

My state of shock and bewilderment worried my cousins. Pavitra and his brother tried to persuade me to go fishing in a small lake near their home. It did not interest me. I sat under a huge olive tree and brooded.

I looked back and tried to understand the mistakes we had made. Had I failed to notice the suspicious looks in the faces of the people who had gathered near our compartment before we boarded the train? I scanned all the faces that I managed to remember. The face of Kala mian, a political colleague of uncle Birendra, raised a doubt. Had he winked at some unknown faces that had boarded the train just as it started moving? Yes, he did. Did I see some faces on the overbridge signalling at the compartment we were boarding? Yes, I had noticed. Why did I not tell my uncle and mother? I realized that my young mind was capable of locating dark clouds but was not trained to analyse if the clouds were storm or rain-bearing. I lacked the ability to interpret events in the present context.

The ghastly scenes that I had witnessed were firmly embedded in my mind and scared me. My palms seemed to still smell of blood. I could often feel the red liquid dripping off my palms. I often thanked father silently for arming me with a weapon that I could use deftly. I wondered how I had the courage to do what I did. Later I realized that adversity does not always dampen the spirits, it also boosts up the will to fight and the struggle to survive.

Father arrived at Ashuganj after about six days.

He was stuck in Dacca as after the Anderson Bridge massacre incident, the train services on this line were suspended. He informed us that political leaders like Jawaharlal Nehru, Prafulla Chandra Ghosh (the chief minister of what had become West Bengal on the Indian side), Shyama Prasad Mukherjee and others had sternly warned Pakistan of serious consequences if the killing of Hindus in East Pakistan was not stopped. There were unconfirmed rumours of Indian Air Force planes bombarding certain areas in East Pakistan. Some papers also carried the Indian threat of marching its troops into East Pakistan if the atrocities were not stopped immediately.

More than these vague and distant news reports the physical presence of father boosted my morale. Behind the calm and friendly façade he was a man of iron will and determination. The only problem with him was that he exercised his determination for the furtherance of his dreams which ordinary mortals failed to understand. Like mother said, most dreams ended up in a bubbling chimera. He looked to us a disillusioned person whose world contrasted as an antithesis to the world crafted by self-seeking politicians. His silent steely mind strengthened my will to fight and survive.

Preparations for our safe return journey home were planned by Dulu on behalf of the pirate Ramzan. Suddenly the baby with mesmerizing eyes, a few curly hairs and a bewitching smile appeared an insurmountable problem. Great-uncle Shome could not ascertain the identity of the dishonoured and slain woman from the local police. Mother rebuffed all questioning looks by replying that this tiny gift of God would be with her. Father nodded in agreement and that clinched the issue.

On our return journey to Kamalpur we used a caravan of three boats—one occupied by us, and the others escorts manned by a mix of great-uncle's labour force and of Ramzan's men. There was no reception party. We quietly boarded cycle rickshaws and skirted the main Bhairabpur village before entering our area. As we crossed the cluster of shops near the sub-registrar's office, several onlookers lined up the street and raised their hands in greeting. We travelled light. Mother's suitcase and my carry bag were lost during the flight to safety. I did not know what valuables mother had lost, but I had lost all my books including Daniel Defoe's *Robinson Crusoe*, a gift from Mano didi before she took the last train to Calcutta. The only possessions that I had left was my precious three rupees and the Sheffield knife.

We were welcomed by Tomtom who broke his leash and ran over half a kilometre. He jumped all over me and licked my face profusely to express his affection. He led the way proudly by incessantly wagging his tail. At home, even before Rahman, Lutfa, Saifi and Jasim greeted us Chandana created a minor whirlwind inside her cage, dancing and prancing. Mother offered her a fresh red chilli. She refused and looked at us turning her neck repeatedly and rolling her eyeballs. I opened the cage and embraced her.

'*Kutahi gechile* (Where did you go)? *Bhoy lage. Bhoy lage* (I was afraid).' She rested her head against my chest and did not resist when I put her back inside the cage.

While Jasim and Saifi embraced me, Lutfa didi ruffled my hair and said a prayer. Rahman prostrated before father and mother and wept, his whole body shaking. 'Let Allah bless you all. Bismillah protect you and punish the traitors and enemies of the people.'

We received a few unexpected guests later in the afternoon. Mehboob Alam and his father accompanied by Moinul Haq, my class teacher, Nazar kaka and revenue supervisor Rashid mian dropped in to empathize with us.

Mehboob called me aside to say that he ran along the train for a while to tell me that there was a gang of killers in the train. Some station staff knew of this and a ticket-clerk had forewarned his father. He, in turn, ran up to the station to warn me.

How could I express my gratitude to Mehboob and his father? They did their best to forewarn us but it was our destiny that forced us to take the fatal journey. The train to Brahmanbaria might have reached there with more dead and wounded bodies thrown out of the compartments. Our journey fortunately ended at Ashuganj.

That night Ramzan visited our home along with Subhan, Nazar and Karamat. Seated in a corner of the empty western court building they sipped tea, smoked hukkas and discussed the security scenario around us.

'Deben karta,' Ramzan pleaded rather apologetically, 'our local people did not attack you even when your home was empty. We all respect you.'

'I appreciate that Ramzan bhai. Our bond cannot be separated by sporadic communal fire and waves of hatred unleashed by the League people. I depend on you.' Father replied in his usual sincere voice.

Mother served a plate of homemade sweets. Her head was covered with her sari pallu. 'Ramzan bhai, you know many people in the surrounding areas. The orphaned baby girl must be from one of the nearby villages. Can you spread the word and try to locate her family?'

'We'll try boudi,' Ramzan stood up to accept the plate. 'Our people will spread the word in the Narsinghdi and Kishoreganj areas.' The dreaded pirate spoke in a respectful voice.

We did not waste time listening to the elders discussing the communal and political situation. The baby kept us busy.

'She must have a name,' stated Lutfa.

'How do we know? Her mother did not tell us,' I replied.

'Suppose we name her?' Jasim asked.

Lutfa favoured the name Pari meaning fairy. Jasim's choice was Champa the fragrant flower and mine was Khushi.

Lutfa said that the name Khushi meaning happiness was appropriate for a girl who had been rescued from a ghastly slaughterhouse scene.

I do not know if the name stuck after she was claimed by her grandparents, an old couple from Narsinghdi near Dacca.

❧

The horror of the journey finally started sinking in after the hullabaloo of the reception was over. I felt I had journeyed through a tunnel of death and destruction. This tunnel was unlike the riverside tunnels Lutfa and I often frequented to contact the swadeshi revolutionaries.

This time I failed to emerge out of the tunnel of my mind which appeared to be a pitch dark labyrinth. Frequent images of human bodies dropping out of the train flashed past my eyes. The frame of a mother, a child clinging to her bosom, repeatedly danced before my eyes. The ashen face and eyes of the young girl standing before the train window and crying for her father haunted me. How could a father leave his young daughter? The answer to this question came to me much later in life when I understood that the animal called man very often failed to live up to the human dharma of protecting his near and dear ones.

I had nightmares. I would often wake up to see if my hands were still bloodstained. In the darkness of night I would flick open the Sheffield blade and examine its sharpness. I would doze off again only to wake up often with loud shrieks. How could I stab a man? How did I manage to survive the shock lying in that bush with dead and injured human bodies? The very sight of that almost naked bleeding woman and her imploring looks revisited me repeatedly. A baby, breast-feeding on a dying mother haunted me and filled me with anger, hatred and fire. My efforts to suppress these feelings were defeated by the lingering smell of blood on my hands.

I did not share my moments of horror with anyone, not even with Jasim and Saifi. I did not attend school. I felt an emptiness gripping me. In this vacuum I was even indifferent to the trees, plants and flowers I adored so much. Jasim noticed it first.

'You have changed. Start going to school,' he pleaded.

'I don't feel like. I lost all the books.'

'Are you still afraid?'

'No. I am angry.'

'Suppress your anger. You're a hero. Everyone in the station, market and village says that you are the only person to have saved your mother and you are the only witness to the whole ghastly event.'

'What does it mean? Do they want to hand me over to the police?' I asked apprehensive that my stabbing that goon might have been reported to the police.

'I do not think so. You are the talk of the town, that much I know.'

∾

Nazar kaka and an employee of the jute mill operated by a British manager approached father. 'Deben bhai, Smith sahib wants to reward your courageous son.'

'What for, Nazar bhai?'

'He is the only person who managed to escape the jaws of death with his mother. People say he saved his uncle also.'

'Why does Smith sahib want to reward him? I don't think it's a good idea.' Father turned down the gracious offer.

'I don't want a reward kaka,' I said, 'I have saved my mother because I am her son. What else do you expect a son to do?' Nazar kaka was amused by my reply.

'Why did you not want the reward?' mother called me aside and asked.

'I am the only person who counted the raining bodies of Hindus. I am the only one who has seen the faces of some of the killers. I am the only person to stab one of the goons. Suppose they attack me again?' My mature reply surprised mother.

'That's okay Nazar bhai. The boy is shaken. Let him rest and start going to school. Please get him another set of text and copy books.'

Nazar kaka seemed to understand the situation and promised to return next day with books and copies.

During dinner, I confronted my parents. 'I won't go to school. I want to go to India. This place is not safe for mother. How can I save her if they attack again?'

'That was an accident.' Father tried to console me.

'No Baba. I have seen the faces of death. Please take us to India.'

'Start going to school, things will be all right. The local people are with us.'

'No. This land is not ours anymore.' I concluded the discussion and left my food. I walked down to Rahman's shed and slept by his side. The resolve to move over to India helped me sleep.

Little did I know that India too was not my home. They had rendered us homeless and robbed us of our identity. The mere word India however, offered some vague assurance of safety. I was not certain if that safety was enough to allow me to finally alight from the train.

However, it was not a scared kid's decision to take the train to India. It was a conscious decision. I had chanced to look into the face of death and escaped it by whiskers. I realized I required more time to live and reshape my dreams in a new world.

I understood that my father hated the idea and my mother was uncertain about the prospects of another journey. The idea of India didn't offer much hope. In my mind I had decided to take the jump into an uncertain hell. My village, my small heaven had already started becoming a part of my memory even before I boarded the final train to India.

thirteen

The Last Burning Train to India

I did not feel like going back to school as I felt I was still travelling in the nightmarish train and had not managed to alight at Ashuganj. I felt I was still travelling and my destination was India. I had started distancing myself from everything and everyone. My stubborn refusal to attend school and even to open the new books and my irretrievable inward journey had pained my parents considerably. While I had decided to escape to India, mother was still indecisive. Father was opposed to it. He still believed that things would improve and as promised by Fazlul Haq, the unrest would settle down and Bengal would be rescued from the Bihari marauders and the fanatics of the Muslim League, Jamait-e-Islami and Ansar Bahini. His optimistic political views were moderated by his links with the brave men of Bengal's 'Agni Yuga' (a period of armed struggle) and his unfazed devotion to Netaji Subhas. He apparently could not reconcile with the political changes that had transmuted the subcontinent for all time to come.

I started realizing his dilemma. There were many. He was not acceptable to the provincial Congress leaders as he was a known critic of Nehru and his ilk. Some Congress leaders in power in West Bengal knew him as a rabid supporter of the United Bengal Movement, spearheaded by Sharat Bose, a brother of Netaji Subhas. He was against Gandhi's alleged failure to influence Nehru and the other ambitious Congress leaders to oppose the immediate transfer of power. To top it all, he was an avid supporter of communal harmony and the unity of Bengal.

Personally, he was not sure what was in store in India. His relationship with his eldest son was far from cordial. He was not certain about his eldest son supporting him at this time of crisis. In fact, he had very little intimate interactions with his children. Perhaps I was the only child who had tried to understand him and forced a relationship by entering into his world of dreams and his vision. Very few people, besides mother and I understood a dervish who never tried to acquire material wealth and tried to follow his ideals and dreams.

He had no home in this strange India. He had not transferred any assets to the other side of Bengal. He was not sure of securing a new career in his chosen vocation. City dwellers were changing over to the more modern allopathic school of medicine. He was not even sure if he could dispose off some landed property and other assets to raise some money for a new start in India.

His hope that the trauma of Partition would die down and traditional brotherhood and amity would occupy the space temporarily wrested by rabid communalists was buttressed by a close band of political colleagues who dreamt of a Bengal for both Hindu and Muslim Bengalis.

Father was not inclined to take the uncertain jump. He was hanging on to a fragile thread of trust and hope. 'Why don't you prevail upon Krishna to go to school? Things are safe again,' father whispered to mother that night.

'I don't think it would work. He has seen too much of the macabre drama of Independence. He saved my life and honour. I feel he is still travelling in that ghost train. I won't stand in his way.'

'You know there are problems. Bijoy is just settling down in his new job in India. I do not know how he would react to our sudden migration to Calcutta. Benoy is still to find his bearings. I am sorry he could not go to college. We don't have a home. I have no job. What would we do there?'

'Don't be so pessimistic. You can get a job in your old college and teach. Ayurvedic medicine is still popular. You can resume your practice. You'll miss the dreams and your political optimism but the reality is that the people over whom we ruled want their revenge. Let's pack up here and make a fresh start.'

'I am too old to start afresh Su.'

'It's never too late in life. Why don't you imagine that you're on a safari and you're changing your course of the journey? Every journey is new and we have to start afresh every time we set foot ahead. Your friends can help dispose off more of our property. I've about Rs 50,000 and some jewellery.'

'Well! If you insist, let's try it out. In any case, there is an end to every journey. I'm afraid of the new India. Its leaders have not been fair to us Bengalis. You know Su, Gandhi and Nehru always suspected C.R. Das and Subhas to be Soviet agents.'

'I know but what is the use of accusing them now? They are the victors. Netaji remains an enigma. All sensible Bengalis know the mischief that the Congress perpetrated on Bengal and Assam. Now let's save our lives. We have no place in Pakistan.'

I realized that father was not happy to quit his ancestral home. His dreams, his life and worship, if not means of livelihood were intricately and inseparably linked to the people of this part of the Meghna-Brahmaputra basin. He was not a city person; he was a man of the soil like the bhuin champa, a fragrant lily that sprouts from the soil and never withers or dies but sprouts every season. What would a man like him do in Calcutta? He had studied at the Grey Street Ayurvedic College but had never tried to set up a practice in that city.

He realized that mother and I had decided to leave the village. He also knew that the newspapers carried ghastly stories of communal riots on either side of the border, and that swarms of Hindus were escaping Pakistan and Muslims were crossing over to East Pakistan in large numbers. It was a time when we had to decide where we belonged. I felt sorry that we had forced a decision on father.

My decision to leave the village for an unknown India was essentially fashioned by my nightmarish experiences on the train ride to Brahmanbaria. I was still struggling with the memories.

∼

My absence from school even after ten days of our return from Ashuganj brought some unexpected visitors. My class teacher Moinul Haq accompanied by Asgar, Mehboob Alam and my mathematics teacher Sadananda Chakravarty turned up at our home. They wanted to know why father had stopped sending me to school. For him to tell a lie was unthikable.

I rescued him from his predicament. 'I lost my books in the train.'

'So what, we could get you new books.' Asgar, a future leader of the liberation movement of Bangladesh spoke forcefully.

'Don't worry. We can help you make up the lost days. You haven't missed much.' Moinul Haq spoke in an affectionate voice. Sadananda Chakravarty approvingly supported him.

That was a decisive moment. How could I tell a lie? I felt ashamed to admit that my mind was unable to accept anything new filled as it was with the horror clips that I witnessed for over two hours. I could imagine nothing but the human bodies dropping into the vast expanse of the Meghna as if they were red pomegranates. I was still travelling.

'Okay. I'll come from tomorrow. Please tell Saifi to pick me up everyday.'

'Good.' Asgar jumped on his feet and almost lifted me up, 'A hero like you should not shy away. You're a courageous boy. We'll fight together.' And that's what Asgar actually did.

Our midday tiffin break was at 12.30. As usual, the chowkidars Jamini and Ibrahim distributed ripe banana and pieces of cake. We stood in the shaded areas and talked about new books and teachers. Asgar suddenly stood up on a table and started addressing the students.

'Dear friends. Today we have with us a hero. Krishna fought with the Bihari brigands and saved his mother. Three cheers for him—hip hip hurray.'

Over two hundred students clapped and cheered.

'Friends,' Asgar continued, 'our Pakistan is home for all Bengalis, Hindus and Muslims. Pakistan does not belong to Biharis and Urdu speaking Ansars. Let us fight them together.'

The students cheered him and I was almost stampeded by them. They rushed to congratulate me. From the corner of my eyes, I saw Headmaster Abdur Razzaq standing in front of his room and watching the drama. From another wing of the school, Maulana Wahidullah and Mufti Hanifuddin watched us intently. Hanifuddin finally came down and addressed the students exhorting them not to be misguided by a former student. Asgar, he declared, was a political activist. He had no business interfering in the affairs of the school. He finally asked the students to shout after him, 'Pakistan zindabad', 'Bangali Bihari unity zindabad.' Some students obliged him but the vast majority sulked and shouted back, 'Asgar bhai zindabad, Bangla bhasha zindabad, Urdu bhasha murdabad.' (Hail Asgar, hail the Bengali language and down with the Urdu language).

I understood the gravity of the situation. I was at the centre of the controversy. The Bihari lobby and the staunch Muslim League followers would not allow this incident to die out within the four walls of the school.

It never dawned on me that Headmaster Abdur Razzaq, an indulgent father figure, would be worried to his bones over this incident. Moinul Haq called me out of the class and escorted me to the headmaster's room. To us this was the room of final judgment. I walked in with deep apprehension, my heart beating faster.

'So, you're the hero!' He said with an amused look.

'No sir,' I managed to croak.

'I know you are. But son, these are bad days. Asgar is a politician. He has big leaders behind him. Stay away from him.' He stood up, patted my back and said affectionately, 'You're a dear student. Your father is a well-known person and liked by all but things have changed. Just concentrate on your studies. Tell your father to see me.'

I was overwhelmed by his affection. I had never seen him from such close quarters, except once, when I had deceived him by feigning a stomachache, to take leave.

After the final bell rang, I went straight to Nazar kaka's music shop where father was examining a patient. He walked down to the school immediately after advising me to go home. He returned at around seven in the evening and told me not to attend school for the next few days. 'Razzaq feels that Asgar's political adversaries might bring in outside Ansars and create trouble. You are the only live Hindu witness to the carnage of 15 February. He feels that it's not safe for you out there.' He patted my back and slowly advised me to study at home and consult friends like Saifi to keep myself updated.

Attending school and being with old friends had partially removed the veil of fear. For a few hours, I had imagined that things would return to normal and that the hours of horror would not revisit me. However, that night a pall of gloom descended on me again. I did not want to be a hero and fight a killer crowd. I knew nothing of Asgar's politics, though I was getting wiser to the fact that 'politics' was the demon that had shattered our dream world.

～

That the school event was a political tussle between the ruling Muslim League and new emerging Bengali nationalist forces did not sink into my mind. I felt sad missing school. I felt cut off from the mainstream of my booming river-port town.

However, the despair was somewhat momentarily lifted by the arrival of a stranger. A man who appeared about sixty, Nabendu Ghosh was from Narsinghdi, a flourishing town nearer to Dacca. He had heard that my father had rescued his granddaughter. Perhaps Ramzan's people had spread the word; perhaps some Dacca Bengali daily had also published a box-item about our escape from the death trap of the Dacca-Chittagong mail.

The tragic story unfolded after our unexpected guest rested for a while and dined with us. His son Dibyendu and daughter-in-law Karuna were blessed with a baby girl. Debyendu worked in a college at Comilla where he was taking his wife and eight-month-old daughter. They were in the ill-fated train on 15 February 1950, a journey that ended with the brutal killing of Dibyendu and Karuna.

Nabendu had heard about his granddaughter Shruti's rescue by my parents and that she was living with us. Shruti, our Khushi, did not fail to recognize her grandfather. Perched on Lutfa's lap she extended her tender arms towards the familiar face of her grandfather and uttered some baby talk. Shruti jumped into her grandpa's lap and clung to his neck. The bereaved father wept loudly and thanked my parents for saving the child.

We felt sad to part with Khushi but her happiness brightened up our hours and moments of despair. Nabendu left for Narsinghdi by a river steamer. Khushi looked at us with her charming black eyes and raised her arm to say bye. The reunion was a relief. It would have been unfair for us to leave Khushi with Lutfa.

About seven days after the school incident Jasim and I were swimming in the family pond. We were collecting mature lotus pods whose seeds made excellent raw or dried snacks. Our family ducks were nonchalantly swimming alongside. We chased them when they dived to hunt fish. It was next to impossible to beat the speed of a diving duck but we mimicked their darting-movement to the best of our ability until we could hold our breath. A fun game that could only be played with ducks that were not scared of us.

Saifi disturbed our game. He came panting from the direction of his village after climbing the steep wall of the dry canal bed. 'Come up Krishna,' he shouted. 'Is your baba home? There's a message for him from my father.'

Father was concentrating on his weighing scale with some herbal powder, and burning in a charcoal oven some gold dust inside a dry mother-of-pearl shell. He called this medicine *makaradwaj* or something like that.

Saifi was in a hurry. 'Uncle, here is a letter from Abba.'

'What's the hurry?' Father spoke in a relaxed manner while pouring the weighed material in a marble mortar. He then perused the letter with a grave look. His normally placid face turned grim. 'Okay Saifi, tell your Abba that I'll be at your home in an hour.'

He went inside, placed the letter under his pillow and went for a quick pre-lunch bath. I took out the letter and read it as fast as I could. Haji Khokan Nizami, Saifi's father, an affluent businessman was a member of the music group headed by Nazar kaka and father. His letter mentioned a meeting at village Kalipur attended by Kala, Dudu, Dhala, Jalil Sarkar, Mufti Salahuddin Qureshi and other important Muslim League leaders. They had decided to attack our village at the earliest opportunity. The last vestiges of our family and our loyalists were acting as the ultimate barrier against the implementation of the policies of Pakistan and the Muslim League. A Hindu-Muslim brotherhood was against the very concept of Pakistan. Khokan asked father to meet him immediately.

We ate lunch silently. I did not betray my nervousness. However, mother broke the silence. 'Is there a problem?'

'No. I'm rushing to Jagannathpur for a meeting at Khokan Nizami's house. I should be back in two hours. Tell Rahman to alert the guards sent by Subhan bhai. No problem but just as a precaution since the huge compound and adjacent gardens are almost empty.'

Father picked up his umbrella and the long baton, which was actually the outer scabbard of a sharp dagger with its knob made of heavy lead and iron alloy. It was a deadly weapon but looked like a long innocent baton.

❧

Father returned around 4 p.m. escorted by two tenants of Jagannathpur. We squatted on a *sheetal pati*, a delicate mat made out of the benchita water weed. Rahman served milky tea.

'How did the meeting go?' asked Mother.

'Khokan has bad news. The Muslim League and Ansar Bahini want to attack our locality and drive out all the Hindus from this part of the village. They think we are inciting the Muslims against Nurul Amin.'

'That's wrong.'

'How can you explain right and wrong to sick minded people. Even after Partition, these people have not run out of the steam of hatred. They have nothing to offer to the people except hatred.'

'What do you propose to do?'

'We go to India.'

'When?'

'Subhan and some other friends are coming this evening. Prepare a meal for them. I'll take a final decision tonight. Some League members and the Biharis are after Krishna's blood. He is the only surviving witness to the February carnage. We'll find a safe place for him.'

The evening gathering was a small one. Besides Subhan, Akram and Nazar kaka the meeting was attended by Matanga Roy, a former Congress leader and now a leader of the East Bengal Awami League. After dinner, they assembled at the community centre over hukkas and paan.

'We're sorry to hear what Khokan has to say. Normally he's right. The League people trust him.' Subhan kaka initiated the discussion.

'Yes Subhan,' father replied, 'I found him to be serious. He offered to purchase my building.'

'Is he after the property?' asked Akram kaka.

'He has the money. I can't sell the entire property. All that I can sell is my own building and some lands that are personal possessions. He offered Rs 50,000.'

'Well Deben,' Subhan kaka added, 'I don't like the idea. We propose you to go over to India for a while. Let this fever cool off. Come back after about six months. We could raise some money for you. Take a train to Agartala at the earliest.'

'It would be better if you raise a loan against my property and give me about fifty thousand against a loan deed. Cancel the deed when I return and pay you back. Take the property if I fail to return.' Father offered a fair deal.

'It's a fair deal Deben. You'll get the money in another seven days. I'll get the paperwork done. Get ready to leave. Let Rahman remain here as custodian. I hope you agree.' Nazar kaka opined as a compromise deal.

'No problem. The very idea of leaving you pains me most. We have grown up together, we have worked, suffered and enjoyed together. I can't imagine my life anywhere else under the sun.'

'Well Deben. History has been rewritten for us. We have been offered a new geographic boundary. This is a wrong alchemy worked out by the League and Congress leaders. We Bengalis have been cursed. Anyway, escape to India for a while.' Akram kaka started weeping inconsolably.

'Compose yourself Akram. We must see Deben off to the safety of Agartala. I have a proposal.'

Subhan kaka explained that those hostile to us might notice our boarding a train from Bhairab. The Leaguers and the Biharis could again attack the train targeting us. He had a better idea—cross Meghna by boat and board the train at Ashuganj. It was a small station and no one would notice us.

'Do you think the route to Agartala is safe?' Father was not sure if that was a sound plan.

'The other alternative is to go to Calcutta via Dacca, cross the ferry at Goalanda and take a connecting train for Calcutta. The Ansar Bahini and the Leaguers are attacking the trains to Dacca and the ferry is unsafe. They pushed hundreds of Hindus to the turbulent waters of the Padma. We know the Agartala route. Our workers can help you escape.'

'I'll go by your decision Subhan bhai. What's the plan?'

'We'd take a boat from Radhepur Ghat, a bit upstream from Bhairabpur. It's a sleepy fishing village. No one would notice. We board the train for Akhaura near the Indian border at Agartala around 1 p.m. In between, there's Talsahar and one more station. Just a run of about one hour and you are there.' Akram kaka sounded very hopeful of his grand escape plan.

We had no other option. The vast majority of the Muslim population was not hostile. They wanted us to stay back but father's close political colleagues and friends were not so sure. Posters and pamphlets circulated by the Jamait-e-Islami, Muslim League and Bihari refugees dispensed pure hatred. Some of the pamphlets depicted pictures of Muslim women being sexually assaulted by Hindu mobs. A few posters depicted mosques on fire.

A particular pamphlet that was circulated in most villages showed Hindus urinating on sacred Arabic words. These efforts to incite Bengali Muslims were fortified by Gazi pat scroll paintings that depicted stories carried to the villages by roving balladeers. They sang in praise of Allah and described the inhuman torture perpetrated on Muslims in Hindu India. They spared no effort to incite the simple Bengali Muslims to attack Hindu villages, plunder their women, appropriate their landed properties and purify the land of Pakistan with Hindu blood. Maulana Qureshi ordained that each drop of Hindu blood would make Pakistan purer.

Such was the ambience that stymied our movements and suffocated our lives. We were fortunate to have people like Rahman and father's friends and colleagues who had not lost faith in the unity of the Bengali people and had not embraced the philosophy of the rabid communalists.

Kamalpur and a few neighbouring villages were an oasis of peace but the heat of raging flames around had started singeing our souls. I for one had no more faith in the capability of our friends to protect the barrage of cordiality and brotherhood against the surge of hatred and perceived vengeance spun in the contorted minds of the people who dreamt of a pure land of Muslims.

Between father and mother and the old faithful Rahman it was decided that Chandana would be set free. Tomtom would be gifted to Jasim and the ducks would remain under the care of Rahman's wife. We would lock the family temple and the gods would be left to fend for themselves. However, Rahman's wife offered to light a lamp every evening on the verandah of the temple building.

It was time to pack up. Mother decided that the total cash of Rs 100,000 and her personal jewellery would be distributed into two parts; each part would be kept in special purses secured under their garments.

Once again, I packed my text and copybooks and the Sheffield knife. I also packed a few storybooks gifted by Mano didi and a cloth towel with designs presented by Lutfa.

∾

13 May 1950.
This was the fated day of our train to India. We consoled
ourselves that it would not be the last journey. Like in 1946
we would be back home again.

Father had planned to leave the house at 5 a.m. and reach
Radhepur Ghat at about 6 a.m. Subhan and the others were
supposed to wait there with a boat ready to sail. It was not
as easy to cut the anchor and sail into the uncertain winds
as we imagined.

We managed to pack fifty-eight year's essential treasures of
father's, mostly his songs, poems and books and handwritten
copies containing ayurvedic formulae and diagnostics in one
tin trunk. The other two contained mother's essential clothes
and only a few earthen and stone handicrafts she had made
over years. My books and clothes were stuffed in a canvas
rucksack.

'Lived with so much and leaving with so little,' father
commented in a pensive mood.

'We're leaving to return.' Mother tried to boost his moral.

'Hope so. People in Exodus do not normally return to die
on the soil where they were born.'

'Why are you so pessimistic?'

His philosophical musings did not amuse Chandana. She
created a big fuss. 'Kuthai jais, kutah brajasi, kuo vadis?
Where are you going?'

'We'll be back soon. Let me set you free. Go wherever you
like.' Mother wept as she opened the cage door. Chandana
refused to come out. She used her claws to cling to the cane
cage. Finally, Rahman brought her out and set her free to fly
away. Chandana refused. She kept on flying over our head
and crying *jais na*, don't go.

Tomtom also rebelled and refused to eat.

Mother walked down to the temple, and prayed for a
while. Father stood at a corner of the eastern court building
and wiped his eyes.

How could I leave without saying goodbye to Saifi, Mehboob, Majid and Kanu? What would Rani didi and Lutfa say if I left without bidding goodbye? Jasim, my shadow and my alter ego, stood by me with wet eyes. How could I leave him?

I stood facing the sprawling eastern court building, wept inconsolably and finally squatted on the ground chanting to myself, 'Some day I'll make a palatial complex like this in the new India.' Mine was a pauper's dream of a sumptuous dinner after weeks of starvation. Rahman touched my shoulder and spoke softly, 'Karta, it's time to go. They would be waiting for us at the ghat.'

'Yes Rahman.' Father broke with protocol and embraced Rahman, our bonded labour and family friend. 'Take care of the house. I'll be back in three months.'

'Inshallah karta, your servant will be here. We have been a part of this family. Just don't forget us.' Rahman embraced me and stepped out on the sprawling green lawns leading to the front gardens. We followed.

Tomtom broke his leash and jumped on me. He managed to bite a corner of my shirt and started tugging at it rather angrily. He was confused and bewildered. Jasim managed the situation by leashing him again. I lost a part of my shirt to the sharp teeth of Tomtom. I did not have the courage to look back.

The tract of the village road to Radhepur ghat did not have a cycle rickshaw. Mother was seated on the backseat of a bicycle, which was pedalled by Rahman. Two family retainers carried our bare possessions of three suitcases. We plodded the rough and hewn village path and narrow gullies, fields ready with mustard, lentils and early jute plants. We skirted Bhairabpur and landed on the ghats of Radhepur, a small fishing hamlet still occupied by Hindu fishermen.

Two boats with winded sails waited on the banks. Subhan and Akram kaka helped us to board the boats and four armed guards boarded the escort vessel. We crossed the mighty Meghna for the last time and hit the shores of Ashuganj, the station where I had landed with mother only a couple of months back. We waited in a Muslim owned shack at the far end of the station to avoid detection by Jamait, Ansar and Muslim League workers. The lady of the home served us ripe bananas, puffed rice soaked in butter milk and sweets made out of ground coconut and gur. The grand breakfast was our last meal on the soils of our dear land. The lady of the house looked poor but was magnanimous in her hospitality. Mother offered her ten rupees as a parting gift.

She refused to accept the gift. 'We live on your land Ma. I cannot take money. Come back soon.'

Mother hugged her and the woman wept inconsolably.

༄

There was no time to waste on emotions. Akram kaka reminded us that the train should be in within fifteen minutes. We marched to the station and climbed up the steep stairs. The train, packed to the limit, turned up an hour late. Subhan and Akram kaka pushed ahead with the help of their men and made space for us in a first class bogie. Their beards and obvious Muslim looks helped in scaring away the frightened Hindu crowd. They made some space for mother to sit with her small bags. Our belongings were shoved under the seats.

The train moved and familiar faces turned into blurred figures as we sped past the outer signal. The absence of Subhan and Akram conveyed the stark message that we were on our own and by leaving our land, we had graduated to the status of refugees. I couldn't relax as memories of my last train journey flooded my mind. I sat tight by my mother clutching the butt of my Sheffield knife. My knife was kid stuff but its very touch gave me a sense of security.

Our train did not stop at Talsahar, a small station where our people normally alighted to visit Sarail. Our family had acquired extensive landed property there. However, the train slowed down considerably after it crossed the outer signal. I was tense with the memory and experience of another train slowing down. I stood up and looked out.

Yes, they were there. About a hundred strong-armed marauders ran alongside the train and tried to board the compartments. No doubt, they were brigands or Ansar Bahini members. They carried Pakistani flags and curved swords. To my horror, I realized that they were Bengali Muslims and not Biharis. My experiences with the Muslims in our area had comforted me that only the immigrant Biharis, Dhakai Kuttis and Jamait and Muslim League sponsored Ansars killed Hindus. It did not dawn upon me that all Bengali-speaking people, whether they were Hindus or Muslims, whether they belonged to Hindustan or Pakistan were not pacifists. Later, in India in 1964 I was to see that sections of Hindus too were no better than mindless butchers.

However, my concern was not the ethnicity of the killers who were running along the train. I was concerned with the speed of the train. I had experienced such deliberate slowing down on 15 February as well.

I squeezed past the crowd and whispered into my father's ear. His secret walking stick was still with him, the last weapon he carried. I had never seen him fighting. His innocent face and his poetic absent-mindedness often created an impression of his incapability to lead and fight. I had had some glimpses of his links with the armed terrorist groups who fought for Independence. I had seen him handling weapons along with his colleagues in the Bengal Volunteer Force. Perhaps his looks were his best camouflage. What he did on that crucial day of the final train journey to India was unexpected.

He climbed up on a seat and shouted loudly, 'Friends, some Ansars are trying to board our train. They want to rob and kill us. Shut all the four doors. Pull down the window shutters. Use any weapon that you have.'

'How can we fight such a large group of Muslims?' someone asked.

'God blesses those who die fighting and God does not open his door to anyone who refuses to fight in self defence. Let us die fighting. Let's save our women and children,' father shouted back.

Some fellow passengers, mortally afraid and emotionally near dead before they physically died, clamoured like a pack of lambs being led to the butcher's abattoir. However, a few young men pulled out their knives and stood guard near the doors. A fat-bellied Marwari with a fatter canvas bag that might have contained loads of money forced past a guarding youth and jumped out to the safety of the land below. He was immediately surrounded by a section of the sprinting mob as if they were feasting vultures. His bag was snatched away and his fat body reduced to a couple of bloody pieces.

Father and two others rushed to lock the doors. Most of the window shutters were pulled down except two. One youngster peeped out of the window. I managed to squeeze my head out and could see the marauding mob.

The Marwari was not the only unfortunate fellow. I witnessed a repeat show of 15 February. I counted eight more bleeding bodies thrown out of the other compartments. Some craftier killers from the bloodthirsty crowd had managed to board a few of the compartments. Our compartment was not spared. A few younger bandits secured themselves on the footboards and banged on the doors with clubs. Catapulted stone missiles broke a few windows. More enterprising robbers and killers managed to hang from the window bars and push through sharp bamboo lances to injure and scare the passengers.

Father shouted at the top of his voice advising every one to lie down on the floor and seats. Some heeded and others started pushing fellow passengers to make safer spaces for themselves. I saw father unsheathing his sleek sword from the innocent looking stick and swishing at a red-eyed intruding face. The sharp blade hit the fingers that had clutched the window bars. The face shrieked loudly and dropped down shouting that there were policemen in that compartment.

The trains to the Indian border often carried a few armed policemen who preferred to ignore the carnage and seemed to derive satisfaction by witnessing human sacrifices at the altar of hatred.

Father's daring action infused fresh blood in me. I took out the knife and stood guard by mother. This show of courage prompted a few other young persons to hit at the hands of those who were trying to climb into the compartment. Fatal hits on a couple of the marauding mob slowed them down. They were nonplussed by the aggressive retaliation. They stopped and shouted: 'Pakistan zindabad, Hindustan murdabad, Allah ho Akbar.'

Someone somewhere in the engine block perhaps concluded that the holy mission was accomplished to the satisfaction of their Allah, and the blood and flesh of a few dozen Hindus had purified the land of the pure they called Pakistan. The train gathered speed with repeated whistle blows, perhaps an expression of glee and satisfaction over the war well fought and won.

That 13 May the sun appeared to be descending faster towards the horizon. We prayed it should keep hanging indefinitely until we crossed over to the safety of India. The train moved at its normal speed and finally entered the Brahmanbaria platform after releasing clouds of steam. Some enterprising passengers disembarked for water and food supplies. Father decided to stay put. His decision was pragmatic. A surge of a crowd tried to board the compartments from all directions, through doors and windows. They kicked, elbowed, shrieked, cried and begged. That was not the time to extend a helping hand to suffering fellow humans. Those were the moments of exhibiting the toughest and deadliest possible animal behaviour. The passengers inside kicked, pushed and abused the people trying to escape death by entering into a compartment that was more suffocating than a chicken coop. They clawed at each other, uttered the foulest abuses and flung dirty epithets involving their mother's and sister's sex organs.

Like soldiers under attack, we stuck to our trench in a corner of the compartment guarding our last possessions. I looked at father and mother in quick succession. Father's face was grim, his eyes red and his body trembled slightly. Mother looked impassively at the surging crowd and instinctively tried to cover me with her body. A mother, I realized, continues to be a mother even when she faces the gravest danger. I had seen another mother, our duck Sonai charging at crows and other predatory birds that tried to pierce her chicks with talons and beaks. At Ashuganj, I had seen another mother breast feeding her baby even as she fought for her last breath.

I comforted mother and said that no one could touch her while I was alive. She smiled. I knew she believed me. She had seen the fighter in me only a few months ago.

∽

The nightmare at Talsahar was not the last bad dream.

The Chittagong Express—our Train to India—gathered steam and ran for a while like a train cutting at the edges of wind. Some windows were opened to allow fresh air in and to remove the stench emanating from perspiring human bodies, soiled clothes and the overflowing toilets.

There was a sudden jerk caused by the application of an emergency brake. Passengers panicked and started howling and crying as if they were pushed to the end of the universe.

I managed to stretch my head out. I could see a few police constables jumping out of the train and cautiously examining the track. I wanted to get out and see for myself. Father stopped me saying that getting out of the train would be easier than getting in again. The compartment was packed to capacity as if it was carrying salted live meat.

The constable in our compartment got down to join his colleagues. He soon returned. 'We want a few young men to help us to remove heavy logs and stones placed on the track.'

'Who would do that?' father asked.

'Don't ask questions. Anything may happen. Obviously, some people don't want you to reach Hindustan. We are here to ensure you reach Akhaura alive.'

A few young men volunteered. As they heaved and pushed the heavy logs and big stone blocks, we saw a group of people rushing at the train from a nearby village. Another determined assault on the train by Jamait and Ansar goons was the natural deduction. This time the train was not moving at all. What could prevent the bloodthirsty mob from boarding the compartments and carrying out mass slaughter? What could a dozen or so policemen do? Were they motivated enough to use their arms against the rioting mob? Perhaps they would stand as mute witnesses and might even demand a share of the booty.

We could see the contours of a crowd as it emerged on the horizon. The dark silhouette now took the shape of human beings, some carrying Pakistani flags, some holding on to their kids and women and others carrying their elders. It was a ragtag crowd of Hindus at the head of which some Muslims waved their hands to stop the train. They soon arrived to be greeted by the arms wielding policemen headed by a sub-inspector.

An aged Muslim with a flowing white beard approached the sharp bayonets. We could overhear him. 'Sir, please allow these wretched people to board the train.'

'Who are they?'

'Sir, we are from Nawabganj village. Nurul Amin's Ansar Bahini attacked the Hindu section of the village two days ago. They killed the teacher, burnt the temple and looted the market. We saved them at great risk. Please take them to Akhaura.'

'We cannot. They have no ticket. Moreover, why did you block the railway line? It is a heinous offence.'

'We know malik but there was no other way to stop the train. The next station Paghachaong is about fifteen miles from here. How could we take the risk of escorting them to the station through Ansar infested villages?'

'I see. You are a great friend of the Hindus.'

'Yes malik, we have been living together for hundreds of years. How can we allow them to be killed by the Ansars? Khuda would not pardon us.'

'You have to pay a penalty for disturbing the properties of Pakistan.'

'Malik, we know that. They have lost everything. Accept this small amount from our poor villagers and take them to Akhaura.' The old villager dressed in a lungi appeared to be the headman of the village. He handed over a bunch of currency notes to the police officer.

'How much?'

'Malik we are poor villagers. Could manage only one hundred. Please take them or the Ansars would kill them and us as well.' To our surprise, the old villager kneeled on the ground and implored the police officer. It was a moving situation. Over one hundred Hindus waited with anxious looks in their eyes, some of them praying with folded hands.

'Their women must be wearing gold. Give us the gold.'

'Malik, they are poor.'

'The poor don't deserve gold. Their gold belongs to Pakistan. Give us the gold if you want them to go to India.'

For the next thirty odd minutes, the aged village headman went about with folded hands collecting gold ornaments from the village women. After collecting the ornaments, he wrapped the precious bounty in a towel and handed it over to the police sub-inspector. The moustached officer examined the booty and asked the headman to line up the fleeing flock and pushed them into the train as if they were goats and lambs to be carried to the abattoir.

The villagers boarded the train after considerable jostling and haggling. The policemen, richer by a couple of hundreds worth of gold, finally boarded the train and signalled the driver. The train chugged and gradually gathered speed. To our great relief it did not stop at Paghachaong station and took a left turn towards Akhaura, the railhead in Pakistan from when we hoped to escape to the safety of India.

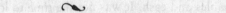

Our train chugged into Akhaura station around 3 p.m.

It was not the joyous ride that we had three years ago when we left the village only to return to its verdant fields. The madness of Jinnah's Direct Action had abated. Then, our elders had again dreamt of a united Independent Bengal. Father and his political friends scurried around in search of the chimera of Bengali unity. It was not that they had not realized the arrival of religion at the centre stage of the Indian political soul. They hoped that cultural, ethnic and linguistic ties could defeat the demon of religion. That was not to be.

Finally, we were at the Akhaura railway platform with its milling crowds. They looked like bewildered and disoriented swarms of ants and bees smoked out of their homes and hives. They shouted, implored and often cried over dead and dying bodies. A few policemen with weapons slung on their shoulders lumbered indifferently, often poking sticks at scared female figures. The police force was not violent but was not helpful either. Some passengers pushed some money into their palms and bought favours such as accessing the food and drink stalls. Some passengers paid heavily to influence the men in uniform to force some rickshaw pullers to pedal them to the safety of India, about three kilometres southeast. Some of those fleeing overloaded with belongings looked like the mules once used in the Wild West of America by gold prospectors.

There was no friend to aid or guide us. We walked past trying to avoid the jostling and stampeding. Everyone was on his own. Family groups managed to stick together by holding hands and by calling out to each other. It was a frightening sight.

Our three-member family struggled out of the confines of the Akhaura platform. Father carried two suitcases on his head and I carried one. Mother managed the sling bags that contained valuables and cash. It was not the time to look at the pitiable condition of my parents. I knew the load father carried was very heavy and he was not in the best of health.

India was still too far. The chaotic sea of humanity milled around haggling, begging and stuffing money into the hands of greedy transporters for a ride to the safety of the Indian border. Thousands of people haggled with rickshaw pullers, horse and bullock cart drivers and drivers of a few rickety buses and open trucks. They charged astronomical amounts from a wretched people whose only thought was of the not so distant border of Indian safety guarded by the armed Tripura constabulary.

Without experience in the art and skill of heckling and bargaining, we felt stranded. My father had defied his family rules and befriended common villagers. However, he too was not in the habit of haggling, imploring and begging. His simplicity and attitude was coated with a fine layer of dignity that made him stand apart from the crowd he liked to keep company.

In that conundrum of confusion, misery and misfortune, he did not know what to do. A soft approach was interpreted as being weak, begging was treated as helplessness. The transport operators behaved as if they were jungle cats waiting to pounce on the helpless herd of confused and frightened animals. No one was ready to show mercy.

One bus conductor demanded Rs 300 per person to give us a rickety ride to Agartala's Gole Market. The tin box was full to capacity with men, women and children crying out like endangered fowl. The humourous conductor suggested that for Rs 300 we could get seats on top of the bus. For getting inside the cage, we were required to pay Rs 500 per head. His jackal-laughter and scornful eyes said it all; he was there to bleed people and make hay out of people's miseries.

We scouted around for a familiar face that might have turned up to receive us. There was none. Father started negotiating with a horse cart driver. He demanded Rs 500 for the longest three-kilometre journey to the safety of India. We were more tired than the proverbial dog. We were hungrier than starving ravens and the burden of the heavy suitcases had taken their toll.

'Karta, what are you doing here?' We heard a familiar voice.

Father turned around and his face lit up when he saw Dhiru Saha, our former family retainer and an inevitable bug in the soup. 'Visiting Agartala for a short while. What are you doing here?'

'It is a bad time for pleasure travel. I'm just helping people in distress. I facilitate the smooth border crossing for my distressed Hindu friends.'

'See you back in the village.' Father placed the boxes at the back of the cart and asked us to board.

'Don't go alone karta. These drivers are thugs. They will kill and loot your belongings. Let me pay off an old debt. Let me ride on the footboard. People in this line know me. They won't dare attack you.' Dhiru did not wait for approval. He jumped onto the footboard of the buggy and asked the driver to drive towards the Indian check post.

The landscape had changed. Most of the trees had disappeared from the roadside and several thatched shacks had come up manned by petty shop owners selling tea, snacks, paan and bidis. The economy, as historians say, flourishes alongside the route the conquering army travels. They did not write that the economy thrives best when there is an Exodus.

The emaciated mule moved slowly. A few lashings and the choicest of abuses connecting the creature's ten generations in incestuous relationships with parents, sisters and other blood relations could not motivate the mule to move faster.

'Karta Ma, who is guarding the house?' Dhiru asked after we had covered barely two furlongs.

'Rahman is there and there are two more men appointed by Subhan bhai.'

'Do you mind if I go back and guard the home. At least being a Hindu I can light the lamps at your family temple and offer daily worship.'

'That would be nice Dhiru. Are you not afraid of going back?'

'No karta Ma. I am a poor man. Who will kill me?'

'Fine, Dhiru. You can take the temple key from Rahman.'

'Give me your side bags. How can I allow my masters to carry loads when I am here?' Dhiru did not wait for mother's approval. He almost snatched three bags from mother's hand and jumped out of the cart.

I did not know what happened to me. I gave the loudest cry possible and jumped on Dhiru. I was no match for the wily jackal. His powerful fist almost floored me. I managed to stand up and whipped out the Sheffield knife. Dhiru took out a much smaller knife but before he could balance the load of bags and the knife, I jumped on him and managed to hit his left hand. He abandoned two bags and ran for the thick woods with the remaining bag. Dhiru's blood had stained my knife and clothes. Human blood gored my hands for the second time.

The spontaneous reaction and the action of hitting Dhiru had stunned me. I realized that a streak of violence had painted my mind with an unseen brush. What had happened to me? Was it my defence mechanism that pushed the violent switch instantly? I stood aghast at the sight of blood on my hands and on the knife.

The cart stopped. The cart owner, a Muslim, parked his mule in a corner and came to my aid. Mother wiped the blood with a piece of cloth and checked the bags that I had managed to snatch from Dhiru. It contained a few ornaments and about Rs 20,000. Dhiru had looted the bulk of the cash, over Rs 80,000 and jewellery worth rupees Rs 15,000, a fortune in those days. His last act of treachery had left us in a dire situation. Dhiru had been a crooked beast from the day I first encountered his act of treachery involving Rani didi. He was a part of the bank robbery that had forced my uncle to flee Pakistan overnight. It never occurred to us that a viper could act only as a viper. His simple guile of going to the village and lighting lamps at the temple had softened mother's heart. Dhiru took advantage of the weakest moment and decamped with our fortune.

There was no time to lament. The cart driver's words wizened us about Dhiru. Our old servant headed a cartel of bag lifters and chain snatchers who cheated people looking for the slightest help from anyone. His was a mixed gang of Hindus and Muslims who had forgotten their religious differences and operated together to enrich themselves at the cost of the miserable people fleeing death and destruction.

We boarded the cart with heavy hearts. Most of our money had been looted and we were yet to hit Calcutta. All our hopes of casting a somewhat smooth anchor somewhere in or around Calcutta appeared dim.

We did not talk. The silence was broken by the tongue and whiplashings of the cart driver, by people marching on foot and the rickety engines of the buses. Our cart reached the Indian checkpoint around six in the evening.

We were surprised to see my youngest aunt's brother Mr Bardhan, an inspector with the Tripura Armed Police, at the post with his men. He spotted and helped us with a decent four-wheeled vehicle to reach us to the Banamalipur residence of my mother's maternal uncle, Brajamohan Dutta.

We were exhausted, desolate and full of despair. I was once again traumatized by human blood, the second and last time I drew human blood. I wondered if I could ever get rid of the salty stench from my hands and my mind. That night I slept on a bare floor after gulping my dinner. I could not sleep. My anger against Dhiru was made worse by fear: Was it the end of our journey? Were my instincts being taken over by violence? In the darkness of the empty room, I tried to look into the shape of our future.

Nothing but darkness mocked me.

fourteen

End of Journey: Another Begining

The Train to India did stop at Akhaura. However, I had not yet alighted from the last train journey to India on 13 May 1950. My body was in Agartala but my mind was not there. Agartala was not our destination and destiny. India's political and geographical boundaries extended to the princely state but to me it was neither a part of Bengal nor a tribal hill state. It had a unique romantic charm. So near to my just abandoned home yet . . .

As I tried to sleep, I made a droning guttural sound. I was not weeping but something inside me was pushing out spasms of pain. Some undefined fire was burning me from inside. It was a queer mix of anger, frustration and utter helplessness. Suddenly I realized that we were the proverbial kings turned beggars overnight by the curse of a witch. The frustration came from my inability to identify the witch. Had the witch appeared in the form of the Muslim League, Congress or the escaping British Raj? Father and his friends were angry with the Congress and the League leaders headed by Nurul Amin and Suhrawardy. To me the dilemma was very complex. I did not know whom to blame. Muslims? How could that be? Jasim, Lutfa, Saifi, Mehboob and Majid were my best friends.

Several branches of our extended family preferred to settle in the new Indian territory. Father dreamt of returning to Bhairab after a couple of months. Mother nursed a faint hope that she would be able to reclaim her mother's property and start a new life in Agartala. I looked forward to reaching Calcutta. In my mind, that was the city of hope and dreams.

I was angry with Dhiru Saha, the family retainer who betrayed us all the way. My hand still smelt of Dhiru's blood. Anger, fatigue and a sense of utter helplessness filled me with a sense of despair. I clutched the handle of the Sheffield knife and tried to vent my angers on its steel.

A series of horrifying cries disturbed my sleep. I woke up frightened only to realize that even on the cold earthen floor I was sweating as if I was being barbecued on a coal fire. To my horror, I discovered that I was trying to shout and hurl abuses at Dhiru and other unfamiliar faces, all dancing around me with swords and knives. But my voice was choked. I had lost my voice! I coughed several times and tried to moisten my parched throat. Some animal grunts came out but no human voice. Had I been rendered dumb? I panicked.

It was no more a horrifying nightmare that had unfolded from the moment we boarded the train at Ashuganj. The human slaughter was real. The cascading stream of stabbed, sliced, injured, dead human bodies that were flung out of the train, the marauding mob that haunted us near Paghachaong station kept on reappearing before my eyes, more horrifically, when I closed my eyelids. The more I squeezed my eyes shut the more rapidly those scenes moved in and out. Some scenes, especially the one of the young mother trying to breastfeed her baby even moments before she breathed her last scared the life out of me. That Ashuganj horror scene montage overlapped by the child trying to suckle on the breast of a nearly dead mother became a permanent vision for the rest of my life.

I forced my eyes open. I could see whatever there was to see inside the dark storeroom and patches of green outside. I preferred to keep my eyes open. Some wet droppings on my chest told me I had company. A few green pigeons nested in the crevices of the wooden ceiling. Their smelly droppings and the chirping of their chicks brought in a whiff of relief. It was better to be drenched by pigeon droppings than to be haunted by the horrific silent slide show.

❧

Mother entered the room after her usual morning bath. The naphthalene smell from her sari indicated that she had opened one of the suitcases. The red-bordered sari matched with the vermilion bindi on her fair face.

'Go and have a quick wash. I'll get us some tea and eats.'

I was surprised by the casual tone of her voice. She looked sad but not down. Like most Indian women, she had learnt to take life in her stride, the way it was presented to her by a male dominated society and family. In spite of her social activism and love for the folk arts, she hardly raised a banner of revolt. I think she had herself drawn a line between her personal proclivities and the social restraints. Most Indian women are experts in the art of composite compromise and absorbing shock and pain. Her unclouded face and steady eyes gave me some courage.

We sat with rest of the family and some other guests over tea and sweetened rice cakes. We ate silently. My great-uncle was an ebullient person. He liked to talk and never tired of expressing his affection. But that morning he was silent.

'You see Deben,' the dialogue was initiated by my great-aunt, 'my father's entire family was driven out by the Muslims. The entire Hindu village of Srimangal in Sylhet was burnt to ashes. I think they should settle down in Agartala.'

'That's natural aunt.' Father replied without trying to read her eyes.

'Sarama, your wife's elder sister who is settled at Johor Baru in Malaysia, has written that Sushama can claim the entire property at Agartala. But we can't leave it now. We have been living here for thirty years. That gives us some right.'

She finished the sentences at one go. She had perhaps rehearsed the dialogue over the years and waited for this moment to deliver it with the right dramatic effect.

'I understand, Aunt,' mother took over the dialogue, 'but we have a problem. I have a right on my mother's properties.'

'That's a matter of law. You two sisters did not claim the property all these years. Your uncle has taken care of it, and added some buildings. He has some rights.'

'We're not here to stake a claim on the house from my mother's brother. However, you must understand that I've as much, if not more right to stay here as you have. Our two sons are in Calcutta, and obviously, Agartala is not my destination. You and uncle know the legal status very well. I'll let you know our decision after talking to Sarama.

'You know Sushama,' my grand-aunt continued, 'Sarama has no children. They have adopted a Chinese girl. They're not coming to claim this property. Perhaps you do not know that your late mother had willed this property to her brother.'

'When did she do that?'

'You and Sarama were young when your mother died and your father took another wife. She willed this property to her brother for bringing you up.'

Father changed the flow of dialogue by lightly tapping mother's shoulder.

'Uncle, I need to go to Gole Market to send a telegram to our sons. They don't know we are here. Once we establish contact we'll be able to finalize our programme.' He did not wait for a reply and set out for the main post office.

Mother went into the kitchen. Later she told me that her maternal uncle had almost touched her feet in the private confines of the kitchen and made her promise on her deceased mother's name not to confront her aunt. The property, he averred, belonged to the two daughters of his sister Srijana— Sarama and Sushama's mother.

I knew my mother. She, like my father, believed more in giving than taking. For the sake of her mother's memory, she said she was ready to give up the claim. After all, she added, she was three and Sarama was seven when their mother died. Her father had promptly brought in a second wife. Her maternal uncle had brought them up before she was married off to the affluent Dhar family of Bhairab. All debts, she added, must be paid, sooner rather than later.

I did not understand the complicated matter but the idea of settling in Agartala did not excite me. Moreover, I was concerned about my voice. I refused to acknowledge that my voice had choked and I could only manage to stammer and croak out unintelligible words. The shame and fear prevented me from admitting the fact.

Why did it happen to me? Was I afraid of Dhiru and the other killers of whom I was not aware? I did not know the medical prognosis of trauma and shock. I took it as a temporary disability that would go away once I recovered from the horrible nightmares that haunted me.

With that infantile hope, I went out in search of my friends Dayal Reang and Mantu Jamatia. They lived in a village near a hillock at the foothills of a vast forest beyond Shivnagar. It took me over half an hour to reach the spot where the village once stood. It was not there. Most of the high grounds were flattened and rows of thatch and tin roofed homes had come up. The verdant forest interspersed with tribal homes, bamboo stockade for cattle and green vegetable patches was gone. Bengali speaking people had replaced the tribal population. They spoke their own dialects, each one distinct from the other. They, in their sense and sensibility of assumed cultural superiority feigned ignorance about Reangs and Jamatias.

'*Eida amamgo Bangali pada* (this is our Bengali locality),' said one person in his Bengali dialect. '*Jungli Jamatiar khabar janina* (we do not know anything about wild Jamatias).'

A shopkeeper said that the hill people had shifted to a respectable distance inside the forested areas. The cultured Bengalis had raised high bamboo barriers to stop the wild elephants straying into their habitats in search of food.

I walked up the forested tracks and reached a Reang hamlet. My enquiries in almost inaudible sounds revealed that my friends had shifted to a nearby hamlet after their lands were either forcibly occupied by Bengalis or were bought out at exorbitant prices. The undulating land was dotted with patches of thatch and tin roofs of the mixed tribal people.

I first spotted Mantu. He was carrying a load of dry wood. Dayal followed him with a load of vegetables. Their carry baskets were hung on their backs and the load was balanced against their foreheads with a flat strap. Both of them stopped when they saw me trotting towards them.

'What are you doing here?' Mantu asked rather tersely.

'We have come over from Pakistan. I came to see you. I find you have shifted your village,' I managed to croak out.

'What happened to your voice? You are croaking like a frog.'

'Just a bad throat. Why are you here?'

'Lakhs of Baangalis have come to our country. They have taken over our lands. We were driven out by Baangalis and the police.' Dayal Reang did not try to hide his scorn or hatred for Bengalis.

'I'm sorry to hear that.'

'Why should you be sorry? Occupy some other village and start selling fish,' said Mantu.

'We don't sell fish Mantu. Why blame me? We are going over to Calcutta. I just came to see you.'

Mantu and Dayal put down their loads and we sat under the shade of a gigantic fig tree.

'So you were also driven out of Pakistan? What happened to your voice? Did you cry a lot?' Dayal noticed the impairment I had developed.

'You have started stammering Krishna. You did not stammer the last time we met.' Mantu looked at me curiously.

I did not feel like recounting the moments and months of nightmare and horror. 'I think it's the stress of the journey and bad weather. Would you like to go fishing again?' I asked.

'No. The lake shores have been taken over by the Baangalis. We are not allowed to fish. We have stopped eating fish. It's so costly after lakhs of fish eaters have taken over our country.' Mantu stood up and straddled the head-load against his head. Dayal followed him.

'Don't come to our village again Krishna. Let's walk down to the market. We have things to sell and rations to buy for the family.' Dayal started walking downhill.

'Why should I not come?'

'Our people hate the Baangalis. It's no good in Agartala. Go over to Calcutta. We might meet again,' Mantu replied.

I walked silently with them. They took a detour to avoid a new Bengali settlement and headed for Gole Market. I felt crestfallen. Within three years Bengali refugees had occupied most of the landmass of Tripura and in turn had created internal refugees. The tribal population was driven out to interior areas and numerically, culturally and economically superior Bengalis had almost taken over the tribal homeland ruled by the Tripuri family of Bir Vikram Manikya Bahadur.

My second tryst with Dayal and Mantu ended abruptly.

My third and final encounter with them was many years later in 1990. They had gained prominence in a left-wing political party and aspired to become ministers. The bitterness of 1950 was not there. However, Dayal reminded me that the unfinished agenda of a happy coalition between the tribal people and Bengalis was yet to be achieved and that was at the root of often-violent manifestations of the political and economic expectations of the tribal people.

I had no reason to disagree.

While my parents waited impatiently for a telegram from my older brothers in Calcutta, I went about renewing my contacts with the posh Gole Market and the palace of the

Manikya Bahadur kings. The Gole Market was still round but its elegance was smeared by scores of thatch huts and huts on bamboo stilts. Bengali refugees had taken over the market area and they acted as intermediaries who purchased commodities brought in by the head-load by the tribals. They were everywhere—on the roadsides, besides the bank of the Gomti River, on the fringes of forests beyond Bishalgarh. They still kept pouring in by train and through the jungle.

I was pained by the disfigurement of the pristine postcard town of Agartala.

My brother Benoy replied by telegram. They were happy to know about our safe arrival at Agartala and advised us to take one of the flights operated by the government and private operators. There was no word from my eldest sibling. We had no idea if they had a roof over their heads and square meals. By nature, Benoy was a silent person. He absorbed pain silently and cried without shedding tears. His quality of compassion and piety surpassed his sense of self-preservation.

Anyway, the hunt started for air tickets that cost forty rupees per head. Some touts, including the inevitable Dukhia of our family pedalled air tickets for Rs 100. He had not forgotten my knife assault on his brother-in-law Bhanu when he was caught in the act of dishonouring Lutfa. He bullied the ticketing agents into not issuing tickets to my father. My father's younger brother, a legal practitioner at the Bajitpur lower court near Kishoreganj, joined father in the ticket hunt. He and his family had also taken a train to Agartala and wished to fly to Calcutta, where his eldest son worked for a Bengali newspaper. My uncle believed that the world stopped at his feet and his self-assumed superiority pierced even the skies.

I met him at a corner of Gole Market sitting beside one of our extended family members who worked as the ticketing agent for a private operator.

'We're flying to Calcutta. What's your father's programme? Does he go back to join his rabble-rousing gang of politicians and folk singers?'

'No idea. Brother has asked us to fly to Calcutta.' I replied as meekly as possible.

'Each ticket costs forty rupees. Do you know we're flying a Globe Master plane loaned by America?'

I knew nothing about aviation. I was more concerned than impressed. It had not occurred to me that father was keen to return home to resume his activities. He was yet to come to terms with the realities of a changed Hindu–Muslim relationship. His group of Muslim friends did not rule East Pakistan. Nurul Amin and his Muslim League goons did.

However, I did not like the tone of my uncle's voice referring to my father as a thumka singer. I swallowed my pride but narrated the encounter at the ticket counter with my enlightened uncle to my parents. Great-uncle Dutta, perhaps prompted by his wife, rescued us. He managed three tickets for us. Coincidentally my uncle was booked on the same flight. We were assured of flying to the real India in another six days.

The sight of two Globe Masters and two smaller planes on the tarmac did not excite me. I was worried. Both father and mother looked worried. Were they hiding something from me? It was a journey into the uncertain city of an unknown India. My only consolation was that I would see Benoy after a year. I wondered how he coped with the world there.

I did not know my eldest brother very well. Only once, he had taken me to Kurmitola, near Dacca, where he was employed as a junior engineer working at the new airbase. In a joint family of over 200 members, it was difficult to strike a friendship even with one's own siblings. Moreover, my eldest brother had left the village seven years back.

However, mother gave me to understand that our temporary address would be the official quarters of my brother-in-law, the husband of my deceased sister. A junior police officer, he lived at a place called Bat Tala, Jorabagan, in north Calcutta. I was not happy to hear this. Even as a child, I knew that my sister's parents-in-law had constantly tortured her for more dowry. My brother-in-law treated her as a childbearing machine. She had delivered six children by the tender age of thirty (only two survived) and died while delivering the seventh stillborn baby. My brief relationship with my sister was very sweet. I missed her and was angry with my brother-in-law when he dumped his children at our village home within weeks of my sister's death and married another woman. The very thought of living at his house brought back memories of my sister. At that tender age, my love for my only sister had blinded me to the fact that my brother-in-law was a virile man and that he needed the company of another woman.

There were no reserved seats in the place. We were huddled like goats and cattle and asked by male stewards to cling to some heavy ropes hanging from stowing compartments and aluminium clips from the roof. I was more interested in looking down into the terrain below, which appeared like a brown desert with hundreds of finger-like rivers crisscrossing the terrain. We were flying over riverine Bengal.

After about two hours, we started hovering over Calcutta and my uncle started pointing out some of the prominent features, often asking if I had seen those earlier. He was full of himself.

The Globe Master landed and we walked past Dum Dum airport. My brothers received us and our uncle's family. Our common destination was the Bat Tala home at Jorabagan police station. The family quarters were big, cloistered, airless and suffocating. All eight of us including five of my uncle's family were accommodated along with twenty other members including my two brothers. We were spared the footpaths of Calcutta, which were occupied by thousands of refugees from East Pakistan. The only comfort we had was the assurance

of two meals a day and time with nothing to do but roam
the streets, count vehicles and marvel at the cloistered city
that frightened me.

Our first few days in Calcutta, crowded with so many
people, cars, trams and assorted vehicles frightened me. I was
not sure if I would be able to cope with the giant city. The
fright pushed me into my inner shell. Moreover, my lost voice
had added to my inferiority complex. I started imagining that
I was still on a train to India, the India I was yet to discover. I
often imagined enemy attacks and flicked open my knife.
I could not explain my predicament to my parents. Mother
was busy cooking for the horde and father was constantly
out in search of a job.

I had lost my books as well as all desire to study. Something
had turned off the fuse in me and I groped in darkness.
Asleep or awake I was constantly haunted by the dropping
human bodies, and the flow of blood. The Sheffield in my
pocket reminded me of the blood of that strange mugger
and Dhiru Saha. I felt a fatal attraction for the blade and
often imagined I could solve all our problems by using the
weapon. I could defeat Hindustan and obliterate Pakistan
with a swipe of the knife.

No one thought of putting me in school. Once I did ask
my eldest brother if I could go to school. He replied rather
tersely that I had better earn some money to augment the
family expenditure. I did not have the courage to ask again
fearing that he might force me to do some job which even
Rahman would refuse to do. I knew he was a much-harassed
man and considered our sudden appearance in Calcutta a
burden. He was looking desperately for a place on cheap rent.
The idea of moving into a ghetto, a basti, a slum did not
sound acceptable to our parents. I did not have the benefit of
overhearing the nightly conversation of my parents because
we slept wherever we could squeeze in. The Bat Tala house

was crammed like millions of shrimp in a bucket full of water. There was no privacy.

∽

Two important events took place in the three months that followed. My uncle who was a lawyer shifted to another location rented by his two sons. His wards found accommodation in decent schools. They had come prepared with transfer certificates and mark sheets. However, the family of eight of my father's first cousin Dhirendra Dhar, the brother of Hirendra who had escaped from Pakistan after the family bank robbery, replaced the departed crowd. Dhirendra's eldest son Satyabrat (Satu), exactly my age, was an enterprising person. Slightly handicapped, he was not academically inclined and preferred to earn some money by working at small trades.

He later acted as my messiah.

The most important event that embittered my eldest brother's attitude towards our father arose out of a vital and moral decision. Migrant Hindus from East Pakistan were forcibly occupying homes deserted by the Muslims who migrated to East and West Pakistan after they were subjected to equally cruel communal riots. The retaliatory 1950 communal riots in Calcutta and suburban areas had allegedly cost over 3000 Muslim lives. Perhaps the same number or more were sacrificed in the eastern part of Bengal during the same period. Plenty of burnt, half-demolished and deserted Muslim homes in the Park Circus, Ripon Street and the Free School Street areas were ready for forcible and unauthorized occupation.

One evening our eldest brother Bijoy, nicknamed Rakhal, took us in a taxi to Park Circus somewhere east of the present tram depot. He forced us into a big charred house, probably of an affluent Muslim family. The empty living room was full of broken glass and black-sooted debris. The house had about six spacious rooms, a few toilets, a spacious kitchen and storerooms. Father examined the rubble and fished out a light blue scarf used by non-Bengali women over their kurta-pajama. Below the pile of female clothes, there were dark thick spots of coagulated blood. The pools of blood could not have been more than a month old.

Besides the pool of blood, he found a woman's foot neatly cut from the ankle, still adorned with a silver ornament. He also fished out a half-burnt book in Urdu. He said it was a copy of the Holy Quran.

He carried the blue scarf and the book and moved around to the other rooms. A piece of rotten female forehand was lying in one corner of the kitchen. The skeletal fingers still had a ring on it and it clutched a rosary.

'Rakhal,' father said to my eldest brother, 'I think lots of human blood has been shed in this house. Lots of women have been disgraced.'

'So what,' Rakhal retorted. 'They killed Hindus in Pakistan and Hindus killed Muslims here in Hindustan.'

'The blood spots are still fresh. Have you seen that severed leg and hand holding the rosary?'

'So what, we have decided to occupy this house.'

'Whose house are you occupying? Don't you require government permission?'

'The land is yours if you wield the stick. Who is going to evict us once we get in?'

Father called our mother aside. Under no circumstances would he occupy a house where women had been tortured, dishonoured and killed. He would not allow her to live in a house where religious books had been burnt.

'No Rakhal, we cannot live here.'

'Where would you go? Go and live in a slum.'

'I would prefer that. I'd rather go back to the village. Don't force me to live in this house of sin.'

We were stunned. Our father, known for his soft and indulgent attitude stood firm like a rock. Mother was quiet.

My eldest brother, not trained in managing a stressful situation, forgot his social and moral training and heaped abuses on our father who stood silently with the burnt Quran and the blue scarf in his hand. His silence was his reply. He was ready to face the worst consequences but not ready to live in a house still exhibiting human blood and bones.

If I understood right, that was the end of the emotional relationship between my father and his eldest son. My brother never pardoned what he thought of as his arrogance. And my father in turn just withdrew into himself. His silence stood like an impenetrable rock between him and his eldest son.

Father's dishonour at a stressful time pained me immensely. I saw him sinking into an abyss of pain and the feeling tugged at my soul. I wanted to share his pain and sink with him. I found it impossible to get out of the cursed train to India and resume studies. A feeling of living in a void and on the mercies of people much smaller to our father in human qualities haunted me incessantly. I felt I was lost for all time to come.

∽

Soon after that ghastly episode at Park Circus, our brother-in-law was shifted to the Shyampukur police station, also in north Calcutta. My parents and I moved as part of his baggage. Father was busy contacting his old friends to secure a job at his alma mater—the ayurvedic institution at Grey Street, and securing school admission for me. He promised to take me to a school nearby.

However, my first encounter with Calcutta culture took place at a playground opposite the police station building. Soccer attracted me more than any other game. Young boys of my age were playing football in a field and some grown-up youths were glued to the radio set broadcasting a football match.

Someone asked me if I wanted to join in. I was game. The position under the bars was my favourite slot and I liked to dive like a circus acrobat.

One of the star players, some Dutta from the venerated Dutta family of Bou Bazaar parried, dribbled and took a tremendous somersault volley at the net from a cool twenty-foot distance. I dived like an acrobat from one end of the pole to the other and deflected the ball away. The cheering crowd was stunned. How could a new kid play that trick, that too on a Dutta aspiring to be a star player in the Mohun Bagan Club?

The Dutta bully charged and started punching me. 'Are you a Bengali from East Bengal?'

'What does that mean?' I managed to ask in a broken and stammering voice.

'How dare you play with us Ghatis (Bengalis from greater Calcutta)? Get out.' Dutta punched me again.

The boys gathered around me and started clapping and singing: *Bangal manushya noi Ure ek jantu, Laaf diye gache uthe, Lej nei kintu.* (The East Bengalis are not humanoids, the people of Orissa are animals, they jump-climb trees, but they don't have tails.)

They made fun of my dialect that we thought of as Bengali. Rabindranath Tagore invented the Bengali language, said one of the boys with an accompanying slap. Ghati Bengali was real Bengali and Bangal Bengali was spurious interpolation.

The moment was humiliating. I croaked and when I could manage a full sentence, I stammered. I felt my trouser pocket. The Sheffield was not there. I felt I could have solved the problem by knifing my way along. I recalled father's advice that the knife could not solve most problems.

I felt I was still travelling on a train inside India that refused to stop. Calcutta did not appear to be the station of destiny. I fumed. To add to my misfortune another unexpected event took place simultaneously. People surrounding a radio set suddenly burst into wailing sounds. Some of them started tearing at their hair and others loudly abused the Bangals for their misfortune.

Someone in the crowd, I think he was one Mullick from the aristocratic family of Burra Bazaar, enlightened me. The football giants, East Bengal, a team of the Bangals, and Mohun Bagan, the team of the Ghatis, were playing a vital league match in Calcutta. East Bengal had just scored two goals against Mohun Bagan sealing its fate to reach the top of the league table.

The lamenting and agitated supporters of Mohun Bagan Athletics Club found a handy object of hate in me. Some of them pounced on me and gave me a sound thrashing, bloodying my nose and bruising my cheek. The fat Mullick boy escorted me out of the ground and advised to be cautious with the Ghati boys. He did not only carry physical weight, he also carried money in his pocket—the propelling power that earned him a spot in the local team.

He explained that his Calcuttan friends were upset with the arrival of millions of East Bengal Hindus and feared stiff competition from them. He added, over a Magnolia ice cream, that Mohun Bagan, founded in 1889 as a national athletics club of elite Hindus of Calcutta had defeated the East Yorkshire Regiment, an all-British club, in 1911 and lifted the IFA (Indian Football Association) shield. For the first time an Indian team had defeated a British team. Mohun Bagan was a symbol of the Calcutta brand of Hindu nationalism.

The other important club was the Mohammedan Sporting Club founded in 1892. It was an exclusive club of the Mohammedans. Often there were Hindu–Muslim skirmishes if the Mohammedan SC happened to humiliate the Mohun Bagan. Hindu–Muslim rivalry had also invaded the soccer grounds of Calcutta.

The East Bengal Football Club was an upstart institution of the Hindus of Bengal. Established in 1920, it was a symbol of East Bengal's cultural presence in the land sanctified by Tagore, Vivekananda, Ramakrishna etc. They were the intruders.

Mullick added that on the day Mohun Bagan won against East Bengal the prices of chingri maach would skyrocket. Prawns were the symbol of the Ghatis. Reversely, the price of hilsa fish would skyrocket when East Bengal defeated Mohun Bagan. He hastened to add that whenever the Mohammedan Sporting Club happened to defeat either the Mohun Bagan or East Bengal some Hindus or Muslims were sure to be stabbed. This was, Mullick added, one of the important cultural totems of Calcutta. Wizened by the kind Mullick boy I returned home with a resolve not to visit the park again and not to be a part of the cultural life of Calcutta. This was something like *Eai paar Bangla and Oi paar Bangla* (Bengal on either side of a perceivable cultural fence).

I continued to travel on my own train all by myself. It was a ghost train; I was the lonely passenger. I did not find a landing ground at the soccer ground of Shyampukur or later at Mitra Institution, a reputed school.

However, I must add that much later I happened to meet the Mullick boy again at Calcutta University pursuing the same course in Bengali literature and language. In the course of my study, I understood that every district of Bengal had its distinct dialect and Calcutta Bengali was actually a dialect by itself, far removed from chaste literary Bengali. Pure Ghati Bengali was as mutilated as Bengali spoken by the Bengalis of Sylhet and Chittagong. Partition had created serious cultural, economic and social fission among the Bengalis of the two Bengals. Perhaps after sixty odd years, those uneven edges have become smoother.

Incidentally, I did not give up playing soccer. I managed to become a minor soccer star. That part of the story unfolded when I psychologically alighted in India from the train in which I was travelling as a lone ghost traveller, distancing myself from the reality around me and still haunted by the bad dreams of February and May 1950.

∽

Father had succeeded in securing a job at his ayurvedic institute at Acharya Prafulla Chandra Street, as a physician at a monthly salary of Rs 250, a princely sum in those days. Although not a regular faculty member, he was happy to find a place in his old institution. It raised our hopes of an honourable survival.

He took me to Mitra Institution, a prestigious school in north Calcutta. The headmaster, a grey-haired elderly person greeted us with a disappointed look. He enquired about father's profession and my former school. Father mostly spoke in our Bengali dialect and the headmaster spoke in English.

'Are you refugee Bangals?' he asked.

'Yes sir, we are from East Pakistan and refugees.'

'Well, you know the standard of education in Calcutta is higher. Do you have a transfer certificate and mark sheets?'

'No sir. We escaped under difficult circumstances!'

'That won't do. How can I admit a child without a TC (transfer certificate) and a mark sheet? And you boy,' he turned at me, 'do you know English?'

I tried to reply. However, only croaking sounds came out and finally I replied in a stammering voice that I had scored well in English in the last class promotion examination.

'I see you stammer. Sorry I can't help your child,' he informed father in a terse voice.

'Please test him sir. He is good at studies.'

'Sorry mister, I don't have time for refugee riffraff.'

We came out and walked silently. I did not vent my anger and frustration. The whole episode spoke volumes about the bias nursed by the headmaster towards refugees from East Bengal.

However, even at that critical moment I noticed that father's body had puffed up considerably. It was not the puffiness of good health. He looked pale and often rubbed his loin region.

'What has happened, Baba? You don't look well.'

'I think I have sugar and kidney problems.'

'Why don't you make some medicines for yourself?'

'Well son. I'm not worried about my health. I know what's going to happen to me. I'm worried for you. You must adjust to the new situation. Give up anger. Nothing can be achieved by anger. You've to win the world through knowledge.'

I did not agree with him. That night I told mother about father's illness. She listened with an impassive face and handed over some money to pass on to father for his medicines. The old man smiled wearily and returned the money by saying that he did not require medicine—he required love and care. He was not merely physically ill; he was dying inside after the Park Circus incident. The wise man was as deep as the sea and hardly allowed anyone to peep into the sea of his sorrow and frustration. My elder sibling had no time for him and he made it clear that the old man's foolishness was responsible for our miseries. I realized that father was not meant for this part of India. His India, like mine, was on the banks of the Meghna and Brahmaputra. I was pained. I could not help unfurl the sails for him and steady the rudder.

∽

Brother Benoy, who worked in some government relief and rehabilitation department on the East Pakistan border, was keen that I should go to school, enrol in a music class and play football. Brother Bijoy had different ideas. He wanted me to join a factory owned by his friend, a person from

Bihar called Tara babu. Tara had a forging factory and he manufactured plastic pens and other plastic kitchen commodities. The factory shed was situated somewhere near a canal, Maratha ditch, in north Calcutta. I had no option but to obey my brother, my breadwinner. Both mother and father opposed the horrendous move and offered Rs 5,000 from the saved Rs 15,000 as incentive to my eldest brother. This created more problems.

He sat down with a piece of paper and pen and demanded a detailed account of the money and other assets our parents carried from East Pakistan. It was difficult to explain that Dhiru and gang had robbed us of major parts of the cash and jewellery. Whatever they could save was due to my presence of mind and courage. His sulking mood told me that he expected more financial help from his parents. I could understand the strain he was put to by our sudden arrival, but I failed to grasp why he could not understand his own parents.

After three days in Tara babu's blazing inferno, I just scooted out with no intention of returning. On the last day of my deputation to his factory, Tara called me aside and offered me a sweet. He drew me near and started inserting his hand into my private parts. I sprang to my feet and brought out the Sheffield and clicked open the blade. Tara screamed out in panic and cried for help. The other employees drove me out of the campus.

Tara's wrath and frustration was taken out on me in the form of several slaps and beatings from Bijoy. He was furious that I had insulted his friend. Like most abused Indian children, I could not explain the shameful act of his friend.

Perhaps he was overwhelmed by the burden we imposed on him. His personality, finances and personal lifestyle were enormously disturbed by our sudden arrival. We were all under stress. Our dreams were shattered. We had no home and were not sure if our host would provide the next meal. I failed to comprehend how a person could be totally devoid of love and respect for his parents. My brother, I later realized, had failed to evolve beyond a certain level in his journey to complete manhood.

❧

Though haunted by destiny I still liked to believe in miracles. A freak incident restored my speech and stopped my stammering. Shorn of school schedules, I used to loiter about in Calcutta. A mere one anna took me to Sealdah railway station by tram.

I was afraid of Calcutta but the city amazed me. It looked like a war zone. Refugees were everywhere. They camped alongside the railway tracks, on footpaths and at all conceivable places. Everywhere there were emaciated half-starved people and miserable looking children. Everywhere the sex-pimps allured the hungry young women. Calcutta was no more the cohesive city it had once been. There were established bhadralok Calcutta people, speaking a Bengali that we somewhat understood. There were Bangals everywhere who spoke Bengali in varying dialects, and there were people from other parts of India who spoke Hindi and a strange Bengali.

The Sealdah railway platforms attracted me. Sealdah did not remind me of Bhairab—it gave me a creepy feeling. I liked to watch the arrival and departures of trains. Being at the station gave me a feeling of oneness with the teeming thousands rushing aimlessly with helpless and vacant looks. They were not sure about the future. Neither was I.

Thousands of refugees who waited for government relief occupied the station's platforms. Families of ten to twelve just carved out some space on the platforms, and on the central verges and footpaths of the main roads. They were everywhere. No centralized camps were set up for them. They raised families, performed marriages and carried out normal human functions. Occasionally I saw Christian missionaries, Ramakrishna Mission and other voluntary organizations distributing food clothes and medicines. However, the rugged and miserable people were getting along with their lives with a glimmer of hope in their eyes.

These observations often tempted me to get down from the imaginary train I was travelling in. What was stopping me? Was it my near-aristocratic past and the secured shelter where I lived? I was afraid of getting down from the train I had boarded on 13 May 1950.

One evening I entered a lane behind the railway station leading to the railway institute building. A hoarding that advertised a missionary school for refugees attracted me. I wanted to explore the possibility of getting admission. It was a deserted lane skirting the Muslim inhabited area of Raja Bazaar.

It happened suddenly. I saw a young boy of about ten running frantically chased by three youths, one of them wielding a knife. The fleeing boy bumped into me and cried out loudly. 'Don't kill me. I am an innocent Muslim. I am innocent,' he begged.

'Who is chasing you? Why?'

'They are Hindu refugees. They want to kill us and occupy our house.'

'Don't worry. Stay put behind me.' I flicked open the knife and stood between the Muslim boy and three attackers.

'Leave him. Are you a Hindu or a Muslim?' one of the invaders asked.

I don't know what happened to me. With loud cries, I swung my knife. Taken aback, the invaders ran back into a nearby lane. But I continued to shout loudly and I suddenly discovered that I was shouting through my own voice box. I folded the knife and tried to talk to the terrified Muslim boy.

To my surprise, I noticed that not only had I got my voice back, I was not stammering. For a moment, I felt like dancing with delight. 'What's your name?' I asked.

'Kamaruzzaman. Yours?'

'Call me Krishna. Where are you going?'

'I go to Mirzapur Street daily to learn the tabla from Ustad Karamatullah Khan.'

'Who is he?'

'He is the greatest tabla player in our country.'

'Will he teach me?'

'Why not? Come with me.'

I walked down to Mirzapur Street with Kamar. The Ustad was busy taking a class. A young girl was singing a classical song. (Later I learnt it was Raga Malkaus).

Kamaruzzaman introduced me and narrated the ugly incident. Ustad patted my back and made me sit by his side. 'You love music?'

'Yes sir. My father is a good singer and composer of Bengali folk songs.'

'Like to learn the tabla?'

'I don't have money to pay.'

'You don't have to pay. Come at least three days a week.' The great maestro initiated me into a new world of music.

My association with him was temporarily snapped when we moved out of Calcutta. However, as an undergraduate student, when I could spare some money by giving tuitions to school grade students, I started attending the Ustad's classes until I left Calcutta to join the civil service. It was a continuous association of nine years. I felt blessed then and even now that I met a friend like Kamar and a teacher like Ustad Karamatullah. My association with them and later with A.K.M. Hassanuzzaman, an undergraduate and post graduate course mate who later became a minister in the West Bengal government, reminded me of my childhood days. In a way, it gave me back some of my days with Rahman, Jasim, Lutfa and Saifi, and my faith in humanity and the oneness of the people of the new India where I was forced to live and perhaps die.

The Kamar incident helped me get off the train, and finally be a part of the new India.

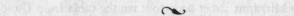

In mid-1951, another change twisted our lives. Our brother-in-law was transferred out of Calcutta to the district police at Uttarpara, a suburban town in the district of Hooghly. Once again, we accompanied him as part of his baggage.

I must admit that our brother-in-law and my sister's substitute were magnanimous. I never thought I could ever love and respect him. His second wife had already produced three kids and was to end up with six. I was not sure if I would ever be able to treat her as my sister. These complicated issues had almost numbed my mind. My perceptions changed vastly when I discovered that my new sister and my brother-in-law were excellent human beings. I had never seen a scowl on their faces and we never had to face the pangs of hunger. They shared our pain equally. Words cannot even begin to describe my respect for their sacrifices.

My brother-in-law was again transferred to another station, and Uncle Dhirendra and his family of eight took over. We were never short of company. We were only short of money and the other necessities of life.

Cousin Satyabrat (Satu) started out with a small business of smuggling rice from across the railway line which was not in the rationing regulation zone. I wandered about aimlessly taking part in sports. Uttarpara, a small town on the banks of the Bhagirathi River looked like a picture postcard. The Ganga, though not so mighty and turbulent, gave me my river back. The town was blessed with several garden homes and orchards from where we could pilfer coveted fruits. The football ground was excellent, just bang on the river and adjacent to the Raj Library where stalwart Bengalis like Michael Madhusudan Dutt and Rabindranath Tagore had spent some creative moments.

To my wonder, I discovered that the young boys of the suburban town were not rabid Ghatis. I was probably the first Bangal boy to live in the centre of town amongst the traditionally aristocratic Mukherjee, Banerjee and Chatterjee families. The young boys accepted me open-heartedly and never mocked me for my dialect. Moreover, my skill under the bars earned me a position in the junior team of the Uttarpara Young Men's Association. Later, I moved to the senior team and earned a place in Bali Protibha, the great neighbourhood club that produced a captain for the Indian Olympic team—S. Banerjee.

I felt at ease. I think the gentlefolk of Uttarpara were more cultured and were not dogmatic about Bengalis from East Bengal. Gradually the small town and its people started accepting me and helped me believe that Bengalis from outside Calcutta were equals.

However, I still carried the knife and suffered from an inferiority complex. All the boys went to school and I was the only one to spend time aimlessly in the libraries and playgrounds.

Father was in bad health. My eldest brother had written me off. Benoy was keen to support me but he was mostly away from what we called home. I was flourishing like a wild weed, my lessons from the streets and not from books and school. That was when I discovered that I could write poems and short stories. With Shibu, a Santhal boy living in our neighbourhood, we started a magazine. I was a regular contributor and Shibu was the staff artist.

My excellence in sports and games and exuberance in writing poems and short stories for the fortnightly magazine could not compensate for the emptiness within me. I felt tempted to get down from the imaginary train and be an integral part of the place.

The desire to walk up to the gates of a school required parental help and some money. Bijoy was so annoyed with me after my alleged misbehaviour with his friend Tara babu that on the slightest pretext he would punish me physically. The distance between Bijoy and me had further widened after my audacious suggestion to the eldest sibling that our father should be taken to a doctor. The Park Circus incident had snapped their relationship. My pleadings had no impact.

My helplessness pushed me more towards sports and music. I tried to forget the pain of distance from the temple of knowledge and the progressive deterioration of father's health by imagining that I had not disembarked from the train that I had boarded on 15 May 1950.

On 12 January 1952, our small town organized an annual sports event. I was a star participant in the 200-metre sprint, high jump and pole vault. I was expected to bag first prizes for the town by defeating competitors from ten other clubs from the Hooghly district.

It was around 11 a.m. Shibu rushed to the ground to inform me that my father had been admitted to the government hospital next door after he fainted on the roadside. I rushed to the hospital. Father was alone but in his senses. Mother had left for home to bring him his midday meal.

He signalled me. 'Come and sit next to me. I want to tell you something.'

'What's happened to you?'

'It's the kidney. Nothing can be done at this stage. I am ready to die as I know that is the only way to walk to freedom.'

'Don't talk of leaving me Baba.'

'No son. Allow me to talk. I've no time. Where is the knife I gave you?' I brought out the Sheffield blade and handed it over to him.

'I had gifted you this to protect your mother and yourself. You've put it to best use. Now you don't require it. Keep it under my pillow.'

'I love it Baba.'

'I understand. But you love me more. You don't require a knife to win the battle of life in this new India. Knowledge is sharper than a sword. Go back to school.'

'Who will take me to school?'

'Find one for yourself. I know you can. It's time for you to get down from the train son. You've been travelling since February 1950. You've reached your destination. Give me your word.'

'Yes Baba. I'll get admission as soon as possible.'

'Here's fifty rupees for admission fees, books, a decent shirt and pants. You know what today is?'

'Yes Baba. It is 14 January.'

'It's a good day, the day of Uttarayana. It is day the sun starts moving to the northern hemisphere. On this day aeons ago grandfather Bhishma had embraced death at Kurukshetra. All these years I fought for everything I felt it was appropriate to fight for against the enemies of the country, my own family members and peoples' prejudices. Since our arrival in India, I've been lying on a bed of arrows, fired by my own blood. Today is the time to go.'

'Don't go Baba. I'll set things right.'

'I know you would, but do that through knowledge. Don't forget that I taught you music, composition and the values of love and caring. That is more important son. Never ever think of taking revenge against people who wronged me. Love them, love their children. Don't measure your wealth by quantity. Measure it by how much you can gift to the needy after assuring a decent living for yourself and your family.'

'Yes Baba.'

'I'm tired. Let me sleep. Take care of your ma.' Father closed his eyes but kept on holding my hand. I sat in silence and watched him. Suddenly his hand slipped out of my grip. I cried out for the nurse. She rushed in, and examined father's pulse and breathing. 'I think he's no more, son. I am calling the duty doctor.'

The junior doctor confirmed what the nurse had said. I walked back home. I did not run. Mother was arranging father's midday meal in a cane basket. 'Good, you are here. Take father his lunch and see that he eats well.'

'Ma, Baba is no more.'

'What did you say? How could he leave without telling me?' She sat down in a corner, the basket of food dropped from her hand. She did not wail, she did not even weep.

'It is the day of his deliverance.' Mother walked down to the hospital with calm and steady steps. She stood by his bed, removed the white sheet and touched his feet in a final gesture to say a silent good-bye after their happy and stormy conjugal life of thirty-five years.

'He was born in 1894 and we were married in 1917. His was a stormy life and he himself invited the storms.'

༄

Three days after the funeral, I approached mother, busy in the kitchen. 'Ma, I want to go to school.'

'That's good. Wait for the rituals to be over.'

'No Ma. I want to go today.' I bowed and touched her feet. She did not stop me.

I approached cousin Satyabrat, readying to pedal down to a market across the railway line for his rice smuggling business. 'Satu, please take me to school.'

'Which one? The government school has closed admission.'

'Take me to any school.'

Satyabrat looked at me and asked me to sit pillion on the seat of his bike. He pedalled towards the twin-town of Bhadrakali. The place, located on the banks of the Ganga, boasted of a high school, besides brick kilns and a famous football ground.

Satyabrat was anything but a shy lad. He dragged me to the headmaster's room and entered after taking permission.

'Sir, here is my cousin. He wants admission.'

'Refugees?'

'Yes sir. I want admission in class eight.' I took over.

Satyabrat tugged at my shirt. 'How can you get in class eight?' he whispered.

'Let me talk. I've lost twenty months that I need to make up.'

'Do you have a transfer certificate and the last mark sheets?'

'No sir. We escaped under attack and had no time to complete the formalities.'

'How can I admit you then?'

'Please let me take a test sir. Give me a chance. I will prove my worth.'

The headmaster, Binod Bihari Bhattacharya, a man from Chittagong, looked at me curiously.

'Are you ready for a test? I see you lost somebody in your family. You'd better come after the mourning period.'

'No problem sir. I'm ready today.'

I did not understand what was going on in the mind of the headmaster. He summoned a peon and called for teachers Ajit Baig and Sadhan Chakravarty. 'Take this boy. Test him for class eight.'

I followed them to a room while Satyabrat waited outside. Ajit Baig set a paper in mathematics and Sadhan Chakravarty in English. They allowed me two hours. After about three hours, Ajit Baig called me in. He told me to come in the next day. Sadhan babu, a gold medallist in English from Calcutta University and a freedom fighter who served ten years in British jails nodded in affirmation. (Ajit Baig was later elected to the Lok Sabha on a CPM ticket).

'Can I deposit the fees today?'

'No problem. Go to the office and complete the formalities.'

Satyabrat and I completed the formalities. 'Date of birth? Any certificate?' asked the office clerk.

'No sir. I don't have a certificate.'

'Date of birth?'

25 January 1937.' Satyabrat stated the date with great authority.

I tugged at his shirt and whispered. 'It's not 25 Satu, it's 13 July. I have to ask mother about the year.'

'It's okay, 25 July is my birthday. What difference does it make if you are one or two years older or younger? Life is not running away. Don't make a fuss else they might cancel your admission.' I was amazed at Satyabrat's audacity.

The date of birth given to me by Satyabrat stuck, for good or bad, for the rest of my official working life.

The next day I changed into normal clothes, discarding the ritual mourning white and walked barefoot to school.

Sadhan Chakravarty entered the class with a register and a cane in his hand. During roll call, he called out roll number twenty-one. I stood up and replied, 'Present sir.'

Sadhan babu looked up and smiled faintly.

I heaved a sigh of relief.

❧

I was in the new India. My train had finally stopped.

I had discarded the knife for books and knowledge. A new journey awaited me and I entered the unknown doors of life that Sadhan babu later explained as doors of forts guarded by many unseen enemies and circumstances, doors to be broken by the power of knowledge and not the sword. He often spoke like my father. Both participated in some sort of struggle for liberation and emancipation.

I must pay obeisance to the old revolutionary who excelled in the language of the enemy he fought. He was the one who taught me English and all the other subjects except Bengali and Sanskrit.

I once asked him about his preference for English. 'To know the enemy better and to defeat him,' he answered.

He helped me enormously to complete my train journey to India. He gave me the feeling that I had arrived and took a paternal interest in me. He taught me to learn more about the new India, not to defeat the country but to defeat my diffidence to accept it as the India of reality.

'Start a new journey boy. Your other journey is over.' Sadhan babu stood like a father figure by my side until I passed out from school and plunged into the brave new world of a new India.

Epilogue

15 August 1947, when the British left India, brought us no freedom. Independence had not blessed us when we escaped Pakistan in 1950. Freedom dawned on us, those who lost our homes, well after 1952, when we, with our own efforts and unspeakable sacrifices, started rooting like desert cacti, on the soil of a new country, one that they called India and we called Swadesh, our own country.

Freedom came not riding the palanquin of fortune; it was thrown on us from the skies. We had no count of how many perished and how many survived. We were the fringe Indians, and those who brokered for power had no plan for us and there was none to chronicle the story of us.

However, sitting on the banks of a water body somewhere near Sylhet, then in East Pakistan, in 1971 and enjoying a frugal dinner with a committed group of Bengali freedom fighters, I smelt the flavour of independence in the sweat and blood of the grim and determined people ready to die for real freedom. They earned it later in 1971. My chance encounter with the son of Lutf-un-Nissa (our Lutfa of Kamalpur), a Junior Commissioned Officer in the East Pakistan Rifles, offered me a chance window to the past. I had heard from him about the historic War of Kamalpur, in which a cavalry unit of Pakistan was destroyed by the Bengali freedom fighters. The memory cells were activated. The steam that propelled the Train to India was coal-fired way back in 1971.

While writing the story, perhaps the first literary rendition of the crumbling down of a composite Bengali society, the impact of decisions taken by the power brokers, vivisection of the country and dividing of minds of the people, I have taken adequate precaution not to pollute the story with my empirical knowledge. I have tried to avoid chronicling certain prejudices I had developed about our extended family members. Hurting anyone was not on the tracks of the rail I was riding.

This decision worked as a handicap as well. I was unable to unlock the mysteries of many events that rocked our lives, made my father and his colleagues determined to fight for a United Bengal and to pursue the dream of Subhas Chandra Bose. In later life, I understood that men with a Mission are not fools. They succeed if the Mission is successful but are dumped by history if their Mission fails.

My later visits to Bangladesh, interactions with several freedom fighters and my professional insight into the seeping back of Islamicized values promoted by Pakistan and embraced by some remnants of the Muslim League and Pan-Islamists, provided ingredients to reassess the spirit of freedom in the Bengali peoples of Bangladesh. A fast flowing and strong current of secularism still flows through the veins of the people who are not afraid of equally strong religious fanatics, parts of the past divisive and destructive chemicals, and who have been fortified with the resolve of jihad in post-Afghanistan mujahedin days. This contradictory strain still troubles my part of Bengal.

Hopefully, the freedom loving people of Bangladesh would be successful in preserving their freedom, the lofty socio-political ideal that came to people like me a good six years after many Indians earned independence. I hope that in India too, we should be able to preserve the bliss of freedom, equality and fraternity despite thundering clouds of separatism continuously haunting us.

Acknowledgements

Forgiveness is a sterling quality but the inability to forget is both a painful pleasure and a nightmare. Certain events are forgettable, most others not. Growing up amidst the bounty of nature and resources, an extended family and with boys and girls beyond the family's societal fence was a unique and blissful experience. Enjoying the bonds of friendship with all segments of society—upper caste and low caste Hindus, Muslims and untouchables was in keeping with my father's lifestyle. Growing up in the cradle of the Brahmaputra–Meghna basin was a dream that was shattered by tragic events that divided our lives, our families and our friendships. Our composite Bengali society gradually splintered as the politics of separatism and nationalism clashed at the precipices of colonial India, waiting for the bleeding birth of two nations. Such cataclysmic separation generates mindless violence and even the sanest people fail to grasp and grapple with the tornado of distrust it unleashes.

Communal violence emanating from power-hungry politicians singed us and destroyed the lives of millions—the storm uprooted us like the famous Bengal cyclone, Kalbaishakhi. Displaced from our country, the India we knew, and forced to escape to a new India, a land that was alien to us. Some like my parents and their revolutionary, political and artist colleagues tried to maintain a semblance of sanity. Establishing roots in a new India was as painful as uprooting from the old India.

My first visit to Bangladesh, to Kamalpur and Bhairab in 1997 after forty-seven years rekindled memories of those historic events. Much to my delight, my friend Jasim, the son of our family retainer Rahman was still around, as was Nazar kaka, my father's artistic companion who still operated a musical instruments shop. Although aged about ninety-two, Nazar kaka, who has since passed on, recognized me. The three days I spent with Jasimuddin, now a businessman, Saifullah, now a retired teacher, and Nazar kaka triggered so many memories. We talked about the village, our childhood friends Rani and Lutfa, and about the sacrifices of my parents and their brave colleagues who were radical political revolutionaries. Nazar kaka inspired me to jog my memory and to tell the story of uprooting and Partition, inhuman massacres and artificial separations of a composite Bengali society.

I fished out the yellowing torn handwritten pages left by my father as well as my old notebooks that recorded major events. It took me ten years to spin the yarns of memory and create the canvas that is *Train to India*. I am grateful to Nazar kaka, Jasim and Saifi. Above all, I am grateful to Commodore Abdur Rauf (Retd) of the Bangladesh Navy, a former freedom fighter, and resident of our neighbouring village Bhairabpur. He perused the book carefully and corrected me on a few points and facts.

My parents Debendra and Sushama played key roles in maintaining equilibrium in a crumbling Bengali society and taught me the basic values of life and the courage to fight untruth, besides my academic education. They were the real teachers and along with teachers like Rani, Manorama and Lutf-un-Nissa they taught me to be a good human being and cope with severe adversities.